Library of
Davidson College

Production, Income and Welfare

Production, Income and Welfare:
The Search for an Optimal Social Order

Jan Tinbergen
Professor Emeritus of Development Planning
Erasmus University, Rotterdam

UNIVERSITY OF NEBRASKA PRESS
LINCOLN AND LONDON

First published in Great Britain in 1985 by
WHEATSHEAF BOOKS LTD
A MEMBER OF THE HARVESTER PRESS GROUP
Published simultaneously in the United States by the
University of Nebraska Press

© Jan Tinbergen, 1985

Library of Congress Cataloging in Publication Data

Tinbergen, Jan, 1903–
  Production, income and welfare.

  Includes indexes.
  1. Economics   2. Production (Economic theory)
3. Production functions (Economic theory)   4. Income.
5. Utility theory.   I. Title.
HB171.T56   1985   338.5   84-28042
ISBN 0-8032-4412-6

Typset in 10/12pt. Times by Mathematical Composition Setters Ltd, Salisbury, UK.
Printed in Great Britain by
Whitstable Litho Ltd., Whitstable, Kent
All rights reserved

To Tine, whose love and wisdom assisted me in all my work

Contents

Foreword ix

Part I. Production 1

1. Market-determined and residual incomes—some dilemmas (with Jacob Kol) 3
2. Production functions with several factors 20
3. Constraints on production functions: essential *vs.* non-essential factors 25
4. Counterproduction. 35
5. On collective and part-collective goods 43
6. Production functions: research lacunae 56

Part II. Income Formation 67

7. On a macroeconomic model of income formation (with Eckhard Wegner) 69
8. The role of occupational status in income formation 78
9. Determinants of manager incomes 85
10. Two approaches to quantify the concept of equitable income distribution 101

Part III. Welfare Functions 111

11. Measurement of social welfare 113
12. The allocation of workers to jobs 123
13. Some neglected determinants of welfare functions 131

Part IV. The Optimal Social Order 143

14. The dynamic welfare maximum 145
15. Some remarks on the optimal tax system 158
16. Optimal education, occupation and income distribution in a simplistic model 169
17. Ways to socialism 174

18. Coexistence: from the past to the future 187
19. Restructuring our societies: international coordination policies 192

Appendix 203
Author Index 205
Subject Index 207

Foreword

This book contains a selection of papers I wrote on production, incomes and welfare (or utility), three concepts to be defined somewhat more precisely in what follows and selected as building blocks of a fourth, the optimal social order.

Production may be defined as the creation of goods or services (goods for short) able to satisfy human needs directly or indirectly (when semi-finished or means or production). This creation requires production factors (natural resources, labour and capital) and the relationship between the quantities of factors used and the production obtained is known as a *production function*. Part I deals with a number of problems encountered when we attempt to quantify production and production functions.

Income may be defined as the flow of products an individual may dispose of in a time unit without reducing his or her wealth. Income formation is the process generating incomes; its most important form is that of paying individuals for the efforts made during a production process. Incomes earned by different individuals depend on their occupation (job), which in turn requires a number of capabilities of different levels. Among the occupations those called *managerial* are among the complicated ones and are given special attention in Part II, which deals with income formation. In all communities incomes are unequal—sometimes very unequal. The question of the equity of unequal incomes looms large in human relationships and political economic discussions. (Chapter 10 deals with the definition and measurement of equity.)

Welfare, in the sense used in economic science, stands for the utility or—more basically—satisfaction experienced by each member of a community. It is the basic concept of economic science, but the way it is used by economists is far from uniform and far from clear. Some of these doubts and the attitude taken by the present author are dealt with in Part III, and also in Part IV.

Part IV is devoted to the *optimal social order*, which constitutes the central theme of the book. Because of the even greater difficulties of defining and identifying this concept, the aim chosen is modest and described as the supply of 'building blocks'. An integration of the subjects dealt with into a textbook is not attempted. This is a drawback, partly compensated for by the possibility for the reader to read each chapter separately. An attempt at greater integration can be found elsewhere, in a book about K. Arrow's work, edited by G. Feiwel. There an attempt is made to tackle the difficult question concerning the costs of institutions. Since institutions are the unknowns of the problem of the optimal order, it is unknown which costs have to be deducted from the benefits we want to maximise. A device must be found which only includes the costs of the institutions that must exist in the optimum order. It may be possible to use the Kuhn–Tucker device in the problem of finding the maximum of some function in a restricted interval. As is well known, this device is based on the algebraic proposition that a product of two factors is zero if one of the factors is zero.

Six of the nineteen papers in this book were not previously available in English: four of them were in Dutch, one in French and one in German. The translation is the author's and has been adapted, as have some of the original English texts, where new facts or insights have changed the author's view; moreover, some errors have been corrected.

Whereas the main orientation of the argument is *economic*, a broad interpretation has been given that feature, in line with the need for *interdisciplinary* thinking. Some of the later chapters—mainly those in Part IV—are on the boarder between economic science and political argument and should be seen as an attempt to defend scientifically the author's political affiliation: a democratic socialist conviction.

The author is a European and may thus have a European bias. This applies in particular to his use of the words 'liberal' and 'socialist', which to many Americans mean something other than to Europeans. But a considerable number of Americans are fully aware of these differences, as is illustrated by the Winter 1984 issue of *Daedalus*, the journal of the American Academy of Arts and Sciences, devoted to 'The Nordic Enigma': Holland has much in common with Scandinavia.

The scientific strategy chosen by the author deviates from that of the majority of economists on some points. This applies in particular to his accepting the possibility of *measuring* welfare or utility. The scientific instruments used are limited by the author's limited command of mathematics, as well as by differences in taste—an almost unavoidable factor. Two features of reality contribute to the necessity of sometimes arbitrary choices of method or strategy. On the one hand, the number of *alternative* theories is very large (for instance on the subject of production); on the other hand, the number of *lacunae* in concrete research is large—as set out in Chapters 6 and 13.

With the aid of our building blocks, and a good deal of intuition, some main features of an optimum world social order may be sketched out.

A comparison with the existing world order is shocking, and commensurate with the fears of many for our future.

Because of technological development, based on scientific development, or even more generally on the development of thinking, the time has come that our planet must be managed as one coherent whole. If we apply management science as developed for objects which are already one coherent whole on our planet, we are forced to conclude that a limited number of very important management decisions have to be taken by institutions in which *all people* living on the earth are represented (cf. Chapter 14).

One of the most recent tasks of world management concerns the maintenance of a clean environment or the cleansing of an already polluted one. It is clear that decisions left to single factories will not do. In most developed and many developing countries national governments have enacted legislation on environmental control. But this is not enough: pollution affects the *world*'s water and atmosphere, and only decision-making at the *world level* will take into account the welfare, in this respect, of world population.

This task seems to be understood better than some of the earlier tasks of world management. In order to deal with these problems, we have created world-wide institutions: the World Health Organisation, the International Monetary Fund, the United Nations Security Council, and others. Similarly, the care of the environment has been entrusted to the United Nations' Environmental Programme. Unfortunately, all these institutions are vested with too little competence and too little power.

Whereas for the management of national problems single countries usually distribute competence and power in an equilibrated way between national and local authorities, this is not the case for the world as a whole. There is an irrationally *lopsided* distribution in favour of national authorities and a near-vacuum at the higher continental and world level. The main reason for this lopsidedness is the concept of *national sovereignty*—the legal aspect of national independence and nationalist feelings. Almost all the peoples of the world have been indoctrinated to attach a very high value to their nationality. In many cases these feelings are connected with the languages spoken or customs and habits. This complex of feelings—and attempts to justify them—has become increasingly dangerous because of the *militarisation* of public life and the development of *armament technology*.

It has been customary in economic science to consider this sector of political activity as a given and this custom has also been followed in this book. Before long it will have become so unrealistic to do so that an *integration* of the military sector into economics will be needed. Important work is already being done by some authors and by the Berlin Science

Centre, especially by its International Institute for Comparative Societal Research, headed by Karl Deutsch. This type of interdisciplinary research is urgently needed now that the danger is growing that for some powerful politicians a substitution of military for economic and social arguments seems attractive.

Some of the further main features of the optimal world order are: (a) no artificial impediments to trade between nations, (b) less inequality of educational opportunities, (c) smaller income differences, and (d) a specialisation of production based on natural endowments—geographical situation, climate, mineral deposits and soil fertility.

The optimal world order's feasibility is a separate problem only while our basic assumptions on human behaviour deviate from actual behaviour. Unfortunately, such a deviation is not large with regard to human selfishness; real man (or woman) does not deviate so much from *homo oeconomicus* (*ica*). It may deviate (and probably does so quite clearly) with regard to the time-horizon. The overwhelming majority of policy-makers and their voters are much more shortsighted than economic science usually tacitly assumes. This applies in particular to the decisions concerning European integration and development cooperation. Both policies are forms of geographical integration and steps in the direction of world management. In comparison with Europe in the Middle Ages, a great deal of integration has occurred, although the process has not been without its setbacks. In European history imposed integration with the aid of military power (Napoleon, Hitler) did not work; the unification of Italy and Germany around 1870 did; while Austria's history shows a different picture. Outside Europe, colonialism in several cases worked as an integrator (USA, India—up to a point, Indonesia). Today's most urgent question is whether some form of integration between communist and non-communist ruled blocs can be found.

Some of the building blocks offered in this book show a scientific level of good quality; the higher we choose the decision-making levels, the more we have to use intuitive thinking and the more that thinking's quality suffers. The need for further research, touched upon in Chapters 6 and 13, evidently is far stronger towards the end of the book, as a supplement to Part IV.

I would like to express my thanks to Wheatsheaf Books for their initiative; to the publishers of the original texts of the chapters, listed below; and to several colleagues whose criticism helped me avoid errors or unclear arguments. Restricting myself to those whose criticisms impressed me in particular, I thank J. de Hoogh, T. Kloek and J. van den Doel for their assistance concerning Chapter 1; P. Hennipman and

D.J. Wolfson for their contributions to Chapter 5; S.K. Kuipers and J. Hartog for their criticism on an earlier version of Chapter 12; and J. Pen for our discussions on income distribution generally. The usual disclaimer applies. The latter is less valid for the case of my two co-authors: J. Kol (Chapter 1) and E. Wegner (Chapter 7).

In terms of hours, by far the largest contribution has been made by Mrs Suze Kleyngeld, who not only gladly and quickly typed the new (translated) chapters, but also showed great inventiveness in adapting existing typescripts to the wishes of the publisher.

J. Tinbergen
The Hague

Part I
Production

1 Market-determined and Residual Incomes—Some Dilemmas* (with Jacob Kol**)

1.1 THE SEARCH FOR INCOME DETERMINANTS

Recently a vast literature has developed about the determinants of various types of incomes and the quantitative impact of these determinants on the incomes considered. Often the incomes considered are earnings or labour incomes (cf. Tinbergen (1977), where a list of authors can be found). In the present essay we shall consider various types of income, including income from different types of labour and incomes from capital. At the same time we shall draw the dividing line (or lines) not only between labour and capital, but also elsewhere. Within the category of labour a number of main occupational groups (derived from the American and Japanese Censuses) will be distinguished; but in addition we shall pay attention to *income types formed on a market* and income types appearing as residuals, to be called *residual incomes*. This is not a new distinction: from the early stages of economic theory the concept of 'rent' has been defined as a residual income. But a number of dilemmas arise when it comes to specifying the incomes that appear as residuals. These entail dilemmas in attempts we propose to make to find the determinants of such incomes and the quantitative impact of the determinants on these incomes. Our main reason for dealing with these subjects is our desire to find the *determinants of manager incomes* as distinguished in the Censuses mentioned. This paper should be considered as a first progress report on this search.

---

* We would like to express our thanks to Nienke Bouma, of the University of Leyden, for computational assistance.
** Erasmus University of Rotterdam, the Netherlands. We wish to express our sincere thanks to Professors J. de Hoogh, T. Kloek, J. Pen and J. van den Doel for valuable suggestions and sources of additional information. All remaining shortcomings are, of course, ours.

1.2 OUR STARTING POINT

We think it useful to start the analyses by a very simple set-up, dealt with quantitatively by Senator Paul H. Douglas (Douglas, 1934) and revisited by him recently (Douglas, 1976). The categories dealt with are two production factors: *labour* and *capital*, for which markets are supposed to exist; whereas a third category, *entrepreneurs*, acting on the demand side of these markets, do not receive market-determined but residual incomes. Capital may—but need not—include 'land' or natural resources. Capital may—but need not—be supplied by individuals who simultaneously supply labour or simultaneously act as employers. Our own preference will be to speak of the *organisers of production* instead of entrepreneurs, in order to remind the reader of the possibility that public authorities may also act as employers, and do so in all countries. In passing we want to remind the reader that in large institutions, especially in corporations, employer activities are performed not by one man who 'runs the affair', but by bodies, both private and public, known as *hierarchies*. Part of the public hierarchy is 'the administration', and in communist-ruled countries private and public hierarchies are amalgamated to a large extent, and include a third, Party hierarchy. We leave it to the reader to decide to what extent our findings may also apply in these countries.

1.3 CONCENTRATION ON THE DEMAND SIDE

In this chapter the supply is given little attention. This is a deliberate exclusion of a subject whose interest was emphasised by one of us (Tinbergen, 1942, 1959). Thus, we are not going to discuss whether or not the supply of factors is elastic, or even shows negative elasticity. Nor are we going to discuss whether or not suppliers are exerting monopoly power. Other *incomes from power*, such as social benefits as part of a social security system, will not be discussed either. This again does not mean that we deny their importance (cf. Huppes 1977; Pen 1971, 1977).

We are not going to deal either with another interesting aspect of our main problem, namely, whether labour productivity is influenced by the way in which production is organised. An increasing interest in this problem has been aroused by those who are in favour of industrial democracy, participation or labour self-management, and an excellent summary of empirical evidence (Stokes, 1978) shows that there is a relation. This implies that the production function is not merely *a technological relationship*. However, we shall hold to the assumption that it is, which is only true if the organisation of production is given and the same for all observations.

The main question we shall pose is whether for managers we can assume that their earnings *are determined by a market*, the difficulty being that they are on both sides of that market. This may lead the economist—and the sociologist—to the suspicion that manager incomes contain an element of monopolism. An *alternative model* to determine manager income may be that they are *residual incomes*. The consequences of this are discussed in section 1.5 and after.

Dilemma I is discussed next.

1.4 THE TRADITIONAL DEMAND MODEL

The core of our exercise is linked to the use of the Cobb–Douglas production function[1]

$$y = dk^{x}l^{\lambda} \tag{1.1}$$

where y is national product, l the quantity of labour hired on the labour market, k the quantity of capital hired on the capital market, and d, x and λ are constant coefficients.

Assuming competition between the organisers of production, the incomes w and i received per unit of labour and capital will be equal to their marginal productivities:

$$w = \partial y/\partial l = \lambda y/l \tag{1.2}$$

$$i = \partial y/\partial k = xy/k \tag{1.3}$$

leading to the well-known statement that the total incomes of labour and capital, W and I are equal to:

$$W = \lambda y; \tag{1.4}$$

$$I = x y \tag{1.5}$$

Consequently the residual income R will amount to:

$$R = (1 - \lambda - x)y, \tag{1.6}$$

implying that it will be $\geqslant 0$ if $\lambda + x \leqslant 1$, that is, positive in the case of decreasing, zero for constant and negative for increasing returns to scale. When considering a nation as a whole we shall add the term 'macro' and speak of *macro returns to scale*.

It has often been suggested that decreasing returns are characteristic of agriculture and constant returns for industries whose optimal unit size is small in comparison to the national or international market. In the latter case, it is argued, increased demand for the industry's product will be met by extending the number of (identical) units. This argument tacitly assumes that a 'reserve' of entrepreneurs of equal productivity is available for such an extension. We may thus formulate as Dilemma II the question *whether such potential entrepreneurs are available* for the majority of non-agricultural activities.

In a situation of *macroeconomic increasing returns* ($\varkappa + \lambda > 1$), permanent losses accompany free competition between private production units. This is an unstable situation, bound to result in cartelisation, public ownership, or both. It applies to a small portion of the economy only. Hence such macroeconomic economies of scale are not likely to play an important role.

Whether by decreasing soil fertility or other geographical factors (e.g. less favourable location), or, finally, by a decreasing quality of entrepreneurs, in the case where $\varkappa + \lambda < 1$ the *residual income is not necessarily determined* by a coefficient, μ, characteristic of *entrepreneurs' marginal productivity*. This is characteristic for residual income, with the only exception occurring if, by coincidence, $\mu = 1 - \varkappa - \lambda$. Part of marginal income is a premium for risk-bearing capital.

1.5 SOME ALTERNATIVE DIVIDING LINES

With the simple scenario set in section 1.4 we are able to represent five different situations by drawing four alternative sets of dividing lines between the types of actors introduced:

(a) Managers and capital-owners are the same individuals, or statistically a separation of profits from interest is virtually impossible. In this case we can even leave out k, i, I, and μ, and a mixed residual income > 0 occurs as soon as $\lambda < 1$. This seems to be characteristic of early capitalism rather than for later periods.

(b) Capital-owners provide part of the labour supply, i.e. this part is not hired. Market-determined incomes are mostly earnings of hired labour, and possibly some capital is hired and paid a market income. Residual incomes include *part of labour income*. This is often valid for small enterprises, and residual income often also includes part of capital income.

(c) Capital-owners constitute a separate group and there is a *capital market*. Market-determined incomes are not only earnings but also interest. The model given in Section 1.4 applies.

(d) Managers become so numerous and preponderant among entrepreneurs that they too can be considered as a *production factor*, receiving a *market-determined manager compensation*. This alternative constitutes the other side of Dilemma I. Indicating the number of managers by m, their compensation by c and their marginal productivity by μ, the production function becomes:

$$y = dk^\varkappa l^\lambda m^\mu \tag{1.7}$$

and manager compensation:

$$c = \partial y / \partial m \tag{1.8}$$

If $\varkappa + \lambda + \mu = 1$, we have another situation of macro constant returns to scale, where quality differences between managers are not recognised. If $\varkappa + \lambda + \mu < 1$, a residual (profit) remains and can be thought of as appropriated by the corporations.

(e) Alternative (d) can be further specified by introducing features of *profit-sharing* which may apply to each of the factors. Profit-sharing must be expressed in *additional equations* in which additional variables occur—the various shares. We do not intend to go into specifics here, but shall mention a type of income determination called *hierarchical*, which is seemingly *unrelated to the recipients' productivity*. Her or his income depends on her or his *level in the hierarchy L* and equals:

$$h = h_0 n^L \tag{1.9}$$

where h_0 and n are constants. This implies that the ratio n between the hierarchical income at level $L + 1$ to that at level L, is assumed constant throughout the hierarchy (Drucker, 1977). This ratio is in the order of magnitude of 1.2–1.4 in private corporations, but higher near the top, and lower in the administrations of democractic countries.

1.6 EMPIRICAL ILLUSTRATIONS FOR THE USA (1959) AND JAPAN (1975): PRODUCTION FACTORS CONSIDERED

In order to illustrate the alternatives mentioned *cross-section estimates of Cobb–Douglas production functions* for the two largest western economies, the USA and Japan, have been made, using US states and Japanese prefectures as the units of observation, the numbers of observations being, as a consequence, 51 and 47, respectively. By coincidence the American figures refer to the year 1959 (1960 Census of Population) and the Japanese to the year 1975, when, expressed in 1975 dollars, *per capita* incomes were $4796 and $4450, respectively, and hence rather similar.[2] As factors of production, we have used four types of labour: (i) professional, technical and similar; (ii) managers, administrators, etc.; (iii) all other workers, except farm labourers; and (iv) farm managers and workers, and *a proxy for capital*, given the group number ix. For the USA, type (iv) has been subdivided into (v) white- and (vi) blue-collar workers. For Japan, type (vii), small enterprises, is distinguished from (ii), and (viii) stands for (ii) and (vii) together. Although many categories of labour for which data are given in the Japanese Censuses seem to coincide with the categories considered in the American Censuses, some of them presumably are not identical, partly as a consequence of structural differences between the two economies. For fear of multicollinearity no regression equations have been estimated with larger numbers of production factors: we may already have included too many.

In the remainder of this section some details about the *proxies* used for *capital* will be discussed. Data on capital per employee were not available to the authors. It was therefore assumed that in each country two types of activities may be distinguished: capital-intensive and labour-intensive sectors. The portion of total manpower employed in the former may be indicated by e_k and this was used as a dummy for the quantity of capital k per employee in the state or the prefecture considered.

For the USA, capital-intensive sectors were represented by transportation, public utilities, mining and manufacturing of durable commodities. Indicating the capital-intensity of these sectors by K_k and that of the remaining sectors by K_l, we can express total capital per employee by

$$k = (1 - e_k)K_l + e_k K_k.$$

Assuming further that $K_k = m K_i$, and choosing K_i as the unit of capital, k can be written as:

$$k = 1 + (m - 1)e_k \tag{1.10}$$

The best estimate we found for m was taken[3] from Hibbert *et al.* (1977) and equals 6. For the USA a similar figure was found.[4]

Since in our regression equations we used natural logarithms of all variables (in order to express the Cobb–Douglas production function by a linear equation), the question to be answered is: what is the ratio between the regression coefficient of $\ln e_k$ and the 'true' coefficient of $\ln k$. Since the regression equation refers to deviations of the variables from their averages we compare, for the logarithms of both proxy e_k and k, the differences between maximum and minimum values among the observations. The results are as follows for the USA:

	Maximum	Minimum	Difference
e_k	0.363	0.078	
$\ln e_k$	−1.013	−2.551	1.538
$k = 1 + 5e_k$	2.815	1.390	
$\ln k$	1.035	0.329	0.706

Hence the 'true' figures relating to capital appear to vary less than the proxies at a ratio of 2.18. The 'true' regression coefficients will then be larger in that same proportion.

For Japan, the capital-intensive sectors taken were transportation and communication, public utilities, mining, pulp and paper, chemicals, petro-chemical industries and iron and steel. The same method as that used for the USA yielded the following results:

	Maximum	Minimum	Difference
e_k	0.149	0.061	
$\ln e_k$	−1.904	−2.797	0.893
$k = 1 + 5e_k$	1.745	1.305	
$\ln k$	0.557	0.266	0.291

Here too the 'true' figures relating to capital appear to vary less than the proxy figures and the 'true' regression coefficients for capital will be 3.07 times as large as the regression coefficients found for the proxies.

1.7 MAIN RESULTS OF REGRESSION ANALYSIS[5]

Table 1.1 shows the main results of our cross-section analysis of the American and Japanese production functions with four or five types of labour.[6]

Two alternatives have been shown for both countries. For the USA the second alternative differs from the first by the omissions of the observations for the District of Columbia which, as a city state, shows some extreme characteristics. The second alternative for Japan is characterised by the combination of the managers, etc. of large organisations and small entrepreneurs. Small entrepreneurs are not shown as a separate group in the USA Censuses. For both countries the two alternatives show a number of similarities which therefore support each other. Even so, the table contains a number of surprises and the rest of this chapter is devoted to their discussion. The most striking are discussed under the separate sections, while the less striking are taken up immediately.

Table 1.1: Regression coefficients obtained in cross-section estimation of Cobb–Douglas function with several types of labour

| Country | $\bar{R}^2$ | Regression coefficients and standard deviations for labour types ||||||| T. of R.C $(\sum \lambda)$ |
		Prof. tech.	Manag.	White-c.w.	Blue-c.w.	Farm	Small e	For cap.	
USA (I)	0.738	0.257 (0.189)	0.090 (0.138)	0.698 (0.224)	−0.225 (0.222)	−0.053 (0.028)		0.194 (0.144)	0.961
USA (II)	0.731	0.237 (0.188)	0.006 (0.150)	0.741 (0.224)	−0.305 (0.229)	−0.072 (0.032)		0.098 (0.157)	0.705
Japan (I)	0.829	0.026 (0.089)	0.028 (0.058)	0.631 (0.120)		−0.080 (0.014)	−0.103 (0.086)	0.043 (0.144)	0.546
Japan (II)	0.838	0.059 (0.083)	−0.214 (0.105)	0.722 (0.111)		−0.087 (0.013)		0.025 (0.135)	0.505

Abbreviations:
Prof. tech   : professional, technical and similar workers
Manag.   : managers, officials, proprietors and similar workers
White-c.w.   : white-collar workers
Blue-c.w.   : blue-collar workers
Farm   : farm managers and workers
Small e   : small entrepreneurs
Cap.   : capital
USA I   : all states, and the District of Columbia,
USA II   : all states
Japan I   : small entrepreneurs shown separately
Japan II   : small entrepreneurs included in managers, etc.
                In both Japanese cases white-collar and blue-collar workers have been combined in order to avoid including too many independent variables.
$\bar{R}^2$: coefficient of determination, corrected for degrees of freedom
$\sum \lambda$ = T. of R.C. : total of all regression coefficients

Although the coefficients of determination $\bar{R}^2$ are satisfactory, the reliability of several of the regression coefficients, as measured by their standard deviations, is moderate only. This may be due to the relatively modest number of observations in each case and has led us to keep the number of production factors as small as possible, without, we think, neglecting our main target. The combination of blue- and white-collar workers into one group, which works in the case of Japan, did not do so well in the case of USA: the combined group obtained a non-significant negative regression coefficient. (The other negative regression coefficients will be discussed in sections 1.9–1.12.)

The only regression coefficients in line with common theoretical expectations and previous experience (cf. Douglas, 1934, 1976) are the larger positive ones for the main types of industrial labour, and their standard deviations are acceptable. Two differences between the USA and Japan seem to make sense: (i) the relative importance of professional, technical and similar workers is much higher in the USA than in Japan; and (ii) the portion of residual in total income is larger in Japan than in the USA. Another way of expressing this finding is that macro decreasing returns are much more evident in Japan than in the USA and the role of small enterprises, often paying lower wages, illustrates this feature of a country whose development is so much more recent and has been so exceptionally rapid over the last 30 years.

The total remuneration of capital must be a larger portion of national income than its regression coefficient of only 0.043. The regression coefficients obtained for capital in the two cases of the USA are of the order of magnitude to be expected: between 10–20 per cent of national income (cf. Kuznets, 1966, pp. 168–9). Admittedly this margin is rather large, though.

1.8 INCOME SHARES AND *PER CAPITA* INCOMES OF FACTORS: THE TRADITIONAL APPROACH

Under conditions of free competition among the organisers of production and validity of the Cobb–Douglas approach to the production function, the coefficients such as those used in equation (1.1) or (1.7), provided their sum total $\leqslant 1$, indicate the *shares of national product* obtained by the factors included. After dividing them by the number of individuals supplying the factors, expressed as a portion of total employment, and multiplying by mean income of all occupations, we obtain, for the market-determined incomes, the *per capita* income for each of these factors. For the United States (1959) we also have the directly observed mean incomes. The comparison of these two estimates is given in Table 1.2 for case I of Table 1.1.

Table 2.1 dramatically illustrates the main points made in the present chapter, namely that in several respects *major deviations from the usual approach occur*, or income is not market-determined at all. Incomes of professionals, technicians, etc. are the only ones for which the indirect estimation is close to direct observation by the Census data. According to Table 2.1 white-collar workers are 'underpaid', and managers, etc., blue-collar workers and farmers grossly 'overpaid'. The interpretation to be given to these surprising figures may be, of course, a rejection of the Cobb–Douglas approach, even as a marginal one, especially for the categories whose λ_i shows a large standard deviation, i.e. managers and blue-collar workers. It may be worth while, however, also to consider the following interpretations.

Table 1.2: Indirect and direct estimates of the per capita incomes of five factors of production for the USA (1959)

	Production factors					
	1	2	5	6	4	
i =	Prof., techn.	Manag.	White-c.w.	Blue-c.w.	Farm	Cap.
Cobb–Douglas coefficient λ_i^a	0.257	0.090	0.698	−0.225	−0.053	0.193
Numbers^b x_i	0.108	0.085	0.198	0.469	0.062	
p.c. inc.^{c} in $	4662	2074	6906	−940	−1675	
p.c. inc. (direct) $	4560	5297	4436	4387	2453	

Notes:
a These are comparable with x, λ and μ in equation (1.7).
b Expressed as portion of total employment.
c Obtained by $y\lambda_i/x_i$, as explained in text, with $y = \$1959$.
  All x_i and y are geometrical averages, since these were readily available. The orders of magnitude are sufficiently close to other means for the crude exercise given in this section.

Abbreviations: See Table 1.1.

1.9 CAUSES AND CONSEQUENCES OF NEGATIVE MARGINAL PRODUCTIVITY

Apart from the standard belief that a production function is a purely technical concept—which we denied in section 1.3—another standard belief among econometricians is that *marginal productivities of factors have to be positive* or, as a limiting case, zero. We think that there are several reasons for believing that in a number of cases marginal productivities can be negative.

A first general reason is that *small independent producers* are making systematic mistakes in estimating costs of production and have a tendency to underestimate or even overlook their own labour input. In addition, they attach a positive value of remaining independent and are willing to sacrifice income, not only from their own labour, but also from their own capital, for independence.

A second general reason is the *structure of society*. With the very large number of people and of activities that characterise modern society there is no escape from the phenomenon that *part of the activities of some individuals or even institutions are counteracting or even destroying the output of other individuals or institutions*. This is the consequence of both decentralisation and administration (or managing) with the aid of hierarchical decision structures. In the case of competition—one of the most important forms of decentralisation—between two firms, part of each firm's activities is to inform prospective buyers of the product concerned that their own product is better than the competitors'. Similarly, if they deal with prospective sellers of raw materials or of factors of production.

This can be vividly illustrated by the well-known experience of the merger of two firms. At the moment that the merger has been agreed by the leadership of the two firms, a difficult process begins of re-educating the lower ranks of both. Instead of telling prospective buyers of the product that the other firm's product is worse than their own, they have to adopt an attitude of solidarity with their former adversary. This is by no means the only way in which activities of some reduce the effect of other's activities. Well-known examples are *rivalries between any part of one administration and the other parts.* The numerous changes in a draft text from a letter to a complete report introduced by a number of successive supervising members of a hierarchy constitute another example.

As a cross-check on the thesis of counterproductivity just formulated, one may ask whether the phenomenon can be eliminated and, if so, how. Proponents of central planning in its extreme 'compulsory' form always maintain that it is exactly this planning that does the trick ('eliminates the anarchy of *laissez-faire*'), but experience has taught all concerned that in a modern society with millions of people and billions of acts complete planning of all details from one centre—so as to eliminate all inconsistencies—is *just not possible.* Single, large firms or administrations even are unable to avoid the phenomenon: it is possible only in very small units. In order to get an idea of the orders of magnitude involved the reader is reminded of the fact that advertising costs in the United States amount to 2.8 per cent of national income (Lindblom, 1978) but are less than 1 per cent in Belgium and France.

In their well-known study, Nordhaus and Tobin (1972) make an attempt to eliminate, from offical growth figures, a number of elements which have something in common with this phenomenon. Between 1929 and 1969 they arrive at a reduction in growth which reduces by about 25 per cent national product in 1969.

Because of the difference in approach none of the figures mentioned is even an attempt at answering our main question, which remains open. But we should mention one highly relevant implication. If indeed actual national product is significantly less than the sum of the products expected to be theirs by its composing production units (firms, authorities, independently working single producers), the incomes paid by the latter cannot be socially justified. A norm for what principle defines incomes which optimise the allocation of production factors cannot be derived from the maximisation of the production as estimated by the composing parts, since in these estimates they do not deduct the harm done to other units. This normative problem is discussed in Chapter 4. The present chapter only claims to give some empirical evidence on negative marginal productivities. It should be admitted, however, that our results may also be due to our assumption—natural in the context—of one production function for each of the two countries. It might be replaced by the assumption of different production functions in different states or prefectures. Such differences may be represented by the introduction of additional variables.

1.10 FARM WORKERS' MARGINAL PRODUCTIVITY IN USA AND JAPAN

A common feature of the results obtained for the USA and Japan we found (cf. Table 1.1) was a highly significant negative marginal productivity of farm production (the term farm workers covers both farmers and agricultural workers). Apart from the features of small independent producers already discussed (cf. section 1.9) we may complete the picture of American farming by two additional features described in detail by Cochrane and Ryan (1976) and Owen (1966). The former, in their Table 9-4, provide us with a highly interesting sub-division of the benefits obtained by six classes of farmers, from those whose gross sales exceed $40,000 to those showing gross sales of less than $2500 for 1964. The lower two classes do not have farming as their main source of income; in fact, these two classes obtain only 20 and 40 per cent of their total net income from farming, respectively. This illustrates the general description of the position of farmers given by Owen (1966), culminating in the statements that a 'negative business result is normal' and that, if farms had shown the same yield on capital as industry, their total net income in 1960 would have been $1.5–2 billion higher.

An impression of Japanese farming can be derived from Denison and Chung (1976), where it is stated (p. 108) that the average farm in Japan is less than 100 times as small as the average American farm; that there are hardly any hired farm workers (p. 86), that income from agriculture (p. 18) is (for 1971) about 0.4 million yen, as compared (p. 23) with 1.30 million yen per person employed in industry (non-residential, non-agricultural). Dynamism of agriculture is restricted, as is illustrated on the one hand by the growth rates (p. 17) and, on the other, by the high level of food prices (Koike, 1979) as compared with other countries.

1.11 BLUE-COLLAR WORKERS IN THE UNITED STATES

It is less evident why, among the negative marginal productivity figures estimated, those for American blue-collar workers also occur, although at a very low level of significance. Yet two phenomena may be mentioned which are able to contribute to an explanation. One is that these lower-paid workers will, more often than other categories, be kept employed as a reserve for a quick increase in production whenever a cyclical change in business requires it. The year 1959 was one of steep recovery after the 1958 recession (cf. Duesenberry *et al.*, 1965, p. 254); part of the reserve may have therefore been present. Another factor that may affect blue-collar workers' marginal productivity is trade union policy. Of the various groups of workers, blue-collar workers are unionised to the highest degree. Several instances are known where unions have been able to compel employers to continue to employ workers even after their jobs had become superfluous as a consequence of reorganisation or the introduction of new technology. A well-known example from the past is the transition from steam locomotives to electrical or diesel traction. An important study (Olson, 1978), brought to our attention by Professor J. van den Doel, has been devoted to this subject.

Finally, part of blue-collar workers are small independents.

1.12 THE COEFFICIENTS FOR MANAGERIAL LABOUR

Tables 1.1 and 1.2 suggest that the marginal productivity of managers, administrators and proprietors, if introduced as a production factor with a market-determined compensation (as indicated in equation (1.8), based on (1.7)), is *not significantly different from zero*. Assuming that manager incomes are part of a residual income, as indicated in equations (1.1) to (1.6) regression equations leaving out the managerial group were estimated. These are shown in Table 1.3 which is comparable to Table 1.1.

The determination coefficients have changed little in comparison to Table 1.1, standard deviations of regression coefficients are somewhat smaller; the sum total of regression coefficients has risen—in Case III of the USA even beyond 1—but not significantly; the coefficient for blue-collar workers has now approached zero. All we can say would seem to be that the assumption of zero marginal productivity of the managerial hier-

Part I. Production

Table 1.3: Regression coefficients obtained in cross-section estimation of Cobb–Douglas function with several types of labour, excluding managerial, etc. and capital

Country	$\bar{R}^2$	Regression coefficients and standard deviations for labour types				T. of r.c. $(\sum \lambda)$
		Prof., techn.	White-c.w.	Blue-c.w.	Farm	
USA (III)	0.737	0.357 (0.159)	0.801 (0.198)	−0.025 (0.162)	−0.032 (0.025)	1.101
USA (IV)	0.740	0.242 (0.165)	0.806 (0.192)	−0.233 (0.191)	−0.069 (0.031)	0.746
Japan (III)	0.825	0.042 (0.081)	0.600 (0.086)	0.600 (0.086)	−0.075 (0.011)	0.567

Notes:
USA III: all states, and District of Columbia.
USA IV: all states

Abbreviations: See Table 1.1.

archy does not provide us with results very different from the market-income approach shown in Table 1.1.

Before drawing some conclusions from the estimates shown it seems proper to repeat the assumptions on which they are based:

(i) the relationship between factor inputs and product (production function) can be described by one and the same function for all states of the USA and for the District of Columbia, and another for all prefectures of Japan;
(ii) as factor inputs, five types of labour and a proxy for capital have been used; the latter has been described in section 1.6; and
(iii) as a first approximation to the production function the Cobb–Douglas function has been applied (i.e. the linear terms of a translog production function).

The main conclusion to be drawn on the determinants of managerial income is that *its relationship with productivity of this type of work* seems to be practically absent. The portion of total product to be attributed to the marginal managerial worker (that is, his productivity) is not significantly different from zero. If managerial income is residual the link with productivity doesn't exist, even in principle. The hierarchical distribution of the total residual—if there is one, as in most cases we considered—according to equation (1.9) has no link with productivity, but one with rank. Elsewhere, one of us (Tinbergen, 1979) has shown that top executive compensation in the United States is biased upward when compared with the hierarchy distribution of equation (1.9).

Our two dilemmas may now be answered as follows: (i) if managerial income is market-determined at all, then it is only to a very small extent; and (ii) in the USA the situation is not very different from what we have called 'macro constant returns to scale' (cf. section 1.4). This suggests that in that country there is an *ample reserve of approximately equally efficient medium* and *small-scale entrepreneurs*, able to run optimum-sized additional enterprises. In Japan, expansion of the number of such enterprises requires the activity of *less efficient additional entrepreneurs*. The low level of marginal productivity of the managerial hierarchy found for both countries supports the growing critical view on bureaucracies as expressed by Parkinson's law.

The impression that bureaucracies have expanded too much is not restricted to bureaucracies in the public sphere. Macrae (1967) sees deconcentration and decentralisation as the coming processes. An example of such decentralisation can be found in the Ministry of Foreign Affairs of the Federal Republic of Germany which has farmed out its bilateral technical assistance to developing countries to the GTZ, a public corporation. Among insiders of large private corporations, too, doubts exist whether the size of such hierarchies will continue to grow. The idea of deconcentration by subcontracting seems to gain purchase *vis-à-vis* the idea of 'empire building'. Thus, Hannah and Kay (1977) conclude their study on concentration by writing: 'We do not think that many benefits would be lost if merger were henceforth a rarer occurrence' (in Nieuwenhuysen, 1978); Fidder and Marcus (1978) point out that information systems in large (business) units leave much to be desired; and Balassa (1978) quotes Varga (1977) to suggest that in Hungary too diseconomies of scale in large firms occur. The reader may be aware of the larger than average size of firms in communist countries than in most western (though not Anglo-Saxon) countries (cf. *Statistisches Jahrbuch für die Bundesrepublik Deutschland* (1971), Wiesbaden, p. 44*–5*).

Finally decentralisation of decision-making by shifting it downwards is increasingly seen as a means of raising job satisfaction, and hence productivity.

NOTES

1. The main reason why we chose to use the Cobb–Douglas production function is its simplicity. Another reason is that we shall apply it to situations where the variables show relatively small deviations from their average, meaning

that the function can be seen as a first approximation to more complicated ones, such as the translog production function, and gives an impression of the situation at the margin of production for the nation considered.
2. These figures have been derived from the *World Bank Atlas* (1977), p. 20, assuming that the growth rate per annum of real *per capita* income of the USA over the period 1960–75 (2.5 per cent) could also be applied to the period 1959–75, and p. 16 for Japan.
3. From the figures mentioned in the article quoted, we estimated figures for 1960 which we combined with Census figures for employment.
4. This figure was obtained by courtesy of Professor M. Sattinger.
5. It seems appropriate to remind the reader of the fact that even incomes which traditionally have been treated as uniform, because they are market-determined, show considerable variation in statistics using the same denomination. Taking as an illustration the most homogeneous group we could find in the 1970 Census of the USA (*Earnings by Occupation and Education* (P.C.(2)-8B) (Washington 1973), p. 77)—mail-carriers, post-office, male, white, 35–54-years-old—18.4 per cent are outside the range $6000–9999—itself a considerable range. In this publication some of the factors making for income differences are shown: apart from colour and age, education is one.
6. Production has been measured as average income *per capita* for the units of observation in both countries. Quantities of labour of the categories shown have been measured as promilles of the labour force for the states of the USA and as promilles of population of the prefectures of Japan. These relative figures have been taken in order to eliminate the differences in size of the states or the prefectures. If absolute figures had been taken they would have been so highly correlated with the size that multicollinearity would have led to fully unreliable regression coefficients.

Since the percentage of total population which is part of the labour force varies between the Japanese prefectures, this percentage might have affected, as an additional independent variable, the dependent variable income *per capita*. Hence alternatives were run for both Japanese regression equations shown in Table 1.1. They showed a very small and insignificant impact on the results. This was understandable from the finding that incomes *per capita* are uncorrelated with the percentage of population in the labour force (the simple correlation coefficient amounting to 0.020). Moreover, the coefficient of variation (standard deviation divided by average) of the percentage in the labour force is 0.011 only and varies between 0.021 and 0.220 for the other independent variables.

REFERENCES

Cochrane, W.W. and Ryan, M.E. (1976), *American Farm Policy, 1948–1973*, Minneapolis.

Denison, E.F. and Chung, W.K. (1976) *How Japan's Economy Grew so Fast*, Washington.

Douglas, P.H. (1934), *The Theory of Wages*, New York.

Douglas, P.H. (1976) 'The Cobb–Douglas production function once again: its history, its testing, and some new empirical values', *Journal of Political Economy*, 84, p. 903.

Drucker, P.F. (1977), 'Is Executive pay excessive?', *The Wall Street Journal*, 23 May.
Duesenberry, J.S., Fromm, G., Klein, L.R. and Kuh, E. (1965), *The Brookings Quarterly Econometric Model of the United States*, Amsterdam.
Fidder, J.A. and Marcus, L. (1978), *'Ineffectieve informatiesystemen in het bedrijfsleven'* ['Ineffective Information Systems in Business'], *Intermediair* 29 September, p. 65.
Hannah, L. and Kay, J.A. (1977), *Concentration in Modern Industry: Theory, Measurement and the UK Experience*, Atlantic Highlands, NJ.
Hibbert, J., Griffin, T.J. and Walker, R.L. (1977), 'Development of estimates of the stock of fixed capital in the United Kingdom', *The Review of Income and Wealth*, 23 (no. 2), pp. 117ff.
Huppes, T. (1977), *Inkomensverdeling en institutionele structuur* [*Income Distribution and Institutional Structure*], Leiden.
Koike, H. (1979), 'Both business and labour unions are starting to assail government's agricultural policy', *The Japan Economic Journal*, 20 February.
Kuznets, S. (1966), *Modern Economic Growth*, New Haven and London.
Macrae, N. (1976), 'The new capitalism', *The Economist*, 25 December.
Nieuwenhuysen, J. (1978), 'Review', *Journal of Economic Literature* XVI, p. 1481.
Nordhaus, W. and Tobin, J. (1972), *Is Growth Obsolete?*, National Bureau of Economic Research, New York.
Olson, M. (1978), *The Political Economy of Comparative Growth Rates*, Conference University of Maryland.
Owen, W.F. (1966), 'The double developmental squeeze on agriculture', *The American Economic Review*, LVI, pp. 43ff.
Pen, J. (1971), *Income Distribution*, London.
Pen, J. and Tinbergen, J. (1977), *Naar een Rechtvaardiger Inkomensverdeling* [*Toward a More Equitable Income Distribution*], Amsterdam and Brussels.
Stokes, B. (1978), *Worker Participation—Productivity and the Quality of Work Life*, Worldwatch Paper 25, Washington, DC.
Tinbergen, J. (1942), 'Zur Theorie der langfristigen Wirtschaftsentwicklung', *Weltwirtschaftliches Archiv*, pp. 511ff. Republished in English (1959) as 'On the Theory of Trend Movements' in *Selected Papers*, Amsterdam.
Tinbergen, J. (1977), 'Income distribution: second thoughts', *De Economist*, 125, pp. 315–39.
Tinbergen, J. (1979), 'Hoogte en beïnvloedbaarheid van inkomens van "managers"' ['Level of and possibilities to influence manager incomes], in van den Goorbergh, W.M. *et al.* (eds), *Over macht en wet in het economisch gebeuren*, Opstellen aangeboden aan Prof. Dr. D.B.J. Schouten, Leiden and Antwerp. (Ch. 9 of this book).

2 Production Functions with Several Factors

2.1 INTRODUCTION

After Jacob Kol and I had published the text of Chapter 1 we discovered the study by Professor Peter Gottschalk (Gottschalk, 1978), who had developed an ingenious method for estimating more precisely production functions containing as independent variables a large number of quantities of production factors. In order to obtain larger t-values of the coefficients, he assumed that the production process considered to be a combination of two simultaneous processes using one of the factors j in common. The other factors are used by one process only. Indicating those used in process 1 (production proper, for instance) by m_h ($h = 1, \ldots, H$) and those in process 2 (administration, for instance) by n_k ($k = 1, \ldots, K$), we have:

$$y = f_1^0 j_1 + \sum_{h=1}^{H} f_h^1 m_h \tag{2.1}$$

$$y = f_2^0 j_2 + \sum_{k=1}^{K} f_k^2 n_k \tag{2.2}$$

$$j = j_1 + j_2 \tag{2.3}$$

All symbols indicate deviations from the variables' averages and these may be considered to be relatively small, permitting us to use linear formulae. Furthermore, y stands for total production, and j_i ($i = 1, 2$) for the quantities of j used by the processes 1 and 2. All coefficients f constitute marginal productivities.

2.2 THEORETICAL MODEL AND ESTIMATION PROCESS

It is useful to make a clear distinction between the theoretical model used by Gottschalk and the procedure of estimation of the coefficients. In the *theoretical model* we must consider as given the coefficients f, and all quantities of factors, that is, all m_h and n_k as well as j. The unknowns are y and the two j_i ($i = 1, 2$). Equations (2.1), (2.2) and (2.3) permit the solution, which is obtained as follows:

$$j_1 = \frac{y - \sum_h f_h^1 m_h}{f_1^0} = b_1(y - \sum_h f_h^1 m_h) = b_1(y - m) \tag{2.4}$$

$$j_2 = \frac{y - \sum_k f_k^2 n_k}{f_2^0} = b_2(y - \sum_k f_k^2 n_k) = b_2(y - n) \tag{2.5}$$

where $b_i = 1/f_i^0 (i = 1, 2)$, $m = \sum_h f_h^1 m_h$ and $n = \sum_k f_k^2 n_k$. Addition of (2.4) and (2.5) yields, writing b for $b_1 + b_2$:

$$j = by - b_1 m - b_2 n \tag{2.6}$$

from which we derive:

$$y = (j + b_1 m + b_2 n)/b \tag{2.7}$$

Substituting (2.7) into (2.4) and (2.5) we obtain:

$$j_1 = b_1(j - b_2 m + b_2 n)/b \tag{2.8}$$

$$j_2 = b_2(j + b_1 m - b_1 n)b \tag{2.9}$$

For a discussion of these results it is preferable to return to the f;

$$y = \frac{f_1^0 f_2^0}{f_1^0 + f_2^0} j + \sum_h \frac{f_h^1 f_2^0}{f_1^0 + f_2^0} m_h + \sum_k \frac{f_k^2 f_1^0}{f_1^0 + f_2^0} n_k \tag{2.10}$$

This formula is identical to Gottschalk's. An essential deviation from Gottschalk's article occurs when we interpret our equations (2.8) and (2.9). These show that j_1 and j_2 cannot be replaced by a linear expression in j and m respectively j and n only; both j_1 and j_2 depend on j, m and n. The coefficients of equations (2.1) and (2.2) cannot be estimated by replacing the j_i ($i = 1, 2$) by j, as done by Gottschalk. We shall call his procedure Method I.

We have to add two assumptions linking the quantities of the production factors:

$$n = A_{20} j + A_{21}(b_1/b_2) m \tag{2.11}$$

$$m = A_{10} j + A_{12}(b_2/b_1) n \tag{2.12}$$

or, substituting either of these relations into Equation (2.7) respectively, and reintroducing here also the f for m and n:

$$y = \frac{1 + b_2 A_{20}}{b} j + \frac{b_1(1 + A_{21})}{b} \sum_h f_h^1 m_h \tag{2.13}$$

and
$$y = \frac{1 + b_1 A_{10}}{b} j + \frac{b_2 (1 + A_{12})}{b} \sum_k f_k^2 n_k \qquad (2.14)$$

It is not easy to give a theoretical meaning to the four coefficients A. Their significance is empirical: A_{10} and A_{12} are the weights to be given to j and n so as to find the best approximation to m; and A_{20} and A_{21} are the weights to be given to j and m, so as to obtain the best approximation to n.

So far we have discussed the theoretical model behind Gottschalk's thesis. We now proceed to the *estimation procedure*. Its task is to estimate four types of regression equations, namely (2.13) and (2.14) that Gottschalk wants to know, in order to derive the fs which are now our *unknowns*, *plus* the equations (2.11) and (2.12), which we need to justify Gottschalk's approach. Writing Bs for the coefficients we have to estimate empirically the regression equations are:

$$y = B_1^0 j + \sum_h B_h^1 m_h \qquad (2.15)$$

$$y = B_2^0 j + \sum_k B_k^2 n_k \qquad (2.16)$$

$$\sum_k B_k^2 n_k = B_{20} j + B_{21} \sum_h B_h^1 m_h \qquad (2.17)$$

$$\sum_h B_h^1 m_h = B_{10} j + B_{12} \sum_k B_k^2 n_k \qquad (2.18)$$

Here (2.15) corresponds to (2.13), (2.16) to (2.14), (2.17) to (2.11) and (2.18) to (2.12). The corresponding pairs show what the theoretical coefficient complexes are which the B represent:

$$(2.15) \equiv (2.13) \text{ yields } B_1^0 = (1 + b_2 A_{20})/b \qquad (2.19)$$

$$(2.16) \equiv (2.14) \text{ yields } B_2^0 = (1 + b_1 A_{10})/b \qquad (2.20)$$

$$(2.15) \equiv (2.13) \text{ also yields } B_h^1 = b_1 (1 + A_{21}) f_h^1 / b \qquad (2.21)$$

$$(2.16) \equiv (2.14) \text{ also yields } B_k^2 = b_2 (1 + A_{12}) f_k^2 / b \qquad (2.22)$$

From the latter two types of relations we derive expressions of the f_h^1 and f_k^2:

$$f_h^1 = b B_h^1 / b_1 (1 + A_{21}) \qquad (2.23)$$

$$f_k^2 = b B_k^2 / b_2 (1 + A_{12}) \qquad (2.24)$$

Introducing these expressions into (2.17) and (2.18) we obtain:

$$\sum_k B_k^2 n_k = \frac{b_2 A_{20} (1 + A_{12})}{b} j + \frac{b A_{21}}{b_1} \frac{1 + A_{12}}{(1 + A_{21})^2} \sum_h B_h^1 m_h \qquad (2.25)$$

$$\sum_h B_h^1 m_h = \frac{b_1 A_{10} (1 + A_{21})}{b} j + \frac{b A_{12}}{b_2} \frac{1 + A_{21}}{(1 + A_{12})^2} \sum_k B_k^2 n_k \qquad (2.26)$$

Confrontation with (2.17) yields:

$$B_{20} = b_2(1 + A_{12})A_{20}/b \tag{2.27}$$

$$B_{10} = b_1(1 + A_{21})A_{10}/b \tag{2.28}$$

$$B_{21} = \frac{1 + A_{12}}{(1 + A_{21})^2} \frac{bA_{21}}{b_1} \tag{2.29}$$

$$B_{12} = \frac{1 + A_{21}}{(1 + A_{12})^2} \frac{bA_{12}}{b_2} \tag{2.30}$$

Equations (2.19)–(2.22) and (2.27)–(2.30), $6 + H + K$ in number, contain the unknowns A, b_1, b_2, f_h^1 and f_k^2, also numbering $6 + H + K$ and admit solution for these unknowns.

2.3 AN APPLICATION TO THE UNITED STATES

As an illustration we consider a production function for the USA using the logarithms of the following production factor numbers:

x_1 = professional and technical workers

x_2 = managers and administrators

x_3 = white-collar workers

x_4 = blue-collar workers

x_5 = farm managers and workers

k = capital, represented by a proxy (described in Chapter 1).

The figures used are those for the 50 states and the District of Columbia in 1959 (*Census of Population*, 1960). Table 2.1 shows the regression coefficients found in Tinbergen and Kol (Chapter 1 of this book), the Gottschalk method, and the Gottschalk–Tinbergen method. For the T–K coefficient standard deviations of the regression coefficients have been added in parentheses.

As an illustration of the improved reliability obtained with the aid of Gottschalk's method, Table 2.2 shows the coefficients and their standard deviations for the two processes used.*

---

* I would like to thank Professor Gottschalk for having computed these equations.

Table 2.1: Regression coefficients for the log of six production factors, USA 1959 (51 observations), and their sum, three methods

Method	x_1	x_2	x_3	x_4	x_5	k	Sum
T–K	0.26	0.09	0.70	−0.23	−0.05	0.19	0.96
	(0.19)	(0.14)	(0.22)	(0.22)	(0.03)	(0.14)	—
G	0.22	−0.02	0.54	−0.24	−0.05	0.07	0.51
G–T	0.30	−0.03	0.87	−0.20	−0.04	0.06	0.95

Abbreviations:
T–K: Tinbergen and Kol (1980)
G: Gottschalk (1978)
G–T: Gottschalk and Tinbergen

Table 2.2: Production functions for the two processes

Technical production:

$$y = 0.48\ x_1 - 0.53\ x_4 - 0.11\ x_5 + 0.17\ k \qquad \bar{R}^2 = 0.69$$
$$\ (0.16)\quad\ (0.23)\quad\ (0.03)\quad\ (0.07)$$

Administration:

$$y = 0.40\ x_1 - 0.05\ x_2 + 0.97\ x_3 \qquad \bar{R}^2 = 0.72$$
$$\ (0.18)\quad\ (0.14)\quad\ (0.19)$$

It is striking that all coefficients, except the one for managers and administrators, have a high *t*-value and confirm the negative marginal productivity of blue-collar workers and farm managers and workers. The explanation may be, for the former, that many enterprises maintain a reserve of blue-collar workers (cf. Hart and Robb, 1980): and for the latter that (i) farming is for many people a hobby, implying that labour costs of family members are strongly underestimated; and (ii) often a maximum crop is aimed at instead of maximum profits.

REFERENCES

Gottschalk, P.T. (1978), 'A comparison of marginal productivity and earnings by occupation', *Industrial and Labor Relations Review*, 31, no. 3, pp. 368–78.

Hart, R.A. and Robb, A.L. (1980), 'Production and labour demand functions with endogenous fixed worker costs', IIM/80-11, *Publication Series of the International Institute of Management*, Wissenschaftszentrum, Berlin.

Tinbergen, J. and Kol, J. (1980), 'Market-determined and residual incomes— some dilemmas', *Economie Appliquée* July, XXXIII, pp. 285–301, (Chapter 1 of this book.)

3 Constraints on Production Functions: Essential *vs.* Non-essential Factors*

3.1 PRODUCTION FUNCTIONS ARE USED FOR DIFFERENT PURPOSES

Production functions have become a subject of rapidly increasing attention for economists and increasing sophistication in econometric procedures. In view of the wide range of subjects covered by Professor Gelting's work, it is a subject with many links to that work.

The main point of focus in this chapter will be the question: what constraints have to be imposed on a mathematical function in order that it may qualify as a production function? Different authors have formulated varying constraints. To a considerable extent this may be due to differences between the purposes for which production functions can be, and are being, used. Thus, there is a different behaviour in short-term and long-term processes. Or, in situations of disequilibrium and of equilibrium, in the labour market compartments involved. The purpose of the use of production functions may be to maximise national income—a question of the choice of branches and technologies—or the purpose may be to study income distribution (cf. Wegner, 1981).

An example of a constraint to a production function is that its first derivatives should be positive (i.e. that increased inputs of production factors lead to increased output). There are situations, however, where this need not be true. In the very labour-intensive process of constructing, say, a dam, increased numbers of workers may reduce total output by the necessity of queuing. The expansion of a hierarchy may create irritation and so reduce production (cf. Tinbergen, 1981). However, it is not the intention to pursue this example further.

---

* The author would like to express his thanks for useful discussions with and information from Professors T. Kloek and J. Hartog, Dr P.M.C. de Boer and Dr E. Wegner.

3.2 GROUPING OF PRODUCTION FACTORS

Strictly speaking, the number of production factors in most production processes is large, even very large. There are very many types of labour and of equipment, and many different materials may have to be used. In order to understand the main macroeconomic relationships it has been found helpful to group similar types of production factors. The early attempts to study production processes (those made by Douglas, 1934, for instance) used very large aggregates, subsuming all production factors into two or three groups. For manufacturing industry only labour and capital, for national production labour, capital and land (or natural resources) were used. In the last few decades, however, a larger number of groups have been introduced, but even so, for a long time that number did not surpass four. Denison's approach (1962, 1967, 1974, 1976, 1979), although not formally presented as a production function, took into account a number of characteristics (working hour, sex, education) for which he corrects, but which does not permit to speak of a 'number' of factors. Bowles (1970) used capital and three groups of labour with different levels of education. Other authors classified labour as blue-collar and white-collar (e.g. Berndt and Christensen, 1973 a and b) and capital in structures and equipment. Alternatively, after energy prices had become a new problem, Berndt and Wood (1974) introduced capital, labour, materials and energy. Ullman Chiswick (1972) used two types of labour (production and non-production workers) and capital. In a later study (1978) she used six factors, distinguishing between modern and traditional sectors for capital and one type of labour (middle-level), considering unskilled and high-level labour in addition. Similar numbers were also used by Gottschalk (1978), who used capital and six types of labour (managers, professional, sales, and 'supporting' workers, craftsmen and operatives). Similarly, Tinbergen and Kol (1980) used capital, managers, professional, white-collar, blue-collar and farm workers.

In a theoretical study, Tinbergen introduced groups of labour with two characteritics, represented by indices (say h and h'), whose quantities or frequencies (ϕ) could therefore be presented in matrix form, using the rows for different values of h and the columns for h'. One example is that h indicates required, and h' actual (or available) levels of education (schooling years). The fundamental reason for introducing two-index labour types may be that some relationship between the two indices is desirable, though not necessarily fulfilled. Clearly, it is desirable that a person's actual schooling approximates to his job's required schooling. This sort of relationship may also be desirable in other cases. A second example is that the indices indicate the locations of the workplace and the home—a short distance is, within limits, desirable. Apart from schooling, personality traits may have to be related to required capabilities, for instance, innate features such as creativity, leadership or physical strength and perseverance.

An interesting corollary of two-index quantities is the possibility of introducing two types of demand or supply elasticities, one in respect with h and one with regard to h'.[1] From the example given, it follows that apart from two, a type of labour may be characterised by four or six indices. In mathematical terms that implies that they can only be arranged into a complex of more than two dimensions (a matrix has two), known as tensors.

3.3 CONSTRAINTS ON PRODUCTION FUNCTIONS: ESSENTIAL *VS.* NON-ESSENTIAL FACTORS OF PRODUCTION

We are now able to take up the main theme of this essay. Production functions can be represented by many different mathematical functions, and in the last few decades a large number have been proposed and tested using empirical data. In section 3.1 we mentioned—but rejected—one constraint often believed to be necessary. In the present section we shall discuss possible constraints on the simplest form of the CES (constant elasticity of substitution) production function. We write that function as:

$$y^{-\varrho} = \sum a_{hh'} \phi_{hh'}^{-\varrho} \qquad (3.1)$$

where y is production per employee, $\phi_{hh'}$, the frequency of the labour type (h, h') and ϱ and $a_{hh'}$ are parameters of the function chosen. From the definition of the ϕ it follows that:

$$\sum_h \sum_{h'} \phi_{hh'} = 1 \qquad (3.2)$$

The constraints we propose to discuss are those on ϱ. This parameter is related to the Allen elasticity of substitution by the relationship:

$$\sigma = 1/(1 + \varrho) \qquad (3.3)$$

Schim van der Loeff and Harkema (1975) formulate the constraint on ϱ as:

$$-1 < \varrho < \infty \text{ (hence } 0 < \sigma < \infty) \qquad (3.4)$$

de Boer (1981) claims that:

$$0 < \varrho \text{ (hence } 0 < \sigma < 1) \qquad (3.5)$$

In this chapter I shall propose that:

$$-1 < \varrho < 0 \text{ (hence } 1 < \sigma < \infty) \qquad (3.6)$$

This seeming contradiction reflects the different purposes for which production functions are used by each of us. De Boer wants the production factor he introduces to be 'essential', i.e. that production becomes zero if such a factor is not used (its input being zero). The production factors to be studied in the present chapter are non-essential, i.e. production may be positive if one or more is not used. Non-essentiality does not mean that they are not relevant. On the contrary, in a number of problems they play an important role. The two-index factors mentioned in Section 3.2 in particular may serve as an example. If the two indices refer to capabilities required and capabilities available, a situation where some capabilities are scarce may make it necessary to employ workers on jobs where capabilities required are greater than capabilities available. If the two indices refer to work and home locations, their difference is important for the study of traffic problems. Yet, a particular value of the distance between the locations may not be 'essential' for the production process the worker considered is engaged in.

The cases we are interested in are those where a quantity of some production factor equals zero, and yet the volume of production is positive. For this to happen we can see from equation (3.1) that the exponent $-\varrho$ of a $\phi_{hh'} = 0$ should be positive: otherwise a term ∞ would enter into the right-hand side and make $y = 0$. Hence the constraint (3.6). This implies higher values of σ than produced by constraint (3.5). Since, as a rule, essential factors will be less numerous than non-essential ones, it stands to reason that their substitution elasticities are lower than those for non-essential factors.

From this it will be clear that all production factors entering into Cobb–Douglas, translog or Leontief (input–output) production functions are essential features.

3.4 ILLUSTRATION OF THE USE OF NON-ESSENTIAL PRODUCTION FACTORS: INTRODUCTION

In order to illustrate the use of CES production functions containing non-essential production factors data of the American Census of Population 1970 have been used, Report PC(1) 1, Table 231, giving a cross-tabulation of 76.5 million workers in 1969 for education (years of schooling) and occupation (main occupational groups). In order to keep the example both manageable and clear, education as well as occupation have been subdivided into three levels, indicated as 1, 2, and 3. For education, level 1 includes up to three years' high school, level 2 from four years' high school to three years' college, and level 3 four or more years' college. For occupational groups we defined level 3 as professional and technical workers, level 2 as white-collar, and level 1 as blue-collar workers. Level 2 consists of clerical and sales workers. Managers, administrators, etc. are the subject of separate treatment: here Cases I, II and III have been distinguished. In Case I, managers, etc. are added to occupational level 2; in Case II they have been included in level 1 because of the capabilities required; and in Case III managers, etc. have been put into the educational levels which they actually attained. All other occupational groups have been considered blue-collar workers. An important assumption is at the basis of the whole exercise, namely that occupational level 1 is in need of educational level 1, i.e that blue-collar workers need up to three years' high school in order to perform well in their jobs); similarly that white-collar workers need level 2 education, and professional and technical workers need level 3 education. Put differently, the *required* level of schooling is level 1 for blue-collar workers; the required level of schooling for occupational groups 2 (white-collar workers) is level 2 and for group 3 is level 3.[2] In other words, we have tried to approximate required levels h by the occupational groups listed, in order to contrast them with actual levels h' of education as defined.

This resulted in two 3×3 matrices, one, Φ, for $\phi_{hh'}$, and one, Y, for the corresponding earnings $y_{hh'}$; both in three versions I, II, and III as set out in connection with the treatment of the managerial group. Both matrices can be bordered; the ϕ with the total of rows and of columns, both of which add up to 1 or 1000 per mille. Row totals refer to the three values of h, and can be written as ϕ_h and constitute promilles in the three occupational groups. Column totals add up for education levels h' and are written $\phi_{.h'}$. They indicate the promilles of the working force with educational level h'. The y matrix is bordered not by sums, but by weighted mean earnings. The corresponding y_h are mean earnings of occupational group h and the $y_{.h'}$ mean earnings of educational levels. Weighted means of both lead to the average earnings of all workers considered, y (cf. Table 3.1).

3.5 ESTIMATION PROCEDURE OF PRODUCTION FUNCTIONS (I, II, III, ϱ)

In this exercise we have chosen the simplest estimation procedure conceivable, where no error terms occur since we have a number of unknowns equal to the number of observations: it may be called nonstochastic. The value of ϱ has been chosen at various levels, satisfying our constraint, $-1 < \varrho < 0$, later reduced to only two levels, $-1/3$ and $-2/3$. The remaining unknowns are the nine $a_{hh'}$, and the nine earnings equations, assumed to be equal to their marginal productivities.[3] These equations may be written:

$$a_{hh'} = y_{hh'} \left(\frac{\phi_{hh'}}{y}\right)^{\varrho+1} \quad h, h' = 1, 2, 3, \tag{3.7}$$

It goes without saying that stochastic estimation methods using, for instance, data for all states or for all state economic areas, are preferable. This would require very considerable data collection, and may be left to later, or to other authors. The illustrative nature of what follows should be kept in mind. Table 3.1 shows the matrices Φ and Y for the three versions of classifying managers, administrators, etc.

Table 3.1: Matrices Φ of frequencies and Y of earnings for the three alternative classifications of managers, etc.

	Φ (in promilles)					Y (in $10 p.a.)			

Version I: Managers classified as level 2 occupations (white-collar)

$h \backslash h'$	1	2	3	Total	$h \backslash h'$	1	2	3	Average
1	300	210	8	518 ϕ_1	1	545	635	827	587 y_1
2	78	220	36	334 ϕ_2	2	640	664	1359	739 y_2
3	9	56	83	148 ϕ_3	3	725	783	1136	980 y_3
Total	387	486	127	1000	Average	567	665	1181	697
	$\phi_{.1}$	$\phi_{.2}$	$\phi_{.3}$			$y_{.1}$	$y_{.2}$	$y_{.3}$	y

Version II: Managers classified as level 1 occupations (professional, technical)

$h \backslash h'$	1	2	3	Total	$h \backslash h'$	1	2	3	Average
1	292	220	8	520 ϕ_1	1	545	635	827	587 y_1
2	51	174	18	243 ϕ_2	2	525	542	1004	573 y_2
3	28	103	106	237 ϕ_3	3	877	936	1238	1065 y_3
Total	371	497	132	1000	Average	567	665	1181	697
	$\phi_{.1}$	$\phi_{.2}$	$\phi_{.3}$			$y_{.1}$	$y_{.2}$	$y_{.3}$	y

Version III: Managers distributed over educational levels

$h \backslash h'$	1	2	3	Total	$h \backslash h'$	1	2	3	Average
1	311	220	8	539 ϕ_1	1	570	635	827	600 y_1
2	51	220	18	289 ϕ_2	2	525	664	1004	661 y_2
3	9	57	106	172 ϕ_3	3	724	783	1238	1061 y_3
Total	371	497	132	1000	Average	567	665	1181	697
	$\phi_{.1}$	$\phi_{.2}$	$\phi_{.3}$			$y_{.1}$	$y_{.2}$	$y_{.3}$	y

Table 3.2 shows the values of $a_{hh'}$, found, as well as their proportion in promilles of their total. These represent the $a'_{hh'}$ if the average a is added as a multiplicative factor when writing the production function

$$y^{-\varrho} = a \sum a'_{hh'} \phi_{hh'}^{-\varrho} \quad (\sum a'_{hh'} = 1) \qquad (3.1')$$

Table 3.2: Values obtained for $a_{hh'}$ and $a'_{hh'}$ for each manager classification and values of ϱ equal to $-1/3$ and $-2/3$

	$a_{hh'}$	I, −1/3	I, −2/3	II, −1/3	II, −2/3	III, −1/3	III, −2/3
$h, h' =$	11	3.107	41.15	3.05	40.78	3.33	43.56
	12	2.854	42.57	2.94	43.24	2.94	43.24
	13	0.421	18.65	0.42	18.65	0.42	18.65
	21	1.486	30.84	0.92	21.96	0.92	21.96
	22	3.078	45.21	2.15	34.13	3.08	45.21
	23	1.885	50.61	0.88	39.68	0.88	29.68
	31	0.399	17.00	1.03	30.04	0.40	17.00
	32	1.458	33.79	2.62	49.49	1.48	33.99
	33	2.750	55.89	3.53	66.08	3.53	66.08
	$\sum a_{hh'}$	17.438	335.71	17.54	334.05	16.98	319.36
	1000 $a'_{hh'}$						
$h, h' =$	11	178	123	174	122	196	136
	12	164	127	168	129	173	135
	13	24	56	24	56	25	58
	21	85	92	52	66	54	69
	22	177	135	123	102	181	142
	23	108	151	50	89	52	93
	31	23	51	59	90	24	53
	32	84	101	149	148	87	106
	33	158	166	201	198	208	207

3.6 PROBLEMS CONSIDERED AND SOLUTIONS FOUND

Having obtained the CES production function—at least, in an illustrative way—we propose to consider some problems which may be solved with it. Seven problems have been selected:

1. If all workers are given an occupation corresponding with their education (i.e. Φ becomes diagonal with values $\phi_{.h'}$) what becomes y?
2. In that same situation, what becomes r, the ratio between y_{33} and y_{11}?
3. If all workers have attained the educational level required by their occupation (i.e. Φ becomes diagonal with values $\phi_{h.}$), what values assumes y?

4. In the same situation as under 3, what becomes r?
5. If, in order to equalise incomes in a situation where all have attained the educational level corresponding with jobs held, how many must have attained a university education (i.e. what must $\phi_{.3}$ be)?
6. As 5, where a difference between education and occupation is admitted.
7. If the ratio r has to be reduced to 1.5, and education level attained corresponds with occupation, how many have to attain a university education (i.e. what must $\phi_{.3}$ be)?

The solutions are shown in Table 3.3 in which, apart from the values given to ϱ and hence to σ, the initial values (i.e. those prevailing in Table 3.1) of r and $\phi_{.3}$ (r^0 and $\phi^0_{.3}$) have been added.

Table 3.3 Solutions of seven problems in six cases (classification of managers and elasticity of substitution), for all of which, $y^0 = 697$

Problems				1	2	3	4	5	6	7
ϱ	σ	r^0	$\phi^0_{.3}$	y	r	y	r	$\phi_{.3}$	$\phi_{.3}$	$\phi_{.3}$
I. Managers classified as white-collar workers										
−1/3	1.5	2.084	0.127	223	2.040	225	1.860	0.295	0.275	0.175
−2/3	3	2.084	0.127	511	2.062	511	1.969	0.519	0.498	0.287
II. Managers classified as professional or technical workers										
−1/3	1.5	2.272	0.237	184	1.954	214	2.305	0.44	0.28	0.175
−2/3	3	2.272	0.237	460	2.106	524	2.287	0.73	0.58	0.287
III. Managers distributed over three education levels actually attained										
−1/3	1.5	2.172	0.172	291	2.27	275	2.111	0.37	0.285	0.220
−2/3	3	2.172	0.172	561	2.22	574	2.140	0.62	0.51	0.700

3.7 COMMENTS AND CONCLUSIONS

Our findings and some tentative conclusions are given under three headings:

(a) Relevance of non-essential two-index production factors
It seems to be clear that the introduction of non-essential production factors makes sense in situations of scarcity of some types of labour (e.g. highly educated), namely, if an educational disequilibrium prevails. Non-essential factors may also occur when deviations between the location of work and dwelling exist.

(b) Limitations of our illustrations
One important limitation is the assumption of only one job characteristic

and corresponding personality trait—the educational or intellectual one. Much would be gained if more information could be used regarding social intelligence, or the capability to deal with people, which play an important role for managers and sales workers. Another limitation consists of the use of the minimum set of observations, assuming that no stochastic components are at work. As remarked before, the use of state or state economic areas may reduce this limitation.

(c) Results of some relevance

Nevertheless, some results of our primitive illustration may be significant. Our range of elasticities of substitution is below those found by Ullman Chiswick, Berndt and co-workers, de Boer and others, because they used a relatively small number of essential factors. Our elasticities are larger than those found for time series, which yield short-term elasticities.

The reduction in y, standing for total production per employee, in comparison to y^0, constitutes an indication that the correspondence between occupation and education is not very rigid—a well-known fact. This also reflects itself in the a-values. Those for $hh' = 12$ are close to 11 and sometimes even surpass it. On the other hand, and understandably, the a_{13} and a_{31} are quite low. In one out of six cases considered in Table 3.2, namely I, $-1/3$, the a-values are unacceptable: $a_{11} > a_{33}$.

The results obtained for Problems 5, 6 and 7 are less easy to comment upon. They all deal with attempts to reduce income inequality by raising educational levels. Depending on the intuitive answers one has in mind, the conclusions—especially for the cases where $\varrho = -2/3$—may be that such an equalisation—or, as in Problem 7, a move into that direction—is impossible (the figures for $\phi_{.3}$ are unrealistically high) or it may be that $\varrho = -2/3$ is not an acceptable value. The usual conclusion that more research is desirable seems to be the only one left. Turning to $\varrho = -1/3$ then, the answers to Problems 6 and 7 indicate that the additional education required is not excessive. This answer does not apply, though, if the recent trend of less interest in education persists.

NOTES

1. This point was made in my book, *Income Distribution* (1975), but errors were made in the elaboration of the concepts.
2. At the time of writing, R.W. Rumberger's 'The changing skill requirements of jobs in the US economy', *Industrial and Labor Relations Review* (1981) 34, pp. 578–90 was not known to me. In this article, Rumberger only mentions the ϕ_h, moreover.

3. We adhere to this neoclassical proposition, even though elsewhere we discuss the evidence against it. (Tinbergen and Kol, 1980; Tinbergen, 1981).

REFERENCES

Berndt, E.R. and Christensen, L.R., (1973a), 'The specification of technology in US manufacturing', *Discussion Paper*, 73–17, University of British Columbia, Dept. of Economics.

Berndt, E.R. and Christensen, L.R., (1973b), 'The translog function and the substitution of equipment, structures and labor in US manufacturing, 1929-1968', *Journal of Econometrics*, 1, pp. 81ff.

Berndt, E.R. and Wood, D.O. (1974), 'Technology, prices and the derived demand for energy', *Discussion Paper*, 74–09, The University of British Columbia, Dept. of Economics.

Boer, P.M.C. de (1981), *Price Effects in Input–Output Relations: A Theoretical and Empirical Study for the Netherlands*, Utrecht, Drukkerij Elinkwijk B.V.

Bowles, S. (1970), 'The aggregation of labor inputs in the study of growth and planning: experiments with a two-level CES function', *Journal of Political Economy*, pp. 68–81.

Denison, E.F. (1962), *The Sources of Economic Growth in the United States and the Alternative Before Us*, Washington, DC, The Brookings Institution.

Denison, E.F. (1967), *Why Growth Rates Differ*, Washington, DC, The Brookings Institution.

Denison, E.F. (1974), *Accounting for United States Economic Growth 1929–1969*, Washington, DC, The Brookings Institution.

Denison, E.F. (1976), *How Japan's Economy Grew So Fast*, Washington, DC, The Brookings Institution.

Denison, E.F. (1979), *Accounting for Slower Economic Growth*, Washington, DC, The Brookings Institution.

Douglas, P.H. (1934), *The Theory of Wages*, New York, Macmillan.

Gottschalk, P.T. (1978), 'A comparison of marginal productivity and earnings by occupation', *Industrial and Labor Relations Review*, 31, pp. 368–78.

Schim van der Loeff, S. and Harkema, R. (1979), 'A note on aggregation of CES-type production functions', *European Economic Review*, 6, p. 97–101.

Tinbergen, J. and Kol, J. (1980), 'Market-determined and residual incomes: some dilemmas', *Economie appliquée*, XXXIII, pp. 285–301.

Tinbergen, J. (1981) 'Contraproduktie', in Eygelshoven, P.J. and van Gemerden, L.J. (eds), *Inkomensverdeling en openbare financiën*, Utrecht/Antwerpen, Het Spectrum (Chapter 4 of this book).

Ullman Chiswick, C.J. (1972), *The Growth of Professional Occupations in the American Labor Force: 1900–1963*, Washington, DC, World Bank (based on Columbia University dissertation).

Ullman Chiswick, C.J. (1978) 'Growth policy and the distribution of income', in Krelle, W. and Shorrocks, A.F. (eds), *Personal Income Distribution*, Amsterdam, New York and Oxford, North-Holland.

Wegner, E. (1981), *Die personelle Verteilung der Arbeitseinkommen: betriebliche Herrschaft und Lohnstruktur*, Frankfurt and New York, Campus-Verlag.

4 Counterproduction

4.1 DEFINITION AND EXAMPLES

In this chapter I propose to discuss a number of phenomena which can be subsumed under one category, which I shall call *counterproduction*. I could also have opted—following physics—for anti-production (similar to anti-matter), because the phenomena under discussion annihilate certain parts of social production, which thus vanish. I opted for counterproduction since this corresponds with the phrase counter-productive, already in use. By counterproduction I mean acts of individuals in the economy which negate other individuals' production, and so reduce social product.

Traditionally, not all activities of an economy's individuals are dealt with by economic science. The latter limits itself to the economic aspects of these activities. For instance, the treatment of criminal acts is left to criminology; acts which damage health are left to medical experts; polluting activities to ecologists; irritation aroused by superiors in a hierarchy with those supervised may be dealt with by labour psychologists; and so on. Each of these activities also implies some counterproduction. Discussing them can be done in two ways. We may discuss them with a criminologist, a medical expert, an ecologist, etc., in which case we are doing interdisciplinary research. This type of cooperation is expanding considerably, and in practical life has played a role for a long time, although perhaps informally. The other way to discuss the phenomena in question is to introduce them into economic science. This type of territorial expansion has been occurring for a long time and, as a matter of course, enhances the degree of realism of economic science. It also facilitates cooperation.

In this chapter attention will be given, among other things, to *competition* between two or more large enterprises, and the activities connected with it. Part of an enterprise's hierarchy is charged with *neutralising*, by advertising or by other types of information, the corresponding activities of similar enterprises. If during a given period the market shares of the enterprises considered do not change, the product of the advertising campaign organised by the marketing personnel of one firm has been neutralised by counterproduction in the other firms.

We shall also discuss other forms of counterproduction, two of which are *bureaucracy* and *independence*. These attempts at enriching economic science sprang from econometric research undertaken (cf. Chapters 1 and 2) to establish production functions for the United States and for Japan in which four or five types of labour and a proxy for capital were introduced.

The introduction into economic science of some forms of counterproduction may indeed constitute an enrichment. In section 4.2 I shall attempt such an expansion. Before doing so, I want to consider the question of whether such an expansion makes sense. It contrasts in a way with the process of specialisation in most sciences; and that specialisation has brought considerable advantages, as has specialisation in production. Can we find a criterion to distinguish useful expansions from less useful ones? To me, it seems that the addition of certain phenomena to the traditional territory of a science is particularly useful—or even necessary—if these new phenomena have a *feedback* on the traditional aspects of that science.

4.2 AN ECONOMIC THEORY ENRICHED WITH SOME CONCEPTS

Jan Pen, in whose honour this chapter was originally written, in his doctoral thesis (Pen, 1950), gives an example of an enriched theory, able to explain the establishment of a *collective labour agreement*. The expansion to be discussed there is clearly of another type. In Pen's thesis a dual monopoly was studied: here a market with limited competition is considered.

In an attempt to integrate into economic theory some phenomena able to cause counterproduction I start from the presentation of the theory chosen in my treatment of economic policy problems (Tinbergen, 1956). In it the concept of 'actor' is used, which is wider than that of 'transactor' used in the construction of national accounts. Actors need not be involved in transactions with others. Even so, they are a part of the total population. The young and the old may not be active in any economic sense, even though we consider *schooling* and *household work* as economic activities. A particular role is played by the use of leisure, part of which belongs to the production process. Actors perform activities which are determined by certain expectations and plans. Important activities for economic theory are those in the *production* process. They may be performed by *independent* actors or by actors *dependent* on others. Independent actors may occur in *small* or in *large* production units: the latter especially may be indicated as the (sociological) group of the *organisers of production*. In that group we also find the leading civil servants.

The dependent actors supply their labour or capital to one or more of the *factor markets*, in which *labour markets* are by far the most important. These are subdivided into labour market *compartments*, for each occupation. The nature of occupation on jobs can be dscribed by *job evaluation*.

An actor may also participate in economic life in her or his *leisure time*. Here (although not exclusively here) *legal* and *illegal* activities may be distinguished; examples of the latter are offences and criminal acts. Examples of the former, political activities; for others either type of activity may be their occupation.

Participation in factor markets can assume various forms, and so we speak of *market forms* (cf. Von Stackelberg, 1934). The individual considered may act on the supply or on the demand side; on the latter we find the organisers of production, mentioned before. A second characteristic of a market is the *number* of demanders or suppliers. If these are very large we approach the situation of *free* or *perfect* competition; at the other end of the spectrum we have *monopoly* or *monopsony*; in between, we may speak of imperfect or limited competition. A third characteristic, important especially in the last market form, is that of *quantity*, *price* or *quality adapter*. This brings us to the question: which *action parameters* or instruments are used by a given individual or group?

An elaboration of the picture essential to our aim consists of a more precise description of what we call imperfect competition. More action parameters exist than are usually dealt with in the theory of imperfect competition (cf. Chamberlin, 1933, 1948; Robinson, 1933; Kuenne (ed.), 1967). In particular, the *counterproductive* aspect of advertising and similar activities is not dealt with; the fact that the persons involved are required to reduce or neutralise the impact of other individuals' activities.

Then, we have to be aware of the fact that not all production is for sale on markets. In particular public administration, which supposedly produces *public goods*, operates in a quite different way. Output is not evaluated by buyers but by governments at various levels and ultimately by parliaments, also at different levels, and in the last resort by voters (cf. van den Doel, 1978).

Large enterprises and public administrations have in common their being *hierarchies*. The actors operate in a system in which counterproductive forces may develop. These forces, the *bureaucracy*, are a phenomenon which have more often been discussed in the last few decades, a well-known example being Parkinson's law. Within as well as between hierarchies many forms of counterproduction occur. One is the question of *competence*. Recently attention has been paid increasingly to the negative impact of a command hierarchy on *job satisfaction* and hence *productivity* at the lower levels. Here action parameters play a role which economic theory has hardly analysed so far. *Duplication of work* is one example, and constitutes a form of counterproduction. Activities not serving the interests of the hierarchy as a whole but only part of it and operating to the disadvantage of the supposed tasks are another. One may think too of the expenditures made, not because the goods bought are needed, but in order to avoid budget reductions of an item next year.

Many actors' tasks are the output or intake of *information*. The importance of this is now generally understood, and we shall discuss it in a more general sense below.

For many activities an *income* is paid. This may vary from *wages* or *salaries*, to the appropriation of a legally-obtained *residual* after deduction of costs from gross revenue, to the illegal appropriation of spoils from theft or blackmail. There are also *institutional* incomes, such as payments based on a system of social insurance. (A wider definition including interest on capital is adhered to by Huppes, 1977.)

A further category consists of *spending* income. Part of this is compulsory, and is transferred to the authorities as *taxes*. But it is well known that this is not always done; income may not be declared. Here we have an example of the supply of *incorrect information*, another form of counterproduction. Non-declaration of income reduces the effect of tax collection by Treasury officials.

Expenditure for consumer goods presents the phenomenon of *overconsumption*, in the sense of consuming more than is healthy; some goods, like hard drugs, even doing great harm to health. Part of this overconsumption may be seen as counterproduction *vis-à-vis* medical work.

Expenditure for investment purposes can also be counterproductive in that it reduces the value of capital goods already in existence (cf. van der Zwan, 1975).

We shall terminate the description of enrichment of economic theory here, since we are not striving for completeness. We have added sufficient examples to those given in the first section in order now to make an attempt to illustrate the range of counterproduction. However, we have not yet mentioned the most important example: military expenditure.

4.3 SOME FIGURES TO ILLUSTRATE THE SIZE OF COUNTERPRODUCTION

In this section some figures will be given to illustrate our thesis that the phenomenon of counterproduction is far from negligible, and that a number of its components are increasing in size. An accurate measurement is not (yet) possible; some of its components depend on expected or planned values of other variables and the measurement of expectation is not (yet) accurate. Occasionally, expectations and plans are the subject of enquiries, but few are published regularly or systematically.

The first illustration concernes *advertising* costs. For the United States, Janus and Roncagliolo (1979) mention figures of $14 bn and $64 bn for 1956 and 1976. (Billions are used here in the American way, i.e. 1 billion = 1 thousand million.) These amounts constitute 3.34 and 3.78 per cent of national income for the years, respectively.

A second illustration refers to *unhealthy consumption.* In the Netherlands tobacco products were consumed at a rate of 2.99 bn fl. in 1976 or 1.53 per cent of national income. This item, as a percentage of national income, has fallen though since 1965, when it amounted to 2.6 per cent. Unfortunately, this cannot be said of the consumption of alcoholic beverages. In terms of pure alcohol, strong alcoholic beverage consumption was 1.89 l *per capita* in 1965, 3.39 l in 1975 and 2.40 l in 1976. The latter figures are twice the 1929 consumption. Beer consumption was 37.2 l in 1965 and rose to no less than 93.9 l in 1976, compared with 28.0 l in 1929.

As a third illustration we take meat. Opinion differs on what is optimal-for-health consumption. The Dutch Health Council considers a daily consumption of 100 g per person to be optimal (36.6 kg *per annum*). Many consumers consider a higher intake desirable: statistics show this. Consumption *per capita* amounted to 46.9 kg and 57.4 kg *per capita per annum* in 1965 and 1976, respectively. (Vegetarians evidently don't share that desire.) The World Health Council considers optimal an even lower figure than 100 g per day. The Dutch Council's optimal figures imply that in 1965 22.2 per cent of meat consumption was excessive, and in 1976, 35.4 per cent. For 1974 that unhealthy meat consumption represented 1.64 per cent of national income.

A fourth illustration can be derived from the compensation paid out by *insurance companies.* In 1970 this constituted 1.9 per cent of national income, and in 1975, 2.2 per cent.

A fifth illustration may be derived from the benefits paid on the basis of *labour incapability*, but this may require closer analysis. The benefits amounted to 1.65 per cent of national income in 1970 and to 3.14 per cent in 1975. (All figures on the Netherlands quoted have been taken from the Central Bureau of Statistics (*Statistical Pocketbook*); national income is at factor costs.)

To finish we quote a few figures on tax evasion and tax avoidance. Here we take Belgian figures, since Professor M. Frank, the well-known expert on this subject, has studied Belgian data with particular care. For

1979 this author concludes that more than 20 per cent of taxable income is non-reported. In the Netherlands tax evasion and avoidance for a long period has been estimated at 10 per cent. Recently de Kam (1977) has reopened the discussion. Final figures have not been arrived at yet.

The figures mentioned so far are only illustrations of the order of magnitude counterproduction may amount to. More systematic research is needed for a better estimation, not to speak of a measurement.

4.4 CAN THE ECONOMY OPERATE WITHOUT COUNTERPRODUCTION?

Impressed by counterproduction among other things, those opposed to *laissez-faire* proposed *central planning* as an alternative. If only all activities were coordinated by one central agency, it was thought, the inconsistencies characteristic of a free economy could be avoided. On closer consideration this only applies, however, to very small communities. Economists often start their theories by considering Robinson Crusoe (admitting at a later stage Friday); or they take the family as their research object.

The dream of the perfect economy occupied many and had an enormous political impact. The attempts to implement it gradually showed its dream-like character. Even the economies of very small nations are too large—as measured by the number of actors and of activities—to observe all activities from one central point. Even 'Big Brother' will not succeed. Thus certain forms of counterproduction have to be accepted. In an industry with some returns to scale, relatively large production units must be maintained, alongside some degree of competition. The alternative would be a monopoly and its non-optimal character cannot be denied.

This does not imply that a number of forms of counterproduction should not be reduced. This is clearly the case for a number of non-economic forms, such as crime, pollution, consumption of unhealthy goods or human errors leading to serious accidents. Most of these forms have economic consequences: some of them can even be considered activities whose extent must be reduced if humankind is to survive. If we share the ecologists' concern that some minimum of tropical rain forests has to be maintained (cf. Myers, 1979), then it might be imperative—more research must be done on this issue—now to consider cutting down these forests as counterproductive and to stop it, for instance in North-Eastern Brazil or in Java.

Next there is growing agreement that bureaucracy should be reduced, that is, the number of hierarchical levels—the 'pyramids' of managers and administrators, in public as well as in private organisations—must be lowered. One of the first to argue along these lines was Macrae (1976), but it is striking how many in the last few years have followed him. Increasingly in their argument job satisfaction, and productivity as a consequence, has been introduced.

These elements are also involved in the explanation of small entrepreneurs' behaviour. According to conventional wisdom these often extend their production beyond the limits of a maximum money income. Looked at in this way their marginal production might even be considered to be counterproductive *vis-à-vis* themselves. Here I feel another interpretation is to be preferred. For small entrepreneurs a 'psychical' income is derived from their independence. They share this preference with others who are not necessarily 'small'. The 'manager disease', another frequently discussed characteristic of today's society, may be seen as an illustration that not only consumption, but also productive activity may be expanded beyond the health limit.

4.5 THE INCOME PAID FOR COUNTERPRODUCTIVE ACTIVITIES

The last aspect of counterproduction to be discussed in this chapter is the question: what income should be paid to those whose work may be seen as counterproduction? (for instance, to sales managers of large enterprises). The problem that arises is that they are paid much more (cf. Gottschalk, 1978) than their macroeconomic marginal product. Presumably the basis of their income is the expected marginal microproduction of their job, where 'micro' refers to the firm level. It remains an open question whether that basis is an expected increase in the firm's income which does not materialise, or whether the basis is—as said above—the degree to which they succeed in maintaining the firm's market share. Some economists doubt whether a basis can be adhered to by the firm that continues not to be fulfilled—an expected increase in the firm's income. If such a doubt is justified, the alternative basis, the degree to which the market share is maintained may be a better one.

The argument presented above, that maintenance of competition is the service sales managers yield to the community, leads to another conclusion. Maintenance of competition may be considered a public good and those producing that public good are entitled to an income equal to that public good. Here we are confronted with the same difficulty applying to other public goods: there is no market for such goods. Their value is implicitly taken account of in the decisions of government, parliament and voters, but not published in a systematic way or with great precision.

For the numerous public goods their prices could be considered to be the dual variables of a programming operation, but its practical implementation is not within reach. The problem remaining is from which source these incomes should be financed. For the time being the answer I arrive at is this: from the residual that flows to successful organisers of production. It is not the final answer, however.

REFERENCES

Chamberlin, E.H. (1933, 1948), *The Theory of Monopolistic Competition*, Cambridge, Mass., Harvard University Press.

Doel, J. van den (1978), *Demokratie en welvaartstheorie*, Alphen aan den Rijn, Samson; English trans. Brigid Biggins (1979), *Democracy and Welfare Economics*, Cambridge, London, New York and Melbourne, Cambridge University Press.

Frank, M. (1979), 'Pour 1979, le fraude fiscal pourrait coûter plus de 200 milliards au Trésor belge', *Cahiers économiques de Bruxelles*, no. 81 pp. 16–29.

Gottschalk, P.T. (1978), 'A comparison of marginal productivity and earnings by occupation', *Industrial and Labor Relations Review*, vol. 31, pp. 368–78.

Huppes, T. (1977), *Incomensverdeling en institutionele structuur*, [*Income Distribution and Institutional Structure*], Leiden, Stenfert Kroese.

Janus, N. and Roncagliolo, R. (1979), 'Advertising, mass-media and dependency', *Development Dialogue*, 1, pp. 81–97, Uppsala, Dag Hammerskjöld Foundation.

Kam, Flip de (1977), *Betalen is voor de dommen* [*Only the Stupid Pay Taxes*], Amsterdam, Bert Bakker.

Kuenne, R.E. (ed.) (1967), *Monopolistic Competition Theory: Studies in Impact. Essays in Honor of Edward H. Chamberlin*, New York, Wiley.

Macrae, N. (1976), 'The new capitalism', *The Economist*, 29 December.

Pen, J. (1950), *Theorie der collectieve loononderhandelingen* [*Theory of Collective Wage Bargaining*], Leiden, Stenfert Kroese.

Robinson, J. (1933), *The Economics of Imperfect Competition*, London, Macmillan.

Stackelberg, H. von (1934), *Marktform und Gleichgewicht* [*Market Form and Equilibrium*], Vienna and Berlin, Julius Springer.

Tinbergen, J. (1956), *Economic Policy, Principles and Design*, Amsterdam, North-Holland.

Zwan, A. van der (1975), 'Dalend rendement op geïnvesteerd vermogen' ['Falling yield on invested wealth']. *Econ.-Stat. Berichten*, 16 July, pp. 680–5.

5 On Collective and Part-Collective Goods

5.1 DEFINITIONS OF COLLECTIVE GOODS

A still useful definition of a *collective good* as distinguished from an individual good is that its consumption by one individual does not reduce the possibility for other individuals to consume it (Samuelson, 1954). Examples are a TV broadcast, the police and a nation's road system (excluding toll ways). The complete set of collective goods will be discussed in section 5.4. Of the three examples mentioned, the TV broadcast is closest to a *purely* collective good; the other two are usually close, but not always. Extended riots may require so much of the police force that the latter is not available to investigate a case of theft. On the first day of a holiday period motorways may be congested and unable to take an additional car. In the latter two cases we speak of *part-collective goods*. These are discussed in sections 5.3 to 5.8.

The definition given may be replaced by *alternative* definitions. For example, that collective goods are the goods produced by public authorities. Accordingly the phrase *public goods* has been used instead of collective goods. This definition may be combined with the statement that one of the reasons why public authorities produce these goods is that public authorities produce them more cheaply than private producers. An extreme case is that either private initiative or private capital is lacking to run the production process under discussion. Three examples may be given. In 1902 the Dutch state mines (DSM) were established to mine coal, since private capital and initiative were too weak. Since 1930 the Dutch state has run a number of farms on newly reclaimed land for a limited number of years; experience with private farming on previously reclaimed land (*Haarlemmermeer*) having shown that the risks were so large that all first owners went bankrupt. The third example is the creation by the Turkish government in 1923 under Atatürk of the 'state economic enterprises' in various branches of industry: at that time private initiative to industrialise Turkey was too weak.

Another alternative definition of collective goods is the one adhered to by most of today's authors on the subject, namely that they are non-excludable and, as a consequence, non-competitive. The subtleties of these qualitative expressions do not affect, however, the mathematical structure of utility functions. Rightly, Samuelson (1981) sticks to the structure of his 1954 treatment.

Alongside purely collective goods, a number of not purely collective goods has been identified by various authors. Thus, Drèze (1974) deals with *semi-collective* goods, of which an interesting example is a collective good that is only available in a restricted geographical area. Goedhart (1975), Wolfson (1979) and several Anglo-Saxon authors, (e.g. Brown and Jackson, 1978), introduced the concept of *quasi-collective* goods, which may be said to have a private component but are made available by public authorities at prices below cost: an important example is schooling.

The category of not purely collective goods to be discussed in the present chapter is different again, and constitutes another aspect already briefly set out. It has some similarity to quasi-collective goods, but cannot be identified with the latter.

5.2 SOME ADDITIONAL CHARACTERISTICS OF COLLECTIVE GOODS

The second definition of collective goods discussed in section 5.1 suggests that their production is required by law. Admittedly, government activities are regulated by legislation, yet at least part of them do not produce collective goods; most state enterprises also produce individual rather than collective goods. In our view (also shared by Goedhart, 1981) collective goods are not necessarily produced by public authorities. A TV broadcast or a highway is usually produced by private associations (in the Dutch system, at least) or private firms. But public authorities do assume some responsibility for them, and this is regulated by law. In what follows we shall consider as the normal case that collective goods are 'ordered' by 'the government', the latter expression being shorthand for public authorities at various levels. Producers are paid for supplying the collective good ordered by the government out of tax revenue and taxes are collected from citizens. Purely collective goods are 'consumed' by all citizens in the same quantity, which is the implication of the definition to which we shall adhere. The tax paid for the availability of a collective good will be supposed to be such that it reflects the marginal utility of that good to the taxpayer. All this will be translated into a simple mathematical model in section 5.8. Parliamentary decisions on the quantities of each collective good to be made available by the government are assumed to be in line with the marginal utilities of each citizen.

This assumption implies that the parliamentary majority's *judgement of these marginal utilities* is substituted for the marginal utilities as experienced by the citizens themselves. This is our alternative to Wicksell's overly idealistic requirement of unanimous decisions on the volume of collective goods to be made available (cf. Hennipman, 1977, 1982).

In the present chapter our main objective is how to introduce into economic theory part-collective goods. As stated above in section 5.1, such goods occasionally are not available to all citizens who want them, and on such occasions the responsible authorities must allocate the availability of the part-collective good under discussion. Such an allocation may consist of some sort of rationing for which they must develop a set of rules—on a congested highway, priority over other vehicles may be given to the fire brigade, to an ambulance, etc. In our model this allocation will also be expressed by a set of equations.

Situations are conceivable in which negative-valued collective 'goods' occur. The best-known example is the 'security' supplied by organised criminals who claim a contribution from shopkeepers. But we shall not pursue this phenomenon.

In most nations minority groups (the parliamentary opposition) are in favour of establishing collective goods not (yet) in existence or larger (alternatively, smaller) quantities of existing collective goods. In the course of history changes in the quantities of a number of collective goods have occurred. This applies to the examples given so far: TV broadcasts, police and highways. It also applies to many of the concrete additional examples to be discussed in Section 5.4. This raises the general question whether collective goods should be restricted to those required by legislation or whether a more fundamental source should be substituted for legislation. In fact, legislation itself is based on more fundamental sources. It is commonplace to consider as the source of positive law ethical or religious principles.

Since this chapter deals with positive economics only and not with normative economics, we leave this question to a later study.

5.3 DEFINITION OF PART-COLLECTIVE GOODS

In section 5.1 we briefly touched upon the possibility that there are goods where the consumption by one individual does not reduce other persons' consumption possibility by the full amount of the first person's consumption, but nevertheless somewhat reduces that possibility, given the total availability of the good considered. This category of goods will be called part-collective. Two examples have been mentioned. In contradistinction to individual or private goods, where the second person's consumption possibility—with a given supply—is reduced by the full amount and purely collective goods, where it is not reduced at all, we have here a category that may be characterised by a continuous parameter related to the *degree* to which other potential consumers have to reduce their consumption.

Two further points must be made. One is that the same good may move within a zone where the parameter mentioned assumes a range of *different* values. The good is not, therefore, identified by that parameter. The other is that *external data* affect the parameter's value. In the police example given in section 5.1, it is the riots which affect police availability for other tasks; in the congestion example, it is the holiday period's beginning which reduces highway capacity to additional cars.

5.4 AN ENUMERATION OF COLLECTIVE AND PART-COLLECTIVE GOODS

The main task of a positive theory of collective and part-collective goods consists of an explanation of the mechanism by which the quantities of all sorts of goods and services produced, distributed and consumed as well as their prices are determined. We shall restrict ourselves to a closed economy and to the short-run statics of the mechanism. By 'goods' we understand goods and services.

One essential feature of a theory and its representation by a model is that it should be *complete* in the sense of containing all goods, all individuals and all firms which together constitute the economy considered. With regard to individual goods, completeness can be checked by statistics of household accounts and of production; with regard to individuals, the census of population statistics, and so on. In order to cover all collective goods we may lack an exhaustive source of information. If we had adhered to the definition that collective goods are those produced by public authorities their combined budgets might have been a source of information. Because of our assumption that government is responsible for the availability of collective goods we may still use that source, keeping in mind, however, that some government products show individual components. We shall have to add some collective goods *not* (completely) covered by legislation, however.

From an inspection of the responsibilities of ministries and their equivalents at lower levels (down to local authorities) we derived the enumeration given below, which contains the examples given before:

internal security (police, justice),
external security (military authorities),
transportation infrastructure, water level control,
information (statistics, libraries, news media including TV, radio, planning),
education, research and publication of its results,
clean air, water, soil,
social security (including working time and labour conditions) (cf. Hartog, 1981),
health services (n.b. *not* considered to be collective by Goedhart),
maintenance of a competitive production and distribution system.

If this enumeration is accepted, a few remarks have to be added.

(i) Purely collective goods are *relatively rare*. Some types of information, working-time and labour conditions are perhaps the best examples.
(ii) As stressed in the preceding text, many of the collective goods listed are part-collective only: this applies to police, transportation infrastructure, social security, health services, and several others.
(iii) The maintenance of a competitive production and distribution system is largely taken care of by private entrepreneurs, but up to a point only. Many markets are oligopolies!
(iv) As stated at the end of section 5.2, the list may be completed by a number of collective or part-collective goods not required by legislation, but by ethical or religious principles. Some examples are, to be a good citizen, a good parent to one's children, and a good partner in marriage.

Most economists today would not include these examples in their lists. Yet there may be good reasons for doing so. But, the subject will be left to a later study, as previously stated.

5.5 THE CONTINUUM OF PART-COLLECTIVE GOODS

As set out in the preceding sections, part-collective goods constitute a range of goods—or rather, of goods in changing environments—between the sharply defined categories of individual and purely collective goods. The essential relationship which distinguishes private from purely collective goods is the one between the supply available u, and the quantities consumed u_i by individuals i ($i = 1, 2, \ldots I$). For individual goods this relationship is:

$$u = \sum_i u_i \tag{5.1}$$

whereas for purely collective goods a set of equations applies:

$$u_i = u \; (i = 1, \ldots, I) \tag{5.2}$$

The question to be dealt with in this section is whether we can find one relation containing a parameter, say ϱ, which covers the complete range of all part-collective goods with individual and purely collective goods as special cases. The answer is yes, and has been inspired by our knowledge of CES production functions, (cf. Kreijger, 1978; de Boer, 1981, where this knowledge is summarised and the initiators of this branch of economics are quoted.) For our purpose a special case is needed:

$$u^{-\varrho} = \sum_i u_i^{-\varrho} \tag{5.3}$$

This relation becomes (5.1) for $\varrho = -1$ and it has been shown that for $\varrho \to \infty$ it converges towards the set (5.2). Its only parameter ϱ is connected with the Allen elasticity of substitution σ_{ij} ($i \neq j$) by:

$$\sigma = 1/(1 + \varrho) \tag{5.4}$$

Since our interpretation of (5.3) is not one of a production function, the Allen substitution elasticity does not enter into our utilisation.

For the study of part-collective goods the most interesting question is the relation between the total quantity of such a good available (u) and the sum $\sum_i u_i$ of the quantities demanded. As an example let us take a simple case where the u_i are the *'quantity' of highway needed for one car*, and let all cars require the same space which we take as the unit. For a total number I of individuals we then have:

$$\sum_i u_i = I \tag{5.5}$$

Using our formula (5.3) to calculate u we get:

$$u = I^{-1-1/\varrho} \tag{5.6}$$

The total number of cars which the highway network's capacity permits to circulate will be:

$$Iu = I^{-1/\varrho} \tag{5.7}$$

From an analysis of formulae (5.6) and (5.7) we may conclude that the relevant interval for ϱ in the particular application is:

$$-\infty < \varrho < -1 \tag{5.8}$$

where $\varrho = -\infty$ corresponds to a purely collective and $\varrho = -1$ to a private good. Some values of Iu are shown below and a numerical example has been added:

ϱ	$-\infty$	-10	-2	-1.5	-1
Iu	1	$I^{0.1}$	$I^{0.5}$	$I^{0.67}$	I
For $I =$ 1 million	(coll.) 1	4	1000	10 000	(priv.) 1 000 000

The value $-\infty$ coresponds with a purely collective good and $\varrho = -1$ with a private good where everybody's car may circulate. Part-collective goods are represented by the range between these two values. Close to $\varrho = -1$ almost all cars and for high negative values of ϱ relatively few are accommodated: i.e. there is congestion.

It is interesting that the interval of ϱ that makes sense for our problem is the one excluded when (5.3) constitutes a CES production function. As set out elsewhere (Tinbergen, 1982), even then it depends on the problem studied which interval of ϱ-values is relevant: it is different for problems in which 'essential' production factors only are considered from problems where non-essential production factors come in.

5.6 A POSITIVE THEORY OF FINANCING THE AVAILABILITY OF COLLECTIVE GOODS

As set out in section 5.2, we consider essential not the production but the ordering of collective and part-collective goods by government. Since we are not dealing with a normative problem, but only with a positive (or analytical) treatment of the role of these goods, the question we want to answer in this section is how governments are financing the collective and part-collective goods ordered. A further restriction is that we only deal with a static theory. This implies that the goods ordered are paid, and the total amount to be paid equals public revenue. Such revenue is collected from taxes in the widest sense, including contributions to the social security system and non-tax revenue.

Finally we make the assumption that taxes paid by enterprises (indirect taxes) are a payment for government services supplied to producers. Admittedly, this assumption is hardly warranted, but in national accounting it has often been made. This reduces the budget we consider to the budget for collective and part-collective goods supplied to consumers and the revenue to direct taxes and non-tax revenue as well as consumer contributions to the social security system. (For a different treatment see Samuelson, 1982, where indirect taxes are the only taxes.)

The main element of choice remains whether equilibrium is interpreted as the equality between total revenue and total expenditures on collective or part-collective goods, or whether some or all of the payments for the K types of such goods we shall introduce into our model are covered by particular types of revenue. In the former case there will appear *one government budget equation*, whereas in the latter there may be more, up to K such equations. The latter would apply in particular if the decision on the ordering of some collective good were taken *jointly* with the decision on the source of financing. In practice this seldom occurs, to the regret of finance ministers; but there do exist special-purpose taxes. In fact they are the best guarantee for rational decisions on public finance.

5.7 THE NEED FOR AN ALLOCATION SYSTEM FOR PART-COLLECTIVE GOODS

The last concept to be elaborated somewhat more than in section 5.3 (where it was first mentioned) is the concept of an allocation system needed for part-collective goods. For purely collective goods no allocation is needed: the quantity available is fully available to all citizens, our example of a TV broadcast illustrates that situation. In section 5.1 we also mentioned circumstances in which part-collective goods may, in contrast, not always be available; and in section 5.2 we mentioned some allocation systems. In the present section some further elaboration is offered. In doing so we shall have in mind other examples than those of the police and the road network. Among the collective goods mentioned in section 5.4 the following provide additional examples: libraries, schools, distribution of research results, maintenance of a clean environment, unemployment, sickness and other social security benefits, and health services.

One method of allocation consists of the establishment of *priorities* amongst categories of different quality. Thus the police force will be used primarily for more serious categories of disaster or crime, and less serious categories may have to be left to later occasions. Water-level control will be exerted first of all in cases of floods; minor adjustments for agricultural purposes constitute a secondary concern. Students admitted to universities may be categorised according to examination results attained in secondary schools; a less attractive system is one of *drawing lots*.

A second method of allocation, applying to equally urgent cases within one category consists of *rationing*. Students of equal ability may receive scholarship of equal amounts, at a level determined by total financial means available. In times of serious depression, unemployment and other social benefits may have to be lowered: another sort of rationing.

Rationing of individual consumer goods in periods of extreme scarcity is a feature of many emergencies.

A third allocation system may be the shifting over time of availability until circumstances become more favourable. In other words, *queuing*, or the establishment of a *waiting-list*. Libraries regularly apply this technique. For individual goods such as motor cars, waiting lists are well known in Eastern Europe.

As a last case we mention the allocation system of *two-part pricing*. In order to obtain the part-collective good desired the person involved may be required to pay a fixed amount (lump-sum) plus a price per unit. This is the system recommended (by Goedhart, 1981, and others) according to the so-called benefit principle. Thus, university students may be charged a tuition fee based on their later incomes: i.e. they are given a loan which they have to pay back in part only, depending on their future income.

5.8 A SIMPLE MODEL AS AN ILLUSTRATION

In this final section the interdependence of the elements discussed before will be shown with the aid of a simple, static, short-run model. In it we use the following subscripts: $i = 1, \ldots, I$, for consumers, $h = 1, \ldots, H$ for producing firms and superscripts $j = 1, \ldots, J$ for individual or private goods and $k = 1, \ldots, K$ for (part-)collective goods. Since the model is meant for the short run, all capital is assumed to be given, as is income C_i derived from capital by person i. The explicit version of the model assumes all production to show diminishing returns. The corresponding supply equations for constant or increasing returns indicate supply to be equal to (given) capacity, or zero, so as to maximise profit or to opt for satisficing production.

The *variables* entering the model and their numbers are listed below:

x_i^j	consumption of individual good j by consumer i	IJ
y_h^j	production of individual good j by firm h	HJ
p^j	price of individual good j	J
λ^i	Lagrange multiplier for consumer i in maximising utility ω_i constrained by budget equation	I
u_i^k	use of (part-)collective good k by consumer i	IK
v_h^k	production of (part-)collective good k by firm h	HK
q_k	price of (part-)collective good k	K
q_i^k	tax paid for (part-)collective good k by consumer i	IK

l_{ix}^j quantity of labour supplied by individual i to produce good j IJ

l_{hy}^j quantity of labour demanded by firm h to produce good j HJ

w^j wage of labour used in production of good j J

l_{iu}^k quantity of labour supplied by individual i to produce good k IK

l_{hv}^k quantity of labour demanded by firm h to produce good k HK

w^k wage of labour used in production of good k K

Total number of (unknown) variables:
$I + 2J + 2K + 2HJ + 2HK + 2IJ + 3IK$

The *equations* of the model are:

Budget equation for individual i:

$$-\sum_j p^j x_i^j - \sum_k q_i^k(u_i^k) + \sum_j l_{ix}^j w^j + \sum_k l_{iu}^k w^k + C_i = 0 \quad (5.1) \ I$$

Demand by i for j: $\dfrac{\partial \omega_i}{\partial x^j} = \lambda_i p^j$ \hfill (5.2) IJ

Demand by i for k: $\dfrac{\partial \omega_i}{\partial u_i^k} = \lambda_i \dfrac{\partial q_i^k}{\partial u_i^k}$ \hfill (5.3) IK

Supply of labour by i for j: $\dfrac{\partial \omega_i}{\partial l_{ix}^j} = -\lambda_i w^j$ \hfill (5.4) IJ

Supply of labour by i for k: $\dfrac{\partial \omega_i}{\partial l_{iu}^k} = -\lambda_i w^k$ \hfill (5.5) IK

Budget equations for government: $\sum_i q_i^k = q^k \sum_h v_h^k$ (Cases 1, 2) (5.6) K

Budget equation for government: $\sum_k \sum_i q_i^k = \sum_k q^k \sum_h v_h^k$
(Cases 3, 4) \hfill (5.6) I

Supply of individual good j: $y_h^j = a_h^j(l_{hy}^j)^{\lambda_h^j}$ \hfill (5.7) HJ

Supply of (part-)collective good k: $v_h^k = b_h^k(l_{hv}^k)^{\mu_h^k}$ \hfill (5.8) HK

Demand for labour to produce good j: $\lambda_h^j a_h^j(l_{hy}^j)^{\lambda_h^j - 1} = w^j$ \hfill (5.9) HJ

Demand for labour to produce good k: $\mu_h^k b_h^k(l_{hv}^k)^{\lambda_h^k - 1} = w^k$ \hfill (5.10) HK

Market equilibrium for good j: $\sum_i x_i^j = \sum_h y_h^j$ (5.11) J

Availability of (purely) collective good k: $u_i^k = \sum_h v_h^k$
(Cases 1, 3) (5.12) IK

Availability of part-collective good k: $(\sum_h v_h^k)^{-\varrho} = \sum_i (u_i^k)^{-\varrho}$
$(-\infty < \varrho < -1)$ Cases 2, 4) (5.12) K

As will be understood, the utility functions ω_i, the production functions and the tax functions $q_i^k(u_i^k)$ are considered to be given.

Market equilibrium for labour producing good j:

$$\sum_i l_{ix}^j = \sum_h l_{hy}^j \quad (5.13) \, J$$

Market equilibrium for labour producing good k:

$$\sum_i 1_{iu}^k = \sum_h 1_{iv}^k \quad (5.14) \, K$$

As shown for equations (5.6) and (5.12) we have distinguished four cases characterised as follows: Apart from the individual goods, we have:

case 1: only purely collective goods, each of them financed by special taxes
case 2: only part-collective goods each of them financed by special taxes
case 3: only purely collective goods financed out of total government budget
case 4: only part-collective goods financed out of total government budget

It will be understood that 'mixed' cases can be easily modelled by combining features of the alternative forms of equations (5.6) or (5.12) or both. In the four cases shown the numbers of equations differ as follows:
Case 1: $I + 2J + 2K + 2HJ + 2HK + 2IJ + 3IK$
Case 2: $I + 2J + 3K + 2HJ + 2HK + 2IJ + 2IK$
Case 3: $1 + I + 2J + K + 2HJ + 2HK + 2IJ + 3IK$
Case 4: $1 + I + 2J + 2K + 2HJ + 2HK + 2IJ + 2IK$

Consequently, in some cases a number of *degrees of freedom* result, to be found as the difference between the number of variables and of equations. They appear to be $K(I-1)$ in Case 2, $K-1$ in Case 3 and $IK-1$ in Case 4. Case 1 appears to be determinate. If degrees of freedom are available, they may be used by the government to impose restrictions on the taxes in order to maximise, as far as possible, some collective utility function. Such additional equations may also specify a particular *system of allocation*, supposed by parliament to be optimal.

5.9 SUMMARY

Part-collective goods are defined as a continuum between private and purely collective goods. Their degree of collectivity is indicated by a parameter as used in a special case of the CES production function. Factor inputs in the latter play the role of quantities available to individuals of the collective good; product in the production function corresponds with total quantity available of the collective good. Parameter values range from -1 (private goods) to $-\infty$ (purely collective goods). External data determine the varying parameter values of a given partly collective good. The latter are in need of an allocation system.

REFERENCES

de Boer, P.M.C. (1981), *Price Effects in Input–Output Relations: A Theoretical and Empirical Study for the Netherlands, 1949–1967*, dissertation, Erasmus University, Rotterdam, Utrecht, Elinkwijk.
Brown, C.V. and Jackson, P.M. (1978), *Public Sector Economics*, Oxford, Martin Robertson.
Drèze, J.H. (1974), *Investment Under Private Ownership: Optimality, Equilibrium and Stability*, Core Reprint, Louvain-la-Neuve.
Goedhart, C. (1975), *Hoofdlijnen van de leer der openbare financiën*, Leiden.
Goedhart, C. (1981), 'Scheefgroei, ombuigingen en profijtbeginsel', in Eijgelshoven, P.J. and van Gemerden, L.J. (eds), *Inkomensverdeling en openbare financiën*, Utrecht and Antwerp, Het Spectrum.
Hartog, J. (1981), *Capabilities, Allocation and Wages*, Institute for Economic Research, Erasmus University, Rotterdam, September.
Hennipman, P. (1977), *Welvaartstheorie en economische politiek*, Alphen aan den Rijn and Brussels, Samson.
Hennipman, P. (1982), 'Wicksell and Pareto: their relationship in the theory of public finance', *History of Political Economy*, Duke Univeristy Press.
Kreijger, R.G. (1978), *Production Functions and Interindustry Analysis*, dissertation, University of Amsterdam.
Samuelson, P.A. (1954), 'The pure theory of public expenditure', *Review of Economics and Statistics*, XXXVI, pp. 387–9.
Samuelson, P.A. (1981), 'Bergsonian welfare economics', in Rosefield, S. (ed.), *Econimic Welfare and the Economics of Soviet Socialism. Essays in honor of Abram Bergson*, Cambridge, Cambridge University Press, pp. 223–66, especially p. 238.
Samuelson, P.A. (1982), 'A chapter in the history of Ramsey's optimal feasible taxation and optimal public utility prices', *Nationaløkonomisk Tidsskrift*, special issue, *Economic Essays in Honour of Jørgen H. Gelting*, ed. S. Andersen *et al.*, pp. 157–81.

Tinbergen, J. (1982), 'Constraints on production functions, essential vs. non-essential factors, *Nationaløkonomisk Tidsskrift*, special issue, *Economic Essays in Honour of Jørgen H. Gelting*, ed. S. Andersen *et al.*, pp. 182–91 (Ch. 3 of this book).

Wolfson, D.J. (1979), *Public Finance and Development Strategy*, Baltimore, Johns Hopkins University Press.

6 Production Functions: Research Lacunae

6.1 WHY WE NEED TO KNOW THEM: SOME EXAMPLES; ORGANISATION OF CHAPTER

Information on production functions is needed for a number of problems in economic science, positive as well as normative. As an introduction we shall mention a few such problems by way of examples, rather than providing an exhaustive list.

Production functions may be the source of information on marginal productivity of production factors, especially labour, by which, under certain conditions, levels of earnings that firms are prepared to pay may be explained. Production functions for goods or services produced by private firms may be compared to production functions for the same goods or services produced by public authorities in order to choose the cheapest supplier. Besides this use in positive economic science we may want to use the knowledge of production functions in normative economics. For example, we may have reasons to advocate some form of incomes policy, and for the proper implementation of such a policy we may need production functions.

Econometricians have devoted considerable efforts in attempts to estimate production functions and an extensive literature has resulted. Some of it will be discussed in the light of the examples mentioned, again without claiming completeness. The main emphasis will be on a number of lacunae we think econometric research shows. We propose to start in this section, with a general characterisation of the work done so far. Each of the other five sections will deal with a neglected area, each constituting a lacuna. The reasons for the neglect are not necessarily the same, as a closer discussion will show.

Starting with a description of what has been done—again without claiming to give an exhaustive picture—we list some of the aspects dealt with.

(1) A large number of mathematical forms of production functions have been tried. The pioneer was Douglas (1934), in close collaboration with Cobb, who advised the well-known linear relationship explaining

the logarithm of production y by a linear expression in the logarithms of production factors x considered. In their earliest attempts, two factors, labour and capital, were used. One generalisation consisted of adding quadratic terms (the translog function), another was the introduction of more than two factors, for instance blue-collar and white-collar workers and equipment and structures (Berndt and Christensen, 1973). The third generalisation was one introduced by Diewert (1974), who proposed a function:

$$y = \alpha_0 \Pi_i \Pi_j \left(\frac{1}{2} x_i + \frac{1}{2} x_j\right)^{\beta_{ij}}$$

The inclusion of more than two factors was often combined with the introduction of two-level functions, with the aid of the well-known CES (constant elasticity of substitution) production functions introduced by Arrow et al. (1961). In its simplest form it may be written as an additive function of powers of the factors explaining the same power of production y:

$$y^{-\varrho} = \sum a_h x_h^{-\varrho}$$

where x_h is the quantity of production factor h, and a_h ($h = 1 \ldots H$) and ϱ are constants.

The two-level idea consists of assuming x_h to be a similar function of sub-factors (blue-collar and white-collar labour or equipment and structures, constituting sub-factors, respectively, of labour and of capital). Such x_h could also be introduced into a Cobb–Douglas function.

The CES function has been generalised in several ways: for instance, by the introduction of larger values of H than just 2, or by the introduction of different powers instead of the same $-\varrho$ for all. The latter generalisation has also been called the addilog function, used by Mukerji (1963).

Still another aspect of the functions proposed is the change over time of technology. The simplest treatment consisted of the assumption that the product obtained from a given quantitative combination of all production factors rises by a constant percentage *per annum*. This example also constitutes a case of so-called unembodied[1] technological change: the change was assumed not to be caused by a change in design of capital goods used or a change in the education level of the labour force; rather, a change in organisation or quantity of equipment per person was thought of. In contrast, embodied technological change is one of the alternatives just mentioned. Somewhat sophisticated discussions have taken place around concepts such as labour-saving or capital-saving changes in technology. These discussions need not be sophisticated if the production process is described in the 'recipe form', usual for short-term changes in production. Contrary to what has been discussed so far, production volume y is then considered to be the independent variable, and the quantities needed of the various production factors are considered to be the dependent variables. The simplest well-known example is the one where all inputs of production factors are proportional to y:

$$x_h = a_h y \ (h = 1 \ \ldots \ H)$$

Technological change may then consist of a change in some of the a_h and a pure case of a labour-saving invention consists of a reduction in $a_{h'}$ if h' refers to labour. Similarly, capital-saving changes can be defined, and savings in any other input. Concepts have to become more sophisticated if substitution between factors is assumed to be possible. We shall not pursue this issue here.

(2) Continuing our sketch of the work on production functions done so far, we can state that in most of this work no intimate link exists between the formulae used and the description of the technology applied. The main exception to this statement is the input–output approach to process industries. But even for non-process industries—construction, say—the input–output method tells us all about the supplies needed, but not very much about how to use the bricks, the timber, the nails, the paint, the glass, etc. in order to build a house. A small group of economists dealing with this subject (e.g. Boon, 1964, 1981) work in some isolation.

(3) In a large part of the research on production functions only a limited number of production factors has been considered, each of them representing, as a consequence, a group of heterogeneous microfactors. Thus, capital stands for a collection of very different types of equipment, from simple tools to railway stations; and labour for a wide range of workers, from labourers to managers.

(4) Empirical testing has very often been limited to macrodata on production, such as all national production, all manufacturing and a restricted number of industries.

(5) Sometimes competitive markets for production factors have been assumed to exist as a justification to use price data as a measure of marginal product, as in Arrow *et al.* (1961).

(6) A special role has been played by the concept of human capital, generalising the concepts of capital as well as education. Through it the hetereogeneity of labour could be expressed in a macroconcept.

6.2 THE NEED TO INTRODUCE MANY TYPES OF LABOUR

After the education explosion of the 1950s and 1960s, labour has become still more heterogeneous. Moreover, income distribution has become a more important component of policy discussions, and the spreading unionisation of all types of labour may make an incomes policy—whether indicative or compulsory—unavoidable. Among the knowledge needed is the marginal productivity of a larger number of worker types from the lowest-paid to the highest. Here we hit on an important lacuna. The number of studies devoted to estimating production functions in which between five and ten types of labour appear as arguments is extremely limited. Besides, the innovative research done by Gottschalk (1978) was barely discussed. The same is true for some of the new problems his results pose. A brief overview seems useful.

Gottschalk estimated the marginal value product for six categories of workers outside agriculture; namely managers, salesmen, professionals, craftsmen, operatives and 'supporting' workers (clerical, labourers and service workers). The terms are abbrevations of the main categories shown in the US Censuses. The ratios of earnings (median) to marginal revenue product he found are shown in Table 6.1.

Table 6.1: *Median earnings E and ratio of earnings/product R for six types of labour* (USA, 1959)

Type	$E(\$)$	R
Managers	8 189	2.03
Salesmen	6 136	2.64
Professionals	6 007	1.12
Craftsmen	4 875	0.35
Operatives	3 797	0.44
Supporting*	3 222	0.55

* Unweighted average of clerical, labourers and service workers.

If free competition had prevailed on the six labour market sectors, all ratios should have been equal to unity, at least if the production function used (which was the Cobb–Douglas function) is correct. It remains a subject for research whether other production functions may lead to different results; and there are many to be tried out, as we have seen. On the other hand, if we accept the Cobb–Douglas function as a correct approximation, Gottschalk's results pose a number of interesting questions to be taken up in section 6.4.

Gottschalk's results find some support by another attempt to estimate production functions for the United States (Tinbergen and Kol, 1980), accompanied by a similar attempt for Japan. In this study, apart from capital, five types of labour were included, and the coefficients of the linear formula for the logarithms of the factor quantities (hence again, the Cobb–Douglas function) estimated. Among the results the following seem noteworthy: (a) significantly negative coefficients were found for farm workers (including farm managers); (b) the coefficients for managers were found to be non-significantly different from zero; (c) significantly positive coefficients were found for manual workers in Japan, white-collar workers in the USA and more or less significantly positive coefficients for professional workers and technicians in the USA; (d) negative coefficients were found for blue-collar workers in the USA, and for small entrepreneurs in Japan.

Theoretical explanations can be given for (a) (cf. Mahmood and Nadeem-ul-Haque, 1981) and (d) (cf. Miller, 1971). These explanations may be briefly indicated as the crop-maximising argument for (a) and the labour-reserve argument for (d). What we want to stress here, however, is the low level of reliability (as expressed by t values) of the Tinbergen–Kol results and the much higher level of reliability of Gottschalk's method, which justifies a brief characterisation of it.

Gottschalk assumes that the production process consists of a combination of two processes (for instance, technical production and administration). More processes are also possible. The two processes use different production factors (types of work), but one factor is used by both. The production functions of each process can be estimated and contain a smaller number of factors. This makes the regression coefficients more reliable: his t-values vary from 1.37 to 14.83 with a median of 3.46. Also the adjusted R^2 are 0.89 and 0.98. Although in my opinion his method contains one technical error, this error can be easily avoided and does not change the essence of the results (cf. Tinbergen 1982a). Thus this method constitutes a considerable contribution to the possibility of including a larger number of types of labour.

6.3 THE PHENOMENON OF COUNTERPRODUCTION

Some aspects of Gottschalk's findings and some features of reality can be understood with the aid of counterproduction, a term which I proposed (Tinbergen, 1981) for a phenomenon identified by others quite some time ago, for instance Mishan (1967), who spoke of the 'costs of economic growth'. What I have in mind need not be linked with growth; it also exists in a stationary economy. In its more extreme forms it is the visible neutralisation of somebody else's production, as with an act of vandalism. Counterproduction also takes more hidden shapes: a driver's error may cause an accident which then requires work by a doctor and other hospital personnel. Still more hidden is the counterproductive character of two competing salesmen or sales managers or just managers. Sales manager A of firm I tries to enlarge firm I's market share, but sales manager B of firm II in the same industry takes action to prevent this from happening. The production of the surplus consumption of many western citizens which makes them suffer from a heart attack is counter-producing the efforts of the medical profession to treat the heart patient.

In an attempt to penetrate to the deeper causes of counterproduction one is confronted with the impossibility of planning every detail of the operation of an economy (production, distribution, consumption, etc.), because our economies are too complicated. But also human behaviour contains elements causing counterproduction: we mentioned vandalism as an example. In addition, the recent development of chemical and radioactive processes has introduced environmental pollution requiring counter-activities.

Production functions should reflect the phenomenon of counter-production and considerable work in this field has been done (cf. Leontief, *et al.* 1977), but much remains to be done.

6.4 DEGREE OF AGGREGATION IN PRODUCTION FUNCTION ESTIMATION

Our example of sales managers A and B in section 6.3 partly explains Gottschalk's findings (p. 374, fn. 29), since his data are for entire manufacturing branches in each state of the United States. This implies that data for single firms are needed if changes in market share as the cause of a salesman's earnings have to be included in a model used for such an explanation. Branch data are already too aggregated. Data for single firms are not available from official statistics and can only be obtained voluntarily from the firms concerned. Presumably the best set-up would be to try to explain company sales with the aid of the numbers of the types of workers employed, including the salesman. A desirable cross-check would be to run the same regression for branch data. In it the coefficients for the other types of labour should not be very different from the ones found with the aid of the firm's data, but those for salesmen should be considerably lower and those for the managers should also be lower, but not necessarily as much as those for the salesmen.

The deviations between coefficients found for the numbers of salesmen with the aid of company data and with the aid of branch data may explain the deviation Gottschalk found between marginal productivity and earnings. The value 2.64 shown in Table 6.1 for the salesmen's R may come closer to 1. The same may happen with the $R = 2.03$ found for managers. It is also possible that the ratios would not become unity, but remain above 1. The remaining ratio R' may then point to a not completely competitive market.

Together with the desirable estimations based on other production functions an extensive programme of data collection and processing appears to be waiting for implementation.

6.5 ESSENTIAL AND NON-ESSENTIAL PRODUCTION FACTORS; REQUIRED *VS.* AVAILABLE CAPABILITIES

Another lacuna in the work devoted to the estimation of production functions may be traced around the distinction between essential and non-essential production factors (cf. de Boer, 1981). An essential production factor is one which must be used in order to obtain the product; if the input of an essential production factor is zero also the quantity of product vanishes. Production factors whose absence does not make a positive production volume impossible are called non-essential. This characterization should not lead us astray. A non-essential production factor may be useful nevertheless, in the sense of showing a positive marginal product. It may be substituted for another production factor which happens to be unusually scarce.

A range of concrete examples exists whose production factors can conveniently be characterised by an even number of indices. The simplest example evidently is one where two indices are appropriate. These may refer to a feature required and the actual feature of the type of factor (say, labour) considered. The feature may be level of education, indicating the required level by an index h and the actual level by h', a quantity $\phi_{hh'}$ of such a 'double-indexed' type of labour may participate in an economy's production process. A concrete example will be found in Tinbergen (1982), where three levels only of education (h, $h' = 1, 2, 3$) are considered: primary, secondary and tertiary education. Data on the required level of some capability are relatively rare; they are available for schooling in the USA thanks to Rumberger (1981), and in the Netherlands, thanks to Zanders *et al.* (1977), and analysed and processed by Hartog (1983).

It is here that the lacuna now to be discussed shows up. Very few data are available when it comes to required levels and levels attained of other capabilities. Job evaluation provides us with required levels of some other features, but the levels attained by those on the job are available only in small samples of special inquiries. For the estimation of production functions such data could be very helpful.

For one category of production functions, namely those describing education processes, a distinction between innate and learnable capabilities deserves particular attention. This distinction itself may be possible only after research on learning processes is directed at it.

6.6 PUBLIC AND PRIVATE PRODUCTION

The last example of lacunae we want to discuss refers to the estimation of production functions for the same good or service, produced in both publicly-owned and privately-owned enterprises. The issue in a way constitutes the main factor of the East–West controversy; that is, its macro aspect. But is has a micro aspect also, since in both social orders the choice is under discussion for narrowly-defined goods or services. There is a vast literature on relative productivity, especially for the United States and the Soviet Union. The evidence we have for individual goods or services in the same country produced publicly or privately is much less organised. Incidental news items seem to indicate that more evidence exists than scientific journals so far published. In addition, incidental political decisions refer to the problem; for instance, the nationalisation and privatisation of steel in the UK.

There are some interesting historial examples. In 1902 the Dutch state mines (DSM) were established in a period when socialist influence on government was minimal. The reason was that no private initiative and capital were available to expand coal mining, considered of vital interest by the government. In 1923 the Turkish government under Atatürk which wanted to modernise the country, created a number of 'state economic enterprises' for exactly the same reason. Today, both DSM and the Turkish state economic enterprises exist. DSM is considered to be a successful corporation which has since abandoned coal mining and produces a variety of chemical products. In the Netherlands state farms also exist, located in newly reclaimed land. The reason for their being state-owned is that after previous reclamations the first generation of farmers went bankrupt because of the particular risks of farming on newly reclaimed soil. After some years the state farms are sold to private farmers.

6.7 SUMMARY

Lacunae in the field of econometric estimation of production functions are listed. There is a need to know (1) production functions using many types of labour, (2) others to better identify the phenomenon of counterproduction, (3) still others to explain the earnings of salesmen,

(4) or of workers with a schooling level deviating from the one required, and (5) for private and public enterprises producing the same goods. The method developed by Gottschalk will be particularly useful in all attempts to include a large number of production factors.

NOTE

1 It seems to me that this word expresses the concept better than the usual word 'disembodied'. Professor James E. Meade agrees with this opinion.

REFERENCES

Arrow, K. et al. (1961), 'Capital labor substitution and economic efficiency', *Review of Economics and Statistics*, XLIII, p. 225ff.

Berndt, E.R. and Christensen, L.R. (1973), *The Specification of Technology in US Manufacturing*, discussion paper 73–17, Dept of Economics, University of British Columbia.

Boer, P.M.C. de (1981), *Price Effects in Input–Output Relations: A Theoretical and Empirical Study for the Netherlands, 1949–1967*, Dissertation, Rotterdam University, Utrecht, Drukkerij Elinkwijk.

Boon, G.K. (1964), *Economic Choice of Human and Physical Factors in Production*, Amsterdam, North-Holland.

Boon, G.K. (1981), *Technology Transfer in Fibres, Textile and Apparel*, Alphen aan den Rijn, Netherlands, Rockville, MD, and a number of other publications, quoted in this study.

Diewert, W.E. (1974), 'Application of duality theory' in Intriligator, M.D. and Kendric, D. (eds), *Frontiers of Quantitative Economics*, vol. II, Amsterdam, North-Holland.

Douglas, P.H. (1934), *The Theory of Wages*, New York, Macmillan.

Gottschalk, P.T. (1978), 'A comparison of marginal productivity and earnings by occupation', *Industrial and Labor Relations Review*, 31, pp. 368–78.

Hartog, Joop (1983), *Understanding Observed Regularities in Wages and Allocation: A Neoclassical Approach*, research memorandum 8316, Dept of Economics, University of Amsterdam.

Leontief, W. et al. (1977), *The Future of the World Economy*, A United Nations Study, New York, Oxford University Press.

Mahmood, M. and Nadeem-ul-Haque (1981), 'Farm size and productivity revisited', *The Pakistan Development Review*, XX, pp. 151–90.

Miller, R.L. (1971), 'The Reserve labour hypothesis: some tests of its implications', *The Economic Journal*, 81, pp. 17–35.

Mishan, E.J. (1967), *The Costs of Economic Growth*, Staples Press.

Mukerji, V. (1963), 'Generalized S.M.A.C. function with constant ratios of elasticities of substitution', *Review of Economic Studies*, 30, pp. 233–6.

Rumberger, R.W. (1981), 'The changing skill requirements of jobs in the US economy', *Industrial and Labor Relations Review*, 34, pp. 578–90.

Tinbergen, J. and Kol, J. (1980), 'Market-determined and residual incomes: some dilemmas', *Economie Appliquée*, XXXIII, pp. 285–301.

Tinbergen, J. (1981), 'Contraproduktie', in: Eijgelshoven, P.J. and van Gemerden, L.J. (eds), *Inkomensverdeling en openbare financiën*, pp. 288–97, Utrecht and Antwerp, Het Spectrum (Chapter 4 of this book).

Tinbergen, J. (1982), 'Constraints on production functions: essential *vs.* nonessential factors', *Nationaløkonomisk Tidsskrift, Economic Essays in Honour of Jørgen H. Gelting*, pp. 182–91.

Tinbergen, J. (1982a), 'Fonctions de production à plusieurs facteurs: une seconde correction', *Cahiers du Département d'économétrie*, Faculté des sciences économiques et sociales, Université de Genève, Cahier 82.04.

Zanders, H.L.G. *et al.* (1977), *Kwaliteit van Arbeid*, Tilburg, IVA.

Part II
Income Formation

7 On a Macroeconomic Model of Income Formation (with Eckhard Wegner)

7.1 INTRODUCTION

The starting point of this chapter is a simple macroeconomic model developed by Tinbergen (1975, 1978) to explain income formation. The main idea of this model is that an important role is played by the difference between the level of schooling attained by a worker and the most desirable level of schooling in order to do his job well. Three levels of schooling are considered: primary (low), secondary (medium) and third (high) level, indicated by $h = 1, 2, 3$. The frequencies (measured as the parts of total employment) $\phi_{hh'}$, where h is the most desirable and h' the actual level of schooling, add up to 1. It is assumed that h is either equal to h' or to the next higher level, hence $h = h' + 1$. This expresses, on the one hand, some flexibility in the choice of a job or a worker for a vacancy and, on the other hand, some scarcity of qualified labour (cf. section 7.4). Thus the labour market is subdivided into (at most) five compartments, whose characterisation by two indices permits the simplest possible separation of demand h and supply h'. The analysis of market forces and their determinants is one of the main objectives of this chapter.

7.2 WEGNER'S CRITIQUE

Wegner (1981) made a thorough, critical analysis of this model and came to the following conclusions: (i) the model is inconsistent (p. 69), because the author overlooked the impossibility for this model to explain a transition to an other less unequal income distribution pretended by himself elsewhere (Tinbergen, 1973); (ii) the role of human capital is characterised erroneously (p. 80); (iii) the consequences drawn for the long-term changes in income distribution are not convincing. Against the background of these criticisms Wegner develops as an alternative a job-oriented model of a type comparable to Tinbergen's. (The meaning of a job-oriented model will be clarified in section 7.6.)

Upon Wegner's initiative his critique has led to a correspondence which showed that, apart from some possible fundamental differences of opinion, a number of misunderstandings and terminological differences could be clarified and this clarification helps to understand better income formation. Since we believe that this net result of Wegner's critique (in Otto Neurath's sense) may interest some of our colleagues, we submit it for discussion.

7.3 TINBERGEN'S ORIGINAL MODEL

The model criticised may be summarised as follows:

Product per active employee is given by the production function:
$$y = k^{\varrho_k}(\phi_{11} + \pi_{21}\phi_{21})^{\varrho_1}(\phi_{22} + \pi_{32}\phi_{32})^{\varrho_2}\phi_{33}^{\varrho_3} \tag{7.1}$$

which may be characterised as a generalised Cobb–Douglas function. The $\phi_{hh'}$ have been defined before. The symbols π_{21} and π_{32} indicate productivity ratios between ϕ_{21} and ϕ_{11}, and ϕ_{32} and ϕ_{22}, respectively. For the individuals concerned they are considered constant; but for the economy as a whole they are variables depending on ϕ_{21} or ϕ_{32}:

$$\pi_{21} = 1 + \alpha_1\phi_{21} \tag{7.2}$$

and

$$\pi_{32} = 1 + \alpha_2\phi_{32} \tag{7.3}$$

where both α_1 and α_2 are > 1. Further, k represents capital intensity and ϱ_k the partial production elasticity of production with regard to capital; ϱ_1, ϱ_2 and ϱ_3 are the partial production elasticities vis-à-vis $h' = 1, 2, 3$. Since they also indicate the portions of income obtained by groups with qualification 1, 2 and 3, respectively, their total equals the labour income quota and ϱ_k the profit quota of total income.

The size of the group with qualification h' is given by $F_{h'}$; hence

$$F_1 = \phi_{11} + \phi_{21} \tag{7.4}$$

$$F_2 = \phi_{22} + \phi_{32} \tag{7.5}$$

$$F_3 = \phi_{33} \tag{7.6}$$

In the normative application of the model the F are considered instruments of education policy, but in the analytical use they are considered given. In the original presentation of the model (Tinbergen,

1975) equations (7.2) and (7.3) are subject to restrictions which have not played a role in our discussion and hence will be disregarded.

Four 'sub-versions' of the model may be distinguished, characterised by:

(i) $\phi_{21} = \phi_{32} = 0$ (ii) $\phi_{21} = 0$

(iii) $\phi_{32} = 0$ (iv) $\phi_{21} \neq 0, \phi_{32} \neq 0$

These distinctions are necessary because the coexistence of groups ϕ_{11} and ϕ_{21} is possible only when individuals with $h' = 1$ are equally satisfied with jobs ϕ_{11} and ϕ_{21}; and similarly for $h' = 2$ with jobs ϕ_{22} and ϕ_{32}. According to the utility functions used (not to be discussed here) this requires:

$$x_{21} = x_{11} + \tau_1 \tag{7.7}$$

$$x_{32} = x_{22} + \tau_2 \tag{7.8}$$

where x are incomes after tax and τ_1 and τ_2 are coefficients occurring in the utility functions. The relationship between incomes before tax l and after tax x are assumed to be:

$$x_{11} - x_{21} = t_1(l_{11} - l_{21}) \tag{7.9}$$

and

$$x_{22} - x_{32} = t_2(l_{22} - l_{32}) \tag{7.10}$$

where t_1 and t_2 are the marginal tax rates.

The relationships between gross income and marginal productivity are:

$$l_{11} = \frac{\varrho_1 y}{\phi_{11} + \pi_{21}\phi_{21}} \tag{7.11}$$

$$l_{21} = \frac{\varrho_1 \pi_{21} y}{\phi_{11} + \pi_{21}\phi_{22}} \tag{7.12}$$

$$l_{22} = \frac{\varrho_2 y}{\phi_{22} + \pi_{32}\phi_{32}} \tag{7.13}$$

$$l_{32} = \frac{\varrho_2 \pi_{32} y}{\phi_{22} + \pi_{32}\phi_{32}} \tag{7.14}$$

$$l_{33} = \frac{\varrho_3 y}{\phi_{33}} \tag{7.15}$$

All 15 equations apply in sub-version (iv): $\phi_{21} \neq 0, \phi_{32} \neq 0$. One or both of the equations (7.7) and (7.8) do not apply in the cases where either ϕ_{21} or ϕ_{32} or both vanish.

7.4 TWO TYPES OF EQUILIBRIUM

It is essential to distinguish the two types of equilibrium. One is that on all market compartments demand equals supply; this may be called *market equilibrium*. The other shows equilibrium for each type of schooling: the level of schooling required by the demand side is actually supplied. In this situation it is not necessary to employ individuals with less schooling than required. This type may be called *educational equilibrium*, and will appear whenever $F_1:F_2:F_3 = \varrho_1:\varrho_2:\varrho_3$. In this case gross income of the three types of labour will be equal. This equilibrium may be a long-term and macro aim of matching education and labour market. Education is then determined by economic needs and not only or necessarily by cultural needs, learning capability and propensity to learn: if some level of education is scarce, it is rational, from the point of view of maximising productivity and profits, to direct education to the scarce type.

7.5 WEGNER'S CRITIQUE

Wegner's critique concerns Tinbergen's (1973, pp. 221ff.) attempt at explaining the appearance of the 'heterogeneous' labour categories ($\phi_{21} \neq 0$ and $\phi_{32} \neq 0$). According to Tinbergen income differences will be larger in the case of educational equilibrium than in the case of market equilibrium, where the heterogeneous groups appear. Wegner correctly shows that this is not true. In the case of educational equilibrium we have

$$\frac{l_{33}}{l_{11}} = \frac{\varrho_3 F_1}{\varrho_1 F_3}$$

For a situation with heterogeneous groups we find, by substituting (7.2) into (7.11) and (7.3) into (7.15):

$$\frac{l_{33}}{l_{11}} = \frac{\varrho_3 \cdot (F_1 + \alpha_1 \phi_{21}^2)}{\varrho_1 F_3}$$

The wage ratio between levels 3 and 1 is larger, since production and total income y are also larger, and the wage difference is larger too.

7.6 QUASI-DYNAMISATION OF THE MODEL

Wegner bases his thesis of the 'model-inherent' impossibility of the transition on a quasi-dynamisation of the model on the argument given by

Tinbergen (1973, pp. 221ff.). Since in essence the model is a static one, we can only speak of a quasi-dynamisation. The latter is undertaken by the introduction of expected values l_{22}^* and l_{33}^*: the employees of schooling level 1 and 2 respectively expect from a job change to a higher level a wage equal to the higher job level. It appears (Wegner, 1981, pp. 71ff.) that in the correspondingly changed model no transition is possible if equations (7.2) and (7.3) remain valid. Individuals changing their job from 11 to 21 (from 22 to 32 respectively) do not obtain a wage slightly below l_{22} or l_{33}, respectively, but (according to equations (7.2) and (7.12), (7.3) and (7.14) respectively) only a wage somewhat higher than l_{11} respectively l_{22}. From this it follows that equations (7.7) and (7.9), resp. (7.9) and (7.10), cannot be satisfied as conditions for the existence of ϕ_{21} resp. ϕ_{32}. To put it crudely: with the production function chosen not all types of labour satisfy the law of diminishing marginal productivity.

Moreover, the model is in fact static only. In essence it only serves the description of empirical situations for long-term forecasting purposes.

7.7 A JOB-ORIENTED MODEL

His criticism induced Wegner (1981, pp. 81ff.) to formulate an alternative model where jobs play the role employees play in Tinbergen's model. The production function is now formulated:

$$y = k^{\delta_k} \phi_{11}^{\delta_1} (\phi_{22} + \beta_{21}\phi_{21})^{\delta_2} (\phi_{33} + \beta_{32}\phi_{32})^{\delta_3} \tag{7.1*}$$

where the δ now constitute the partial production elasticities with regard to the job categories $h = 1, 2, 3$.

Moreover, it is assumed that the productivity of employees working on a job for which they have not been educated is lower than the productivity of those who were educated for that job:

$$\beta_{21} = \text{const} < 1 \tag{7.2*}$$

and

$$\beta_{32} = \text{const} < 1 \tag{7.3*}$$

Equations (7.4) to (7.10) of Tinbergen's model remain valid.

For the relation between gross income and marginal productivity of the employees we now have:

$$l_{11} = \frac{\delta_1 y}{\phi_{11}} \tag{7.11*}$$

$$l_{21} = \frac{\beta_{21}\delta_2 y}{\phi_{22} + \beta_{21}\phi_{21}} \tag{7.12*}$$

$$l_{22} = \frac{\delta_2 y}{\phi_{22} + \beta_{21}\phi_{21}} \tag{7.13*}$$

$$l_{32} = \frac{\beta_{32}\delta_3 y}{\phi_{33} + \beta_{32}\phi_{32}} \tag{7.14*}$$

$$l_{33} = \frac{\delta_3 y}{\phi_{33} + \beta_{32}\phi_{32}} \tag{7.15*}$$

In the framework of this model a transition from a situation of an employment only determined by h to one of market equilibrium becomes plausible; and the reduction in income differentiation can be shown. It can also be shown that the demand side will take advantage from employing people with a level of education below the one required: in every situation where $\partial y/\partial \phi_{33} > \partial y/\partial \phi_{22}$ production per employee average labour productivity can be raised when individuals with $h' = 2$ work on jobs for which $h = 3$.

7.8 AN ALTERNATIVE ANSWER TO WEGNER'S CRITIQUE

Another possibility to escape from Wegner's objection is to replace the generalised Cobb–Douglas function (7.1) by a CES function with a substitution elasticity $\sigma > 1$. For simplicity's sake we only consider explicitly the average income per employee, indicating it by z; for total product per employee we then obtain $y = z/(1 - \varrho k)$.

For labour income we now assume (since $\varrho = \frac{1}{\sigma} - 1$):

$$z^{-\varrho} = \sum a_{hh'} \phi_{hh'}^{-\varrho} \tag{7.16}$$

For marginal productivities and so for gross wages it follows that:

$$l_{hh'} = a_{hh'} \left(\frac{z}{\phi_{hh'}}\right)^{\varrho+1} \tag{7.17}$$

This relation may be verified by replacing the a by the l:

$$z = \sum l_{hh'} \phi_{hh'} \tag{7.18}$$

We still have one degree of freedom, which may be used to choose ϱ, on the condition that:

$$-1 < \varrho < 0.$$

It can now be shown that income inequality in the case of labour market equilibrium is smaller than in the case of educational equilibrium

($h = h'$). As criterion we again use the wage ratio l_{33}/l_{11}. For market equilibrium we derive from (7.17):

$$l_{33}/l_{11} = (a_{33}/a_{11})(\phi_{11}/F_3)^{1+\varrho} \tag{7.19}$$

For $h = h'$ (educational equilibrium) we find:

$$\bar{l}_{33}/\bar{l}_{11} = (a_{33}/a_{11})(F_1/F_3)^{1+\varrho} \tag{7.20}$$

Since ϕ_{11} is part only of F_1, we have $\phi_{11} < F_1$, and hence, as long as $1 + \varrho > 0$:

$$l_{33}/l_{11} < \bar{l}_{33}/\bar{l}_{11} \tag{7.21}$$

7.9 EMPIRICAL EVIDENCE AVAILABLE AND DESIRABLE

Since Tinbergen's model was built with the intention of reflecting reality for forecasting purposes, it is clearly desirable to aim at a fully empirical production function instead of the semi-empirical function (1). Such has been the aim of later work by Tinbergen and Kol (1980) and Gottschalk (1978). In these studies the authors find that—formulated briefly and hence somewhat superficially—better-paid groups are overpaid and lower-paid groups underpaid.

These results may be interpreted as exploitation by human capital or, alternatively, as the consequences of the power relations in a hierarchical division of labour, which work out as differing appropriation possibilities (cf. also Wegner, 1982a).

Wegner's (1981, pp. 172ff.) results which show wage gaps in favour of the higher performance groups can be interpreted, compared with the other empirical results, in a limited way only, since they are based on an institutional wage structure imposed by collective bargaining. It seems desirable that Gottschalk's, and Tinbergen and Kol's results be checked with the Federal Republic of Germany's data on performance groups (*Leistungsgruppen*).

7.10 POSSIBLE CONTRIBUTION OF HIERARCHY MODELS

On the theoretical side, the question arises whether or not hierarchy models may contribute more to the explanation (cf. also Tinbergen,

1981) and constitute a more reliable basis of the forecasting capability of a theory. In this connection it remains to be discussed whether or not the nature of the objective for which we use the models conflicts with the realisation of a theoretically conceivable equality of marginal productivities and hence of labour incomes (i.e. to be a system for the production and profitable use of goods and services and simultaneously a system of domination). It cannot be excluded that because of this side condition to the economic system limits are imposed to the reduction in income inequality, namely whenever the hierarchical division of labour is endangered (cf. Wegner, 1981). This may be a stronger argument than the fear that the maintenance and development of the national labour force would be endangered; a problem, which could be solved by an integrated, qualification-oriented transfer-tax system.

7.11 CONCLUDING REMARKS

In the preceding sections the elements of Wegner's critical analysis have been discussed extensively and, we believe, largely clarified. Wegner rightly pointed out that in the original model income inequality under market equilibrium surpasses inequality under educational equilibrium. With the aid of his alternative model it appears that the criticised result is essentially connected with the model specification. Furthermore, it has been shown that with a CES production with an elasticity of substitution above unity these difficulties can be avoided. The question remains how Tinbergen's opinion that exploitation by human capital today has become more important than exploitation by physical capital must be understood. Some comment may be added. In the Netherlands and comparable countries less than 10 per cent (in 1962 20 per cent) of national income is income from physical capital. Among the capital-owners social insurance institutions are important. Dividends, which are mainly income to the richer groups, amount to about 2 per cent in the Netherlands.

High incomes are received to a larger extent by highly educated individuals such as the free professions (doctors, architects, lawyers, etc.), and also managers. The 'managerial revolution' shifted, in Tinbergen's opinion, the power centre from capital-owners to managers. One should not overlook, however, that the hierarchy as the organisational form of the division of labour and with it the managers in principle are oriented on the objectives of capital owners. To what extent, after all, they exert direct power depends on how concentrated capital ownership is.

REFERENCES

Gottschalk, P.T. (1978), 'A comparison of marginal productivity and earnings by occupation', *Industrial and Labor Relations Review*, 31, no. 3, pp. 368–78.
Gottschalk, P.T. and Tinbergen, J. (1982), 'Methodological issues in testing the marginal production theory', *De Economist*, 130, pp. 325–35.
Tinbergen, J. (1956), 'On the theory of income distribution', *Weltwirtschaftliches Archiv*, 77, pp. 155–75.
Tinbergen, J. (1973), 'Labour with different types of skills and jobs as production factors', *De Economist*, 121, pp. 213–24.
Tinbergen, J. (1978), *Einkommensverteilung* (revised German translation of *Income Distribution*, 1975), Wiesbaden, Gabler.
Tinbergen, J. (1981), 'Skill scarcity, monopoloid and hierarchical incomes in some western countries', in Assorodobraj-Kula, N., Bobrowski, C., Hagemeijer, H., Kula, W. and Łos, J., *Studies in Economic Theory and Practice, Essays in Honor of Edward Lipiński*, Amsterdam, New York and Oxford, pp. 155–62.
Tinbergen, J. and Kol, J. (1980), 'Market-determined and residual incomes—some dilemmas', *Economie Appliquée*, XXXIII, pp. 285–301.
Wegner, E. (1981), *Die personelle Verteilung der Arbeitseinkommen. Betriebliche Herrschaft und Lohnstruktur.* [*The Personal Distribution of Labour Incomes. Intrafirm Power and Wage Structure*], Frankfurt and New York, Campus-Verlag.
Wegner, E. (1982a), 'Ursache und Vermittlung von Einkommensungleichheit in kapitalistischen Unternehmungen', [Cause and legitimation of income inequality in capitalist enterprises], in *Mehrwert. Beiträge zur Kritik der Politischen Ökonomie*, 22, pp. 70–85.

8 The Role of Occupational Status in Income Formation

8.1 INTRODUCTION

During the last decade numerous attempts have been made to estimate the impact of various explanatory variables on individual income. There is a tendency away from the purely stochastic approach, whose latest representative probably is Christopher Jencks (Jencks, 1972). Among those interested in this search into the income formation process Professor Pieter de Wolff has supplied us with an interesting study on the impact of years of schooling, differentiating between years with a smaller and years with a larger impact (de Wolff and van Slijpe, 1972), and using Torsten Husén's (1969) material. In the present chapter another part of the income formation process will be tackled.

Among the variables included by a number of authors on the subject (e.g. Jencks, 1972; Bowles and Nelson, 1974) the one called occupational status (O) appears. One of the advantages of using this variable is its relative reliability, in the sense that people of differing social position and consulted in different time periods do not show very diverging opinions on it. What is less clear in some of the empirical analyses performed is the precise role O, according to the authors, plays in the income formation process. One can imagine three rather different roles. Two of them assume that O has an immediate impact on incomes; and this impact may be of a different nature. One way in which O influences income may be that O is a measure of *psychical income*, adding to the job-holder's satisfaction alongside money income. The other is that O is a measure of an effort to be made to perform the job. In the former case money income I will have to depend negatively on O; in the latter case it will have to depend positively, since the effort needs a compensation.

The relationship we are now discussing is known as *earnings function*; it expresses income (here assumed to be identical to earnings) as a function of a number of degrees to which the individual income recipient possesses certain qualities relevant to do the job satisfactorily.

Elsewhere (Tinbergen, 1975a) I went into the question of the nature of the earnings function. In terms of economic analysis this function is a price equation, that is, expressing a price in terms of supply and demand factors. The variables appearing on the right-hand side of the function are usually only supply factors, however. This does not mean that the earnings function is a supply equation; for then, the numbers employed should also appear in it. The reason why demand factors are often not explicitly shown is that the group for which the function has been estimated faces one and the same market. Demand factors are constant, therefore, and their impact is hidden in the intercept and the coefficients of the earnings function. The best-known supply factors considered are years of (various types of) schooling and years of experience on the job (see e.g. Mincer, 1974). One theme of this chapter is whether, in addition, ocupational status is one of the supply factors, and which of the two alternative interpretations of it seems more likely (cf. section 8.3).

An additional theme we shall deal with only makes sense if O constitutes a measure of effort. Assuming that effort compensation leads to 'justifiable' income differences, in contradistinction to differences due to scarcity rents, we may obtain a very crude impression of the relative importance of justifiable income differences (cf. section 8.4).

The third role of O we propose to deal with is to attribute to O an altogether different role, namely that of a factor co-determining the choice of the length of the *education process*. This implies that the impact of O on income is an indirect one. To test this alternative we make an attempt to explain years of schooling S with the aid of occupational status O, adding one or more other independent variables (cf. section 8.5). This implies that a *different path* of causation is introduced, where occupational status is planned before or during the educational process, and the latter, apart from depending on other generally accepted phenomena, also depends on occupational status sought.

8.2 MATERIAL USED

Our study is meant as an illustration of how to proceed and its results are highly tentative. This is because the material available at the time of writing is the best available, but lacks information on a number of supply factors of a non-cognitive character which may well be relevant. For this reason—and possibly for other reasons as well—the multiple correlation obtained for the earnings function is 0.595 only; that is, the variance explained only 0.355. This is very close to the results obtained by de Wolff and van Slijpe for Husén's total sample, amounting to $R^2 = 0.332$. The material used is that of Duncan, Featherman and Duncan (1968) as shown by Bowles and Nelson (1974). It has the advantage of covering, for the four age groups considered together, about 10,000 persons.

Bowles and Nelson supply a correlation matrix for the age groups 25–34, 35–44, 45–54 and 55–64 years, respectively, and our estimations have been entirely based on their Table A.1. Readers interested in the considerable number of details added as footnotes to that table are referred to that source.

8.3 EXPLANATION OF INCOME WITH THE AID OF FOUR AND TWO INDEPENDENT VARIABLES

As a first test, an attempt was made to construct an earnings function (or explanation of income), with four independent variables, namely, occupational status O, years of schooling S, childhood IQ (Q), and socioeconomic background (B). In standardised variables the multiple linear regresssion for the age-group of 45–54 years equation runs:

$$I = 0.43\,O + 0.00\,S + 0.03\,Q + 0.22\,B;\ R^2 = 0.355 \qquad (8.1)$$

Our choice of independent variables is based on the direct relationship Bowles assumes to exist in his path analysis (containing S, Q, B), adding O as another independent variable, representing either effort or psychical income, as announced. In comparison to Bowles's result, R^2 increases from 0.255 to 0.355, but the positive algebraic sign of O excludes it interpretation as psychic income. Only on the assumption that O constitutes an effort can we accept (8.1). The virtual absence of an influence exerted by years of schooling remains an unsatisfactory feature of (8.1), however.

By dropping Q and B as directly affecting variables we obtain an alternative result:

$$I = 0.48\,O + 0.12\,S;\ R^2 = 0.323 \qquad (8.2)$$

which is only slightly less in explanatory power, but again shows an (even increased) impact of O in its role of an effort index.

Exclusion of O as an explanatory variable, and taking as the only independent variable S, we obtain:

$$I = 0.44\,S;\ R^2 = 0.197 \qquad (8.3)$$

which implies a considerable fall in explanatory power.

The evidence so far shown gives more support to O as an effort indicator than as a representative of psychological income.

As a check on the preceding result equation (8.2) has also been estimated for the other age groups considered by Bowles and Nelson. For the four groups we obtain Table 8.1.

Table 8.1: Regression coefficients and R^2 for O and S: four age groups

Age group	Regression for O	Coefficients for S	R^2
25–34	0.41	0.03	0.184
35–44	0.50	0.10	0.324
45–54	0.48	0.12	0.323
55–64	0.41	0.11	0.242

The material used, of course, limits the possibilities of experimenting. Various alternative ways of explaining income variance are conceivable, if one had access to measured independent variables whose appearance in the earnings function would make sense. From a Dutch sample of a few hundred higher employees a wealth of other variables has become available. Whereas a full analysis of this new material is to appear elsewhere, one feature may be mentioned here. In contradistinction to actual years of schooling, years of schooling required for the jobs held appear to explain about 85 per cent of income variance. With this in mind, one may wonder whether there is not a high correlation between occupational status and schooling required. Introduction into equations (8.1) or (8.2) of that variable might therefore change the algebraic sign of O and hence leave room for the psychical income assumption. We shall not pursue this issue however.

8.4 'JUSTIFIED' INCOME DIFFERENCES: THOSE COMPENSATING FOR EFFORT

Elsewhere (Tinbergen, 1975a) I have introduced a theory of 'justice' with regard to income differences and proposed to consider as justified income differences those constituting a compensation for effort. Other components of income, especially scarcity rents of inherited capabilities or inherited wealth, are not considered elements of an equitable incomes-and-jobs distribution. On the assumption (i) that our variable O constitutes a proper measure of effort connected with each type of job, we may use our results in order to estimate which portion of income variance is justified in the above sense. Using standardised variables x_i (exogenous) and y (endogenous) and assuming (ii) that the variance l of the latter can be completely explained by a number I of variables x_i we have:

$$l = \sum b_i r_i \qquad 1 \leqslant i \leqslant I \qquad (8.4)$$

where b_i are the regression coefficients in:

$$y = \sum b_i x_i \qquad (8.5)$$

and r_i is the simple correlation between x_i and y. To any one of the x_i we can then attribute a contribution $b_i r_i$ to the unit variance of y. Further assuming (iii) that the b_O we found in our incomplete ($I = 2$) regressions are the same as the ones needed in the complete regression (8.5), we find for the contribution of O, as a percentage of total variance, 18, 28, 27, and 20, respectively, for the four age groups mentioned in Table 8.1. The reader will be aware of the heroic cumulation of assumptions used, however.

8.5 OCCUPATIONAL STATUS AS A CO-DETERMINANT OF EDUCATION CHOSEN

We shall now tackle the third subject mentioned in section 8.1. This means the attribution to O of a different role in the path analysis presented by other authors, namely the role of *co-determining the length of the schooling process*. This exercise will be carried out for a number of alternatives. First, O will be used as the only exogenous variable determining the number S of years of schooling. Secondly, various second exogenous variables will be added, in turn: to begin with income I, considered as 'income aimed at'; next, parents' income P, socioeconomic background B and father's education E. Thirdly, three exogenous variables will be used, namely O, P and E. The material used did not permit to estimate other three-variable regressions, or a four-variable one. The results obtained are shown in Table 8.2.

Table 8.2: Schooling 'explained' by (a) occupational status (O) only, (b) by O and income I, (c) by O and parents' income P, (d) by O and father's education E, (e) by O and socioeconomic background B, (f) by O, P and E, (g) by P and E, for four age groups. Regression coefficients are shown in column headed by exogenous variables used. Variance explained is indicated by R^2 (regression coefficients and R^2 in per cent)

Age	(a) O	R^2	(b) O	I	R^2	(c) O	P	R^2	(d) O	E	R^2	(e) O	B	R^2	(f) O	P	E	R^2	(g) P	E	R^2
25–34	74	55	73	1.5	55	60	28	61	63	23	59	56	33	62	56	23	16	63	42	33	42
35–44	73	54	70	6.5	54	60	23	57	62	23	58	54	30	59	54	17	19	60	42	34	42
45–54	63	48	62	9.4	46	52	30	53	58	28	53	47	39	57	49	22	21	56	45	28	39
55–64	63	40	59	8.8	41	47	35	49	54	24	45	44	36	49	43	30	15	51	46	25	38

The following conclusions can be drawn.

(1) In nearly all cases somewhat more than half of the variance in S can be explained.
(2) The regression coefficient for O is in almost all cases 0.5 or more.
(3) The multiple correlation coefficients obtained are highest for the youngest group and in all cases falling with rising age.
(4) The impact of parents' income and of father's education is practically equal; that of socioeconomic background clearly somewhat higher.
(5) Occupational status O contributes significantly to the explanation of schooling S: additional variance explained can be read from cases (f) and (g) and amounts to 21, 18, 17, and 13 per cent, respectively, for the four age groups considered. Practically the same results are found by comparing results under (e) with the single correlations between S and B, not mentioned in the table.

As a further check on conclusion (5) a few more estimates were made for the age group 25–34 only. An explanation of S was attempted using O, childhood IQ (Q) and socioeconomic background (B) and another one without including O among these exogenous variables. Variance explained by the inclusion of O amounts to 0.64 as compared with 0.46 without O. The regression coefficient for O was 0.52. Thus, as the main conclusion of this section we may retain conclusion (5).

8.6 CONCLUSIONS

Our exploration of the role to be attributed to occupational status O using Duncan, Featherman and Duncan, (1968) material suggests that:

(i) if O is assumed to co-determine income it is a measure for effort needed in performing one's occupation rather than a measure for psychical income;
(ii) the latter possibility can only be opted for if income is determined to a high degree by schooling required as distinct from actual schooling, and if a high correlation exists between occupational status and schooling required;
(iii) assuming, on the basis of (i), that O represents the effort needed to perform the occupation chosen, we can estimate what portion of income variance is justified in the sense of section 8.4; and this portion would then be of the order of 20 to 30 per cent;
(iv) if O is assumed to be a co-determinant of the years of schooling rather than of income, its role appears to be significant: its addition to other determinants such as income, parents' income, father's

education socio-economic background or childhood IQ raises the portion of variance explained by some 18 per cent in the various cases studied.

REFERENCES

Bowles, S. and Nelson, V.I. (1974), 'The inheritance of "IQ" and the intergenerational reproduction of economic inequality', *The Review of Economics and Statistics*, LVI, p. 39.

Duncan, O.D., Featherman, D.L. and Duncan, B. (1968), *Socio-Economic Background and Occupational Achievement: Extensions of a Basic Model*, Washington, US Department of Health, Education and Welfare.

de Wolff, P. and van Slijpe, A.R.D. (1972), *The Relation between Income, Intelligence, Education and Social Background*, Institute of Actuarial Science and Econometrics, University of Amsterdam.

Husén, T. (1969), *Talent, Opportunity and Career*, Stockholm.

Jencks, C. (1972), *Inequality*, New York.

Mincer, J. (1974), *Schooling, Experience and Earnings*, NBER, New York.

Tinbergen, J. (1975a), 'Substitution of academically trained by other manpower', *Weltwirtschaftliches Archiv*, 111, p. 466.

Tinbergen, J. (1975b), *Income Differences: Recent Research*, North-Holland.

9 Determinants of Manager Incomes

9.1 INTRODUCTION

In today's western societies managers are probably the most powerful social group; their power surpasses the power of capitalists, i.e. capital-owners. This is not a new idea and has already been recognised in the phrase 'managerial revolution'. In essence it means that in large enterprises the managing board rather than the shareholders' meeting determines the enterprise's policy. Similarly in the public sector the Cabinet has a greater impact on current affairs than parliament.

It is far from easy, however, accurately to define the group of managers, especially if one wants to choose as a basis what Censuses of Occupations or of Industries offer us, as an 'as careful a description as possible' of real business life. In such Censuses a separate group for agriculture and other forms of small enterprises that characterises these forms of productive activity is the one of 'cooperating family members', where the head of the family is counted among the '(small) *independents*' together with the '(free) professions', whose income often is not 'small'. Most attention has been given to the continually growing numbers of *dependants*, those working in somebody else's service. The latter criterion has increasingly been used by Marxist-oriented ideologists as an indication of *exploitation*, even without asking what the ratio between incomes of the employer and his employee is. The latter quantitative criterion initially has been—correctly—the criterion for exploitation. In order to define what officially is now known as the *position in the enterprise* two additional criteria have been needed, namely the limitation of what constitutes an enterprise and, subsequently, of heads of enterprises. The concept of enterprise has been given a technical and a juridical form. So the concept of *technical unit* has resulted as distinct from a (juridical) *enterprise*, and a large enterprise may contain far more than one technical unit, the latter being determined by the production technology. Even a geographical aspect has to be added by the introduction of the concept of *local establishment*, because an enterprise may have a variety of establishments at different locations. An example is a retail enterprise with local affiliations; but also a production enterprise with a sales office located elsewhere. Corresponding with all these definitions of production units, heads of firms may be enterprise heads, heads of technical units or heads of local establishments.

An additional complication is the existence of *cooperatives* and *limited companies* whose managing directors are also employees. Thus, in various Censuses independent heads of enterprises, managing directors of limited companies and of cooperatives are enumerated separately.

The last complicating element brings us to the essential subject of this chapter, which we shall indicate by the concept of *hierarchy*. In large enterprises a distinction can be made between a number of levels of leading personnel, who together form a *pyramid*—a metaphor often used. Below the level of the heads of enterprises and managing directors of limited companies or cooperatives, we find several levels, down to foremen and workers. The latter are subdivided into *production* workers and *non-production* workers, including clerical workers, etc. Production workers may be skilled, and some *levels of skill* may be distinguished. The hierarchy structure probably originates from military and administrative structures and has penetrated increasingly into material production units when they became larger. The three types are also characterised as *bureaucracies*. In communist countries they tend to be large—because economies of scale impressed communist thinking—and another hierarchy, the party bureaucracy, is added.

A feature we shall emphasise in this chapter is that the management of these large units is done not only by 'the' head of an enterprise, but jointly by the *upper part of the pyramid*, organised in tiers and characterised by *line functions* as distinct from *staff functions*, which, as a rule, do advisory work, including research and scientific work, also to be found in the world of free professions and the education sector, especially in tertiary education.

To the extent that management of production or government implies the exertion of power, the upper part of the pyramid described is more important than the top of small business. The word 'manager' accordingly is used to indicate the top of the pyramid rather than heads of enterprises of all sizes. The American Census of Occupations, comparable to the European Census of Enterprises, reflects this fact by a different subdivision of the active population into main occupational groups. The second main occupational group 'managers, officials, proprietors, etc.' consists of this upper part of the pyramid rather than of the chief executives who will be dealt with in this chapter. The first main occupational group 'professionals, technicans, etc.' is similar to what in Europe are called the free professions. In the other main occupational groups, (craftsmen, salesmen, farm managers, etc.) a considerable number of heads of smaller production units are included. Data on the social position in the productive sector have to be taken from the administration of social insurance, in the USA a much more recent institution than in Europe, especially Germany, where Bismarck introduced social insurance in the late nineteenth century, in order to compete with the Social Democrats.

The clear difference between, on the one hand, independents and, on the other hand, the top of the hierarchies is also shown by the different quantitative development of their numbers as a percentage of total working population. Over the last few decades the number of independents decreased, whereas the number of managers, etc. increased relatively.

As indicated briefly only by its title, this chapter principally deals with the income of *chief executives*: its level as well as the *determinants*, implying the possibilities of *influencing* that income. The importance of the subject has been clarified—if necessary—by the French economist Serge-Christophe Kolm (1977). His vision is that the level of top-manager incomes is hard to explain with the aid of economic factors and, rather, needs an explanation by sociological factors. He thinks this group is in a monopoloid position, characterised by a kind of solidarity. In a sense—but possibly somewhat exaggeratedly—this group may be said to be able to determine their own income share from the total gross revenue of big business. The aim of this chapter is to summarise the results of research directed at this state of affairs and to identify some possibilities of further research. Since the subject is by no means a new one we shall have to consult, first, the existing literature.

9.2 SOME DATA TAKEN FROM EXISTING PUBLICATIONS

It is not our intention to present a complete survey of the existing extensive literature: rather to summarise briefly the relevant *quantitative* information. Two very important sources are Newcomer (1955) and Lewellen (1968). The former provides us with a number of data on 1900, 1925 and 1950, including the growth of assets of 214, 238 and 428 corporations in those three years. It is not clear whether and in what way these are representative. Assets of the median corporation grow from $45 million in 1900 to $147 million in 1950. The data show some characteristics of the 'chief executive officer' which we shall discuss later. For 1950 an interesting survey of the incomes of these top managers is given, as far as these could be traced from reports of shareholders' meetings, composed of earnings and profit shares, subdivided according to size of the corporations' capital. Table 9.1 reproduces these data.

88   Part II. Income Formation

Table 9.1: Incomes in 1000$ of chief executives of corporations of different size (assets in $ m)

Incomes	Assets ≤ 100	101–200	201–500	> 500
≤ 50	29 %	28 %	21 %	11 %
51–100	41 %	39 %	35 %	38 %
101–200	29 %	30 %	34 %	38 %
> 200	1 %	3 %	10 %	13 %
	100 %	100 %	100 %	100 %

Lewellen (1968) provides us with many more details, using *c.* 550 persons and *c.* 50 largest corporations (according to *Fortune* magazine's ordering in 1964). Incomes of chief executives are shown for the person with the highest income as well as for the average of the five highest paid. Options on shares are transformed into income: the incomes are after tax and show the development over time, reproduced in abbreviated form in Table 9.2 (taken from Lewellen, p. 129).

Table 9.2: Incomes after tax in $1000 of (A) the highest-paid and (B) the average of the five highest-paid; selected years

Year:	1940	1945	1950	1955	1960	1963
A	102	62	123	214	222	187
B	60	41	79	125	133	121

The composition of these incomes is mentioned for most of the years as well under the headings (1) salary and bonuses, (2) pension, (3) profit share and postponed earnings, and (4) options on shares. From 1950 on pension provisions play a more important role than before, and categories (3) and in particular (4) from 1955 onwards. For 1955–63 options on shares account for, on average, 51 per cent of computed income before tax. The author adds (p. 186) that, after correction for price movements, no change in real income occurs between 1940 and 1963. For top executives' gross incomes of the 500 largest corporations Burck (1976) estimates that these showed no real change, whereas the index of real wages rose 39 per cent during that period.

Lewellen continues his analysis by the statement that in 1940 as well as in 1963 number 5 from the top executives after tax received some 40 per cent of what the top executive was paid. In addition, no change occurred in the portion of total income out of salaries and bonuses. He states in addition (p. 299) that in the period covered turnover, capital and profits grew more quickly than the incomes of top executives. Nominal incomes after tax of the top executives increased by a factor 2.1, as compared to 2.4–3.2 for the best-paid professions (medical experts, lawyers), 3.6 for blue-collar workers and 5.0 for young graduates. The author ascribes this change to the publicity given by the Securities Exchange Commission to incomes of chief executives.

In what follows we shall formulate alternative assumptions.

For the United Kingdom and the United States, Smyth, Boyes and Peseau (1975) published additional figures and added some results of econometric research. For the UK they compared the various methods to define a firm's size. For the years 1971–72 sales, assets, employment and share capital of the 1000 largest enterprises were compared. The squared correlation coefficients (r^2) between any pair of measures vary from 0.50 to 0.74 and so are fairly but not very high. For the 500 largest corporations in the UK and the USA also the elasticities between any pair of measures are mentioned. Sales in both countries show elasticities below unity; the only elasticity > 1, but 1.06 and 1.07 only is for assets with regard to employment (for the USA and the UK, respectively). These results are not very interesting. Much more interesting is a series of attempts to express, among other variables, the top executive's income EC as a (linear) function of profits P and sales S. With the aid of a device to eliminate multicollinearity the best result obtained is:

$$EC = 100108 + 1.07 P + 0.025 S$$

For a relation between EC and sales only the result is:

$$EC = 149456 + 0.023 S \qquad (9.1)$$

Incomes do not contain, however, 'postponed compensation' and options on shares. Both formulae use \$1 as unit for EC, but \$1000 for P and S.

For other than the two Anglo-Saxon countries, some figures of chief executives are available for Japan and the Netherlands, in both cases from tax returns. For a comparison, the definitions of income must as a matter of course be taken account of. In 1977, according to the *Japan Economic Journal* (8 May 1978, p. 3) in Japan 136 persons had an income over 200 million yen. A list of the twenty highest incomes shows that only few non-business men are in that group. A second factor to take into account is that Japan's population is about half that of America's. (This is why we compare Japanese figures for 136 persons with the 272 highest-paid business men in the USA.) Their lowest income, as reported by Burck (1976) in 1975 was about \$220,000. This, however, is only their labour income (earnings), amounting, according to Lewellen (1968), to 12 per cent only of their total income. The latter may then be estimated at more than eight times the income mentioned, hence $1.76 million. The lowest total income of Japan's 136 richest amounts to 167 times the average income in Japan. For the USA $1.76 million amounts to some 250 times the average American income. According to this (very crude) comparison Japan shows *less inequality* than the USA, a result also obtained by other authors from other data.

For the Netherlands in the income statistics of the Central Bureau of Statistics, derived from tax returns, managing directors of limited companies are shown separately. In order to make a comparison with the USA here we follow a different way and concentrate on labour incomes as part of the total incomes of the managers considered. In 1966[1] 2121 of these managing directors had a total income over 100,000 fl. For the group of all who had an income beyond that amount labour income was 79,365 fl. The population of the United States having been 150 million as compared with 13 million in Holland, the comparable rank to 2121 in Holland was 30,836. An attempt to rank the labour income of executives in the USA (Tinbergen, 1977) yielded for the period 1970–75 and in dollars of that period an estimate of $51,000. In 1966 prices this is $36,400 (132,000 fl.), that is 166 per cent of the income of 79,365 fl. Incomes *per capita* in the Netherlands were 5446 fl. in 1966 and, for the USA $3400 (12,300 fl.), i.e. 226 per cent of the Dutch figure. According to these estimates then, in the Netherlands high incomes are relatively more moderate than in the USA.

It seems interesting to add a comparison between the United Kingdom and the United States. For this we take the relation between chief executive incomes EC and sales S, discussed before for the United Kingdom. With the aid of Burck's (1976) data for American corporations a similar (linear) relationship was estimated:

$$EC = 191300 + 0.011\,S$$

Table 9.3 shows some results for various values of S:

Table 9.3: Labour incomes of chief executives (in $1000) EC of large corporations in the UK and the USA for some values of sales S (in billions of $)

Sales in billions of $	20	5	1
EC in the UK in $1000	609	264	172
EC in the USA in $1000	411	246	202

The figures (which may not be strictly comparable) suggest that the largest corporations in the UK pay quite a bit more to their chief executives than those in the USA, but the smaller ones less than in the USA. This may be a consequence of the more progressive income tax in the UK.

9.3 POSSIBLE INFLUENCES OF POWER

The concept of power has various components: thus, a physical component exists—structural or revolutionary *violence*—alongside the component of *tradition* or *habit*. There are also two components of *economic* power or *scarcity*: the power of *natural* scarcity and that of *organised* scarcity. The latter may take the form of a complete or partial monopoly (monopolistic competition). It may also exist in less overt ways, if a sociological group acts in solidarity without formal agreements, or has, for instance, easier access to the government hierarchy, whose upper layers feel themselves members of one group: a certain mobility between business managers and the top tier of civil servants. This mobility has been studied extensively by Lindblom (1977) and, incidentally, by this author (Tinbergen, 1979).

Drucker (1977) states it is 'nonsense' to interpret the high incomes of chief executives as the price the market is forcing the organisers of production to pay. He discusses the possibilities of avoiding taxes and of the *internal logic of a hierarchy* as the determinants. He starts his description of that logic with a foreman who earns $15,000 without and $20,000 with 'fringe benefits', that is, the advantages business life pays in kind to its top people. Every next higher level in the hierarchy then must earn some percentage more. This thesis shows some similarity with Tuck's (1954) ideas. This will be given a numerical shape in section 9.6.

Power elements can be reduced to their economic minimum and so, for many, justify them, when *natural* scarcity only of the capabilities needed properly to do the job of the various forms of leadership are shown. We shall deal with this way of income formation in sections 9.4 and 9.5. We then come back to the theory and practice of hierarchies and to some possible checks of the two theories set out.

Before concluding the present section we want to set out another concept of an *equitable income distribution*. The definition of an equitable income distribution adhered to by many is the distribution resulting from free competition on both sides of the market. This means the elimination of monopoloid elements (including those in a hierarchical structure). We consider such a free competition distribution to be appropriate or efficient for the operation of an economy, which is also optimal in a sense. But for us (cf. Pen and Tinbergen, 1977) equitable income distribution contains a further element, namely an equal satisfaction or welfare of the various social groups. The optimal income may yield a higher level of satisfaction to those in charge of interesting, fascinating or challenging work than to those whose work is dirty, dull, heavy or monotonous. That depends on whether the challenging work implies a burden of responsibility that is experienced as a negative satisfaction. More information is needed here.

9.4 THE MARKET'S DEMAND SIDE: THE INTENSITY OF REQUIRED CAPABILITIES

In the economist's usual view of a market with free competition (especially on the demand side) the price the *organisers of production* are willing to pay for a well-defined occupation (or job) equals the *marginal productivity* of the implementation of the tasks required. The crudest approaches of this method were those where a small number of production factors were distinguished—for instance, natural resources, labour and capital, or even the latter two only, if product is interpreted only as the value added to the material inputs. The price of labour was then expressed as a function of the quantity of labour and that of capital used. The simplest production function was the one formulated by Cobb and Douglas (Douglas, 1934), which was soon enriched by an element of *technical progress*. In later research the latter was split up into a changing quality of labour as well as of the capital goods used. If capital goods did not change, but the quality of labour or the organisation of production did, it became customary to speak of 'disembodied' technical change, although 'unembodied' seems a better expression. Technical change in which capital goods only changed their quality was called 'embodied' technical development.

In these early attempts to establish production functions all labour was considered as a *homogeneous* production factor of which the quantity was only a determinant of the product obtained. It is clear that this is too crude a picture where many essential problems have been eliminated *a priori*. Most of the important problems of the labour market and certainly the ones connected with manager incomes are connected with differences in the quality of labour.

For practical purposes this has been understood decades ago and resulted in what is known as *job evaluation* or *classification*. For a large number of occupations or jobs a number of *qualifications* have been identified and the *intensity* or degree of each necessary to do the job adequately. Such intensities usually have been expressed in rank numbers (for instance, from 0 to 9), comparable to scores in competitions of certain games or to marks as given to students. The scales have been calibrated so as to match with standards defined for some basic jobs and classification performed in cooperation with representatives of employers and employees. Starting with the occupations in single industries and with the simpler jobs, the system has gradually been extended to more industries and to more difficult and complicated jobs, and the system has also increasingly been made more uniform, so as to make possible *inter-industry* comparison. For the highest functions various different methods still are applied by differing corporations. A well-known starting point for managers may be the analysis by the famous economist Schumpeter (1912) who characterised a good entrepreneur as the man who was able to think of 'new combinations' and to implement them. In recent years this capability was lacking in quite a few enterprises, as exemplified by the rigidity with regard to products made: textile producers, for instance, who wanted to manufacture textiles only instead of textile machines, or combination of textiles with plastics (two concrete examples of combinations in the Benelux countries, which thereby saved the enterprises which invented the innovations).

Among the authors who have tried to characterise the essential features of managers Barron (1930) sees *thoroughness* as one such feature, and he feels that much formal schooling adds too little of this quality to their students. Maccoby (1976) and Harrell (1973) elaborate on this aspect, and as early as 1970 Muller elaborated the system used by Shell, Europe's largest corporation (in terms of assets—if employment is taken as the criterion, Philips is the largest).

One of the difficulties of the problem of defining the evaluation criteria for managers is that the organisers of production have to define the criteria on which they will be selected themselves.

It is difficult to deny that the required itensity of any one capability will be higher for the same occupation in a larger corporation than in a smaller; this is an argument in favour of some sort of hierarchy in their organisation. But this raises the question, however, of what the optimal size of an enterprise is. As long as economies of scale are a clear technological feature (as in chemical industries, or steel-making), a larger enterprise will be the more productive. This tends to monopoloid situations, however, with the possibility of negative economic consequences. But there are also enterprises which are larger than necessary—the product of 'empire builders' (cf. van den Doel, 1971), with unnecessary hierarchies. The latter may reduce job satisfaction and hence productivity, as set out for the German Democratic Republic by the communist dissident Bahro (1977), partly as a consequence of the irritation created by supervision.

The central question arising in the search for the causes of the hierarchy element is whether the chief always contributes more to production than his subordinates. It is not always self-evident that the chief must be able to do all his subordinates do—and somewhat more; the 'somewhat' that entitles him to 20 per cent more income. If a subordinate is a very able specialist, it isn't necessary for the chief to be so; it is sufficient if he is able to assess the assumptions made by the specialist and the significance for the enterprise of the results obtained. His common sense must be equal to or higher than the specialist's; his specialised knowledge or ability may fall short, and that may be scarcer than common sense.

For good leadership in a small or medium-sized enterprise the *ability to deal with people* is important. For a large enterprise this may be less so and more abstract capabilities—Muller and van Lennop's so-called *helicopter view*—is important. It implies an ability to survey the totality of problems the enterprise is faced with, as well as a *sense of proportion*: the relative importance of the individual problems.

An important aspect of the required intensities of capabilities is the extent to which they are *innate* and the extent to which they can be *learned* or developed by learning. Where the latter applies the scarcity of the category of employees or leaders may be influenced by the organisation and *expansion of learning facilities*. As early as 1955 Newcomer pointed to the then recent institutions of *business schools* as an indication that the capabilities required can, at least partly, be learned.

One attempt to estimate a *production function* from which the demand for three types of labour can be derived was undertaken by the author for the United States. The types of labour considered were (1) professionals, technicians, etc., (2) managers, officials and proprietors, and (3) all others. The type of function estimated was a so-called translog production function, where the logarithm of total product is a quadratic function of the logs of the quantities of production factors; in this case the three types of labour. For this function is is possible to express the *share* in total income λ_i ($i = 1, 2, 3$) as linear functions of the logs of the quantities L_i. The expressions found for 1969, with symmetry imposed, were:

$$\lambda_1 = 0.3748 + 0.1041 \ln L_1 + 0.0028 \ln L_2 - 0.1069 \ln L_3$$

$$\lambda_2 = 0.1764 + 0.0028 \ln L_1 + 0.0001 \ln L_2 - 0.0029 \ln L_3$$

$$\lambda_3 = 0.4488 - 0.1069 \ln L_1 - 0.0029 \ln L_2 + 0.1098 \ln L_3$$

The interesting feature of these results is that λ_2 appears to be *practically constant* (if rounded to two decimal places). If the numbers of managers supplied were considered to be autonomous, and in particular only weakly affected by earnings, then an increase would result in an inversely proportional fall in earnings, as a consequence of the demand resulting from this production function. Supply elasticities have not been estimated accurately, as far as known to the author, but positive as well as negative elasticities have been found. The position of zero elasticity (autonomy) seems to be realistic.

9.5 THE SUPPLY SIDE OF THE MANAGER MARKET: THE CAPABILITY INTENSITIES ACTUALLY AVAILABLE

As observed, the required capabilities' intensities are *partly innate*, or inherited. In family enterprises much knowledge and many assumptions will be passed on from parents to children. However, the best leadership will not always be supplied by parents. In a number of cases this will have to be attracted from outside. Both Newcomer's and Burck's data show that the need for formal training as a supplier of entrepreneurs' services has gradually increased. Newcomer (1955, p. 68) mentions that in 1900 25 per cent of the older managers had grammar school education only (in 1950 of the younger managers no more than 2.5 per cent). In 1900 35 per cent had attained secondary schooling (1955, 17 per cent). A university degree was found for 5 per cent in 1900 and in 1950 for 20 per cent of the younger executives of corporations. Of the chief executives of the 500 largest corporations dealt with by Burck (1976) more than 50 per cent had a university degree. Increasingly the *business school* supplied their training. Sturdivant and Adler (1976) inform us that 'some college' had been taken in 1900 by 40 per cent, and in 1975 by 96 per cent.

The social background from which the 500 top executives were recruited also changed. In 1900 45 per cent were reported as 'rich', in 1976 this was the background of only 8 per cent.

The intensities of capabilities are not usually available from generally accessible sources; mostly on the files of personnel departments. A limited number of enterprises only were prepared to make that information available. In the Netherlands AKZO corporation was most helpful (cf. Hartog, 1983). More recently an extensive inquiry was made by Rumberger (1981a and b, 1983), who used various editions of the *Dictionary of Occupational Titles* to estimate, for a large sample of the American labour force, the level of schooling required for their occupation. Similar attempts for non-cognitive capabilities have not come to my attention.

9.6 THE DETERMINANTS OF EARNINGS: IDEAL METHOD TO TRACE THEM AND SOME PROVISIONAL DATA: THE HIERARCHY FRAMEWORK

For an economist the ideal method of tracing and verifying the determinants of earnings consists of (i) constructing theories on demand for and supply of the category of labour under discussion (here, managers); (ii) assuming that, in the somewhat longer run, equilibrium between demand and supply will be approached and require an equilibrium level of earnings. The *earnings equation* expresses this equilibrium by equating demand and supply and mathematically expresses earnings in terms of *demand factors* and *supply factors*. In the preceding sections we have discussed some of the variables that may co-determine the demand for and the supply of managers, hence some of these demand and supply factors. As stated before, we do not know statistical figures for all relevant variables yet. This applies in particular to the variables required intensity of *non-schooling capabilities* essential for the adequate performance of a manager's tasks. We should add that these non-schooling capabilities are given different headings by different authors, e.g. leadership, ability to survey the totality of problems to be faced, sense of proportion, ability to deal with people. These concepts may partly overlap.

Top executives, who are most typically the managers of advanced developed countries, operate within the framework of a hierarchy and some authors have developed a theory of hierarchies, already briefly described in section 9.3. We shall now enter into some more detail of a *stylised* version of this, but without discussing whether the assumptions made can be based on economically meaningful arguments (cf. Lydall, 1959, who was the first who formulated a number of assumptions; and Wegner, 1981, who mentions and criticises the arguments used by a series of authors in favour of these assumptions). The stylised version still leaves us with one degree of freedom, hence one parameter to choose; moreover, we shall find that that version deviates from observed versions.

The stylised version assumes that the hierarchy consists of N levels (numbered from 1 for the lowest to N for the highest level) and that each person in any level supervises m persons of one level lower (the *control span*) whereas his or her income y is h times the income of the supervised person, hence:

$$y_l = h y_{l-1}$$

where l is an arbitrary level. The income of the person at the top of the pyramid ($l = N$) y_N will then be:

$$y_N = y_1 h^N \tag{9.2}$$

where y_1 is the (lowest) income at level 1.

The total number n of persons working in the hierarchy will be:

$$n = 1 + m + m^2 + \ldots + m^{N-1} = \frac{m^N - 1}{m - 1} \tag{9.3}$$

The value of N for a given number n follows from this relation:

$$N = \{ln(nm - n + 1)\}/ln\, m \tag{9.4}$$

Since from (9.2) we may derive:

$$ln\, y_N = ln\, y_1 + N\, ln\, h = ln\, y_1 + \frac{ln\, h}{ln\, m} \{ln\,(m-1) + ln\, n\} \tag{9.5}$$

if we neglect the 1 in (9.4), which is permitted for large n; we may rewrite (9.5):

$$ln\, y_N = \left\{ ln\, y_1 + \frac{ln\, h}{ln\, m} ln\,(m-1) \right\} + \frac{ln\, h}{ln\, m} ln\, n \tag{9.6}$$

or

$$ln\, y_N = a + b\, ln\, n \tag{9.7}$$

where

$$a = ln\, y_1 - \frac{ln\, h}{ln\, m} ln\,(m-1), \text{ and } b = ln\, h / ln\, m.$$

For the 150 largest European corporations we estimated n as a function of sales S (derived from *Vision*, October 1977, pp. 49ff.) and (9.1) for the United Kingdom (which connects y_N with S) in order to estimate numerically equation (9.7). The result was:

$$ln\, y_N = 5.43 + 0.1532\, ln\, n \tag{9.8}$$

For some values of m between 5 and 10 we then obtain values of h between 1.28 and 1.42.

Actual incomes of individual $Nr\, 5$ in the hierarchy for a long period amounted to 0.4 times the income of the top executive. For values of m between 5 and 10, however, $Nr\, 5$ is only one level below the chief executive and the ratio of 2.5 of his income to that of $Nr\, 5$ is much higher than 1.42. So we attain as a first impression that *near the top income inequality is much higher than the stylised model indicates.*

Since little empirical research on the degree of realism of the assumptions at the basis of the stylised model has been done, our main conclusion must be to stress the necessity of such empirical research; and to do so we need more data on the intensity of non-schooling capabilities needed for the occupations in the upper part of hierarchies. The subject will be taken up in more detail in the next section.

9.7 SOME POSSIBLE TESTS OF THE POWER THEORY OF CHIEF EXECUTIVE INCOMES

We now propose to discuss some conceivable tests of the theory we have suggested, namely, that chief executives' incomes are higher than the incomes that would result in a market with free competition; in other words, that they are expressing a monopoloid element.

One method is that set out at the end of the preceding section, where we stressed the desirablility and also the lack of empirical data to perform that test. Its essence is that from a *production function* containing as one of the inputs the chief manager an estimate of his marginal productivity is made and compared with his income. In order to avoid the complications of counterproduction contained in manager incomes (cf. Chapter 4) the production function should be estimated from *single-firm* data.

A second method is that based on Lewellen's (1968) and Burck's (1976) findings that top manager incomes have not changed in real terms since 1940 or 1952, whereas average incomes have increased considerably. From them we may conclude that at least in 1940 and in 1952 these incomes were relatively much higher than those accepted in 1976 by top managers, but that their jobs have nevertheless been done. This may be interpreted as indicating that managers are willing to do their work at relatively lower incomes than in 1940 or 1952, and that therefore they did have a *monopoloid* position in these years. It does not follow that they also had such a position in 1976, unless more recent figures show a further reduction. Compilation of these more recent figures therefore constitutes a second method of testing.

A third method consists of a *comparison* with incomes of persons who do similar work in a competitive market. This may be the case with the employees of *consulting* firms. For the Dutch consulting firm Logica Nederland B.V. the 1975 and 1976 annual reports cite incomes of the professional staff of $27,000 and $20,800. The 1960 Census of Population PC(2)8B reports incomes of (white) sales engineers aged 35–54 years in 1959 of $15,590, of operations and systems researchers and analysts of $13,500, and of economists of $17,848. Subject Report PC(2)–7F states that considerable numbers of accountants, industrial engineers and sales managers earned less than $50,000. For these American figures it is less clear whether they worked as consultants, although they are included in the free professions. Here again a more systematic inquiry is recommended.

9.8 DETERMINANTS AND PROSPECTS OF MANAGER INCOMES

From the preceding analysis, and in particular from sections 9.4 and 9.5, we think we may conclude that incomes of top managers may be influenced to some extent. We base this conclusion on the possibility of *developing capabilities* needed by a learning process, in particular in business schools—we observed that this institution has been expanded considerably. Just as Goldberger's (1976, 1977, 1978) research enhances the plausibility of an *overestimation* by several authors of the inheritable component of cognitive abilities, the innate element of other capabilities required by managers seem to have been overestimated, as the history of many family enterprises illustrates.

Our conclusion then is founded on the suspicion that manager income formation contains elements of *monopoloid* character. This originates from a certain solidarity between members of the same sociological group, who find themselves on both the demand and the supply side of the market for managing personnel. That element may also express itself in the traditions prevailing in hierarchies, discussed in section 9.6. We admit, however, that more extensive and more convincing research is possible and hence desirable. For the practice of incomes policy we do not see much danger for western economies, since *psychical* income from prestige and challenging tasks also plays its role, and constitutes a sort of reserve, permitting a limitation on *money* income.

In addition to these factors for the future, *changes* in demand and supply will also exert their impact on manager incomes. On the demand side there will be a shift towards *service* industries, where the average size of the enterprise is smaller than in manufacturing industries. There also tends to develop—and here we follow Macrae (1976)—in manufacturing industry, a higher degree of *decentralisation* since some doubt has arisen regarding the productivity of large hierarchies. Bureaucracy has become a dirty word—perhaps rightly so—even though the need for coordination of production continues. Finally, the desire for more autonomous decision-making in the lower part of the hierarchy is a reality and has become possible as a consequence of better education: this will enhance job satisfaction and hence productivity.

On the supply side more schooling will work out and raise supply, especially for well-paid jobs, and so reduce monopoloid forces.

Demand as well as supply factors are moving in the direction of smaller income differences. In recent decades in both the United States and the Netherlands this has been clearly visible.

NOTE

1 Since this year is close to the year of Lewellen's data I did not try to update the following figures. Income distribution in the Netherlands have become much less unequal since, certainly more so than in the USA.

REFERENCES

Bahro, R. (1977), *Die Alternative* [*The Alternative*], Cologne, Frankfurt am Main, Europäische Verlagsanstalt.

Barron, C.W. (1930), *They told Barron*, New York, p. 298.

Burck, C.G. (1976), 'A group profile of the Fortune 500 chief executives', *Fortune*, May, pp. 173ff.
Douglas, P.H. (1934), *The Theory of Wages*, New York, Macmillan.
Drucker, P.F. (1977), 'Is executive pay excessive?', *The Wall Street Journal*, 23 May.
Goldberger, A.S. (1976), 'Jensen on Burcks', *Educational Psychologist*, 12, pp. 64ff.
Goldberger, A.S. (1977), 'Twin methods: a sceptical view', in: Taubman, P. (ed.), *Kinometrics*, Amsterdam, North-Holland.
Goldberger, A.S. (1978), 'Pitfalls in the resolution of IQ inheritance', in Morton, N.E. and Chung, C.S. (eds), *Genetic Epidemiology*, New York.
Harrell, T.W. (1978), interviewed by Boertje, J.C.B. *Sociaal-Economisch Management*, 27 May, p. 17.
Hartog, J. (1983), *Allocation and the Earnings Functions*, research memorandum 8205, revised, February, Dept of Economics, University of Amsterdam.
Kolm, S.-C. (1977), *La transition socialiste*, Paris, Cerf.
Lewellen, W.G. (1968), *Executive Compensation in Large Industrial Corporations*, New York.
Lydall, H.F. (1959), 'The distribution of employment incomes', *Econometrica*, 27, pp. 110–15.
Maccoby, M. (1976), *The Gamesman, the New Corporate Leaders*, New York.
Macrae, N. (1976), 'The new capitalism', *The Economist*, 26 December.
Newcomer, M. (1955), *The Big Business Executive; the Factors that Made Him*, New York.
Muller, H. (1970), *The Search for the Qualities Essential to Advancement in a Large Industrial Group*; an exploratory study, Utrecht.
Pen, J. and Tinbergen, J. (1977), *Naar een rechtvaardiger inkomensverdeling* [*Towards a More Equitable Income Distribution*] Amsterdam and Brussels, Elsevier.
Rumberger, R.W. (1981a), 'The changing skill requirement of jobs in the US economy', *Industrial and Labor Relations Review*, 34, pp. 578–90.
Rumberger, R.W. (1981b), 'The rising incidence of overeducation in the US labor market', *Economics of Education Review*, 1, Summer, pp. 293–314.
Rumberger, R.W. (1983), *A Conceptual Framework for Analyzing Work Skills*, project report no. 83–A8, Institute for Research on Educational Finance and Governance.
Schumpeter, J.A. (1912), *Theorie der wirtschaftlichen Entwicklung* [*Theory of Economic Development*], Leipzig.
Smyth, D.J., Boyes, W.J. and Peseau, D.E. (1975), *Size, Growth, Profits and Executive Compensation in the Large Corporation*, London.
Sturdivant, F.D. and Adler, L.D. (1976), 'Executive origins: still a gray-flannel world?', *Harvard Business Review*, November/December, 125ff.
Tinbergen, J. (1977), 'How to reduce the incomes of the two labour elites', *European Economic Review*, 10, pp.115ff.
Tuck, R.H. (1954), *An Essay on the Economic Theory of Rank*, Oxford, Basil Blackwell.
van den Doel, J. (1971), *Konvergentie en evolutie* [*Convergence and Evolution*], Assen.
Wegner, E. (1981), *Die personelle Verteilung der Arbeitseinkommen*, [*The Personal Distribution of Labour Income*], Frankfurt and New York, Campus-Verlag.

10 Two Approaches to Quantify the Concept of Equitable Income Distribution

10.1 ALTERNATIVE DEFINITIONS OF EQUITY

In sociopolitical discussions the phrase 'equitable income distribution' constitutes a central concept. It may even be maintained that the background of conflicts on incomes is the belief that incomes show differences that surpass equitable differences. The solution of such conflicts might be furthered if more precise concepts than just feelings could be developed. Best of all, of course, would be the elaboration of measurable concepts and actual measurement. This chapter tries to clarify some recent contributions made to such an elaboration by the author, in collaboration with various colleagues (Bouma *et al.*, 1976; Pen, 1977; Berkouwer *et al.*, 1978; van Praag, 1978). It seems desirable to introduce the subject with the statement that there is no agreement among social scientists about the definition of an equitable distribution. In addition the reader should be reminded of the necessity not to consider incomes only, but at least some characteristics of the source(s) of income too, in particular efforts that have to be made in order to obtain that income. So in what follows it will be assumed, often tacitly, that the distributions considered are those of income and effort.

Disregarding the simplistic thesis that to arrive at an equitable distribution we only have to eliminate income from capital, it seems that three definitions of an equitable distribution are most frequently defended. Definition I maintains that an equitable income distribution is characterised by equality of each person's income to the contribution she or he makes to national product. This may be called the liberalist definition. It implies that incomes from capital, socioeconomic status of parents, and from exceptional inherited endowments with personality traits are all considered equitable. The implication that nature is equitable especially deserves attention.

Definitions II and III may be dealt with by the introduction of the concept of admissible income differences, which is just another way of describing an equitable income distribution. The two definitions have in common that income differences compensating for differences in effort are acceptable and sometimes called compensatory differences. Definition II also considers admissible differences due to a prevailing scarcity of productive personality traits. These differences are instrumental in allocating qualified individuals to the jobs where they will be most productive. For the adherents of Definition II this is a reason for accepting such differences as equitable. Adherents of Definition III do admit that 'scarcity rents' are useful for the most productive allocation of the individuals concerned, but do not agree that this makes such differences equitable. Their definition can only be presented in the form that an equitable income distribution equalises welfare among all individuals: those who make greater efforts are compensated by income differences which in fact means that everybody is, then, equally 'happy'. This argument should be restricted to those factors of happiness that can be socially organised. It excludes degrees of happiness due to purely personal elements such as religion, friendship, love or physiological handicaps of a serious nature.[1]

This chapter is based on Definition III; this is a value judgement and should therefore be explicitly stated as such. It is useful to be aware, however, of the possibility that society develops in such a direction that Definitions II and III may converge (cf. Tinbergen, 1977). Such a convergence would be attained if, by a sufficient expansion of education and training, all existing scarcities could be eliminated. This elimination would be reached if for every job to be filled in society a person could be found whose productive personality traits are identical to the traits required. Whether scarcity can be overcome again depends on the extent to which the relevant personality traits can be learned, given the inherited traits. The answer has to come from education research.

10.2 A PRECONDITION: MEASURABILITY OF WELFARE OR UTILITY

The application of Definition III of an equitable distribution crucially depends on the possibility of measuring welfare (or, in older economic language, utility); in other words, quantification of the concept of equitable income distribution requires quantification of welfare. Whereas in Pigou's opinion (Pigou, 1920) such a quantification should not be excluded, most economists until recently followed Pareto (1896) in denying it. Partly as a consequence of the general tendency of many sciences to expand beyond their original territory (Tinbergen, 1980) some economists have reintroduced the measurement of welfare as part of their discipline. This chapter deals with two approaches undertaken recently, admittedly both still in their infancy. As an introduction to the subject the present section discusses some elements appearing in a welfare (or utility) function. To the present author it seems appropriate to distinguish between variables, parameters and coefficients, with some important subdivisions. The main feature of the three elements is the degree of changeability. As the name indicates, variables are changeable entities. Parameters, as usual in mathematical terminology, are constants for individual observations (in our case for individuals or for households) but need not have the same constant value for all observations. Rather, they characterise the observed individual. Coefficients, finally, are constants and characterise the impact of variables and parameters on utility. Ideally they would characterise the human race, but occasionally one may want to limit this characterisation to parts of the human race or the human race in a certain cultural setting or stage.

As usual each attempt to classify elements has its limits or limitations. Thus, for practical purposes we may call some elements a parameter, but at closer look they may be variable when we consider a longer period of time. Family size provides an example.

This brings us to the practical aspect of mentioning by their concrete name a number of usually important elements. For our subject important examples clearly are income and job or occupation, the latter characterised by job evaluation variables which we shall also indicate by the phrase 'intensities of required capabilities'. Capabilities is a qualitative concept (e.g. intelligence, manual or physical strength or flexibility) but what matters in addition is the intensity or degree of that capability required to do the job 'properly'. What we shall add to job evaluation is the 'learnability' of the required intensity. The philosophy behind this concept is that, in order to attain a certain intensity of a qualification, an individual starts from an innate component inherited from her or his parents and is able during a learning process, to raise that intensity. The philosophy at stake is the tool that we hope will help us to integrate the educational aspect and the labour market aspect of a socioeconomic analysis of income distribution or of a policy to change income distribution. The learnability also has a time aspect: capabilities that can be easily learned can also be quickly learned. This opens up the possibility that some capability intensities are variables, where others are parameters, or, as we may also formulate it, are variables only in the long run.

Some of the most important parameters are the *innate components of productive capabilities* (intelligence, leadership, persistence, etc.); others are health, creativity and family size.

10.3 UTILITY MEASUREMENT FROM BEHAVIOUR: 'REVEALED' UTILITY

In principle, at least two methods of observation of some entity are available, which may be called direct and indirect measurement. In the case of utility direct measurement so far has only been attempted by asking the individuals involved how 'happy' they were, clearly after some explanation of the yardstick to be used. This method may be called an 'opinion poll', comparable to the public opinion polls held nowadays by Gallup institutes and their like. For reasons of exposition of some consequences of utility measurement we shall deal with the direct method in Section 10.4, even though this is slightly illogical. The indirect method does not measure the entity directly, but derives it from observed behaviour. The result will be indicated by revealed utility, in line with well-known similar expressions ('revealed preference', for instance). In cases such as our subject where a natural, generally accepted yardstick does not (yet?) exist, both methods have a drawback which precisely is the reason why many members of the profession deny the possibility of measurement. The drawback of the indirect method, now to be discussed, is that some assumptions have to be made which need not be made for the application of the direct method. We may even add that alternatives to the method exist where, with weaker assumptions, only partial information is obtained. Thus in Frisch's (1932) study the weak assumption is made that sugar is a non-substitutable commodity, but Frisch's measurement only aims at estimating the flexibility of the marginal utility.

The approach offered in this section is more ambitious; it aims at defining an equitable income distribution, assumed to be identical with a state where all individuals have the same level of utility or welfare. Accordingly, we have to start from a stronger assumption. This is that utility does not depend on the values of the parameters in the utility function. Less strong forms of this assumption are (a) that utility depends only weakly on parameter values, or (b) that our assumption only sets a limit to actual values of utility; namely, that a person with higher parameter values (variables being equal) has a utility level not lower than a person with a lower parameter value. All this is based on the further assumption that parameters are measured in such a way that rising values indicate characteristics usually considered attractive.[2] Among the examples of parameters mentioned at the end of section 10.2, only family size may have to be measured negatively.

Application of the method requires the availability of an earnings equation expressing earnings in terms of a number of variables and parameters.[3] Notwithstanding the considerable volume of research done on earnings equations, not many examples can be found which satisfy this condition. The main reason is that in the more successful results of estimating earnings equations so many dummies are used that it is not clear whether they represent a variable or a parameter. More generally, it is the lack of direct measurements available of what the real parameters are.

One of the best examples known to us is to be found in the revised version of a recent study by Berkhouwer et al. (1978, p. 9) where earnings y of AKZO's higher personnel before harmonisation[4] are expressed in terms of:

- x_1: general education required
- x_2: specialised education required
- x_3: experience required
- x_4: leadership capability
- x_5: capability for establishing external contacts
- x'_1: actual general education of individual
- x'_2: actual specialised education of individual
- x'_3: actual experience of individual

Only two non-cognitive capabilities were included since factor analysis carried out by Hartog (1978) seemed to show that two such factors are relevant. AKZO's practice is to use seven of these, because their denominations are more satisfactory to the persons involved. There thus remains the clear possibility of a considerable degree of overlapping between these seemingly different denominations.

Of the eight independent variables (in the statistical sense of that phrase) mentioned we consider as the variables in the terminology of this chapter x_1, x_2 and x_3, representing the job chosen. In contradistinction x'_1, x'_2 and x'_3 can be considered as parameters characterising—certainly in the short run—the individuals' intellectual capabilities, both the innate components and the (largely innate) learning capabilities. We are also inclined to consider x_4 and x_5 as largely innate capabilities, although this is not certain and needs further investigation. The material available does not permit a decomposition of these variables into a variable component and a parameter component, however.

The earnings equation runs:

$$y = 0.125\,x_1 + 0.313\,x_2 + 0.177\,x_3 + 0.218\,x_4 + 0.247\,x_5 +$$
$$(2.97)\quad (6.14)\quad (6.27)\quad (8.30)\quad (9.67)$$

$$0.073\,x'_1 + 0.138\,x'_2 - 0.010\,x'_3$$
$$(2.58)\quad (3.59)\quad (0.41)$$

$$\bar{R}^2 = 0.861 \quad (10.1)$$

where all variables have been normalised (average = 0 and standard deviation = 1), and *t*-values have been given in parentheses. Since the individuals observed were free to choose their job and the corresponding income, it follows that the coefficients in front of the variables x_1, x_2 and x_3 constitute the trade-offs of these variables against income y. Therefore an equitable distribution (or a system of acceptable income differences) will be defined by:

$$y_E = 0.125 x_1 + 0.313 x_2 + 0.177 x_3 \tag{10.2}$$

In order to judge whether the actual income distribution (10.1) is or is not equitable we compare the standard deviations of both distribution (10.1) and distribution (10.2). The variance of y_E can be calculated from (10.2) if we know the correlation coefficients between x_1, x_2 and x_3, which are:

$$r_{12} = 0.842, \ r_{13} = 0.219 \text{ and } r_{23} = 0.423.$$

The standard deviation σ_E of y_E turns out to be 0.517. This is about half of the standard deviation of y, which is unity, as observed. Changing the strong assumption that parameters do not affect utility into a weaker one, where parameters do (positively) affect utility, we arrive at the conclusion that an equitable distribution is considerably less unequal than the actual distribution: at least 40 per cent.

In order to avoid misunderstanding we shall list once again the assumptions underlying our example:

(i) we defined equity to prevail when welfare or utility is equalised among the individuals considered;
(ii) we assumed that parameters do not affect welfare negatively (or, in the case of family size, positively);
(iii) we assumed that all relevant parameters and variables were included in our analysis;
(iv) we restricted our exercise to the sample of AKZO employees, which does not include less qualified employees usually called workers.

10.4 DIRECT MEASUREMENT OF UTILITY

As stated in section 10.3, we shall now discuss the other method of utility measurement, the essence of which is that individuals are asked to express their degree of satisfaction or welfare in terms of a number of verbal classifications, customary in public opinion polls. We mentioned social indicators as a similar method whose application has spread widely in the last decade or so (cf. Thierry et al., 1977). These authors join us in making a distinction between actual and required indicators, comparable to our distinction between supply and demand intensities of qualifications. McKennell (1978) joins us in making a distinction between cognitive and non-cognitive components of well-being.

Van Praag and his colleagues have concentrated on the impact of income on satisfaction or utility and have collected a vast amount of information on how the individuals approached think they would evaluate incomes different from their actual income. They extended their questionnaire over nine different states of satisfaction, defined verbally from 'very badly-off' to 'very well-off'. The use of words to characterise intensities of satisfaction entails the possibility that the same word may not have an identical meaning to different persons. But since human language constitutes the two most important means of communication between human beings, among other purposes to implement socio-economic policies, the approach is the best available. Moreover the use of nine different verbal indications reduces the possibility of misunderstanding. Another danger may be the one of simulation. This is minimised by replacing the individual's name by a number and by guaranteeing confidentiality. Whenever similar questioning is applied by official institutions, the danger of simulation may be reduced by announcing the use of material for at least two different purposes in which opposite interests play a role.[5] For the present purpose these problems are irrelevant, however.

An important next step in the method now under discussion is the quantification of the answers by the scientists who organised the data collection. In this a divergence of some importance exists between van Praag and this author. Van Praag has chosen the cumulated lognormal probability distribution. This implies, first of all, that all utility levels are between 0 and 1. Moreover, it implies that each of the nine income figures correspond with the nine deciles between 0 and 1 (i.e. with equidistant figures from 0.1 to 0.9). Finally, it facilitates the mathematics of a number of interesting further uses of the utility function carried out by van Praag and his co-workers. The present author prefers a logarithmic function of income corrected for the impacts of a series of parameters and variables, hence $a \ln(y - b)$ where a is a constant, y income and b an agglomerate of relevant parameters and variables as defined before.

Research done by van Herwaarden and Kapteyn (1979) shows that among the two-parameter functions tested the two alternatives just mentioned show the best fit. An economic argument in favour of the logarithmic function is that it shows decreasing marginal utility throughout, whereas the cumulated lognormal distribution does not. In a few applications made by the present author the former function is more convenient (see Chapter 16).

Van Praag's function—often written as

$$N\left(\frac{\log X - \mu}{\sigma}; 0, 1\right)$$

admits a satisfactory interpretation of μ with the aid of actual income, and family size. It was used to define an equitable income distribution in the following way (Bouma et al., 1976). Two tests were taken with the aid of the 2663 observations taken form members of the Dutch Consumer Union in 1971. One consisted of testing a theory of utility:

$$\omega\left[E(\log X - \mu)\sigma\right] = F(X, s, v, w, t)$$

where: X = income after tax, s = occupation, v = years of schooling, w = capability to take independent decisions and t = age.

The material on X, v and t was of satisfactory quality. The material used for s and w was very crude, for lack of better data. The variable s was measured as one of the three quartiles of the v-material for each of ten occupational groups into which the sample was subdivided. The parameter w was taken as equal to 1 for wage and salary earners, to 2 for lower and middle executives, teachers, professional experts and agricultural workers, and 3 for the professions and for commercial occupations. Two forms of functions were taken for F.

The second test consisted of the establishment of an income equation (similar to an earnings equation), expressing X or its log in terms of s, v, w and t, or their logs. In both types of test either the difference $s - v$ or the log ratio $\log s/v$, both squared, were added for reasons irrelevant to the present chapter.[6]

In all, seven type I and twenty type II tests were taken. The R^2 (coinciding practically with the $\bar{R}^2$ because of the large number of observations) were not impressive: they varied between 0.198 and 0.258 for type I and between 0.315 and 0.400 for type II. Most of the σ_b-values are satisfactory. For the actual income equations they have been added in Table 10.1. For the equitable income equations they are similar. From these equations five pairs were available showing the same independent variables expressing (i) equitable incomes, and (ii) actual incomes as the dependent variable, or their logarithms. These pairs are reproduced in Table 10.1.

If we forget for a while the doubtful quality of our independent variables, one feature of Table 10.1 deserves mention. The ratio between the coefficients of a given independent variable appearing in the X_E equation to that appearing in the X_A equation is not, on average, very

Table 10.1: Equitable (E) and actual (A) incomes or their logarithms in the five comparable pairs

Cases 1/11 $\log X_E = 0.27 \log v + 0.10 \log w + 0.50 \log t$
             $\log X_A = 0.44 \log v + 0.24 \log w + 0.71 \log t$
             $\quad\quad\quad\quad (0.04) \quad\quad\quad (0.02) \quad\quad\quad (0.02)$

Cases 2/12 $\log X_E = 0.14 \log s + 0.12 \log w + 0.47 \log t$
             $\log X_A = 0.38 \log s + 0.23 \log w + 0.67 \log t$
             $\quad\quad\quad\quad (0.04) \quad\quad\quad (0.03) \quad\quad\quad (0.03)$

Cases 6/16 $\log X_E = 0.245 \log s + 0.28 \log (s/v)^2 + 0.010 \log w + 0.48 \log t$
             $\log X_A = 0.54 \ \log s + 0.46 \log (s/v)^2 + 0.12 \log w + 0.67 \log t$
             $\quad\quad\quad\quad (0.04) \quad\quad\quad\quad (0.09) \quad\quad\quad\quad (0.02)$
             $\quad\ (0.02)$

Cases 4'/34' $0.001 X_E = 0.23 \ v + 0.00 \ (s-v)^2 + 1.28 \ w + 4.38 \ t$
               $0.001 X_A = 0.54 \ v + 0.39 \ (s-v)^2 + 2.85 \ w + 7.31 \ t$
               $\quad\quad\quad\quad\ (0.06) \quad\ (0.10) \quad\quad\ (0.35) \quad\ (0.29)$

Cases 9/39 $0.001 X_E = 0.24 \ v \quad\quad\quad\quad\quad + 1.28 \ w + 4.38 \ t$
             $0.001 X_A = 0.67 \ v \quad\quad\quad\quad\quad + 3.63 \ w + 7.39 \ t$
             $\quad\quad\quad\quad (0.05) \quad\quad\quad\quad\quad\quad (0.26) \quad (0.30)$

different between v, w and t. In our terminology schooling v was assumed to be closer to a variable—something open to choice—whereas ability to take independent decisions was thought to be chosen to a parameter—something innate, or nearly so. In principle the latter should be clearly more scarce than the former. This appears not to be the case. That finding hints in the direction that w is to a lesser degree innate than often thought. The conclusion we draw is that it is highly desirable to collect better material on the variables and parameters in order to use it in the future samples of the van Praag type: material of the quality of the AKZO material discussed in Section 10.5.

As a final observation we want to repeat that this chapter is an attempt to illustrate two approaches to quantifying the concept of equitable income distribution and stress the word *illustrate*, hoping that we may have whetted the appetite for the collection of better and more extensive data on the phenomena discussed.

NOTES

1 It may contribute to modesty for economists that, according to an inquiry by Levy and Guttman (1975), a happy family life, satisfactory leisure time, living

within a satisfactory social group and good health contribute more than two-thirds to the variance in happiness, and the two most important economic factors (income and job satisfaction) 13 per cent only. Of the variance explained by the six most important factors the contributions are, respectively, 84 and 16 per cent. All factors explain two-thirds and all economic factors one-third of the variance.
2 Admittedly this way of measuring parameters makes the assumption as formulated under (b) very close to a tautology, but it remains meaningful.
3 This implies that we restrict ourselves to labour incomes. In developed countries those cover an overwhelming part of total primary income.
4 The situation before harmonisation of the salary scales used in the sixteen enterprises of which AKZO was composed seems to be a better representation of a free market.
5 Thus, an inquiry into the number of rooms available to each of the households in a Dutch city in wartime was announced to be undertaken with two purposes: (i) for the rationing of coal and (ii) for the obligatory quartering of people whose houses had been destroyed by bombing.
6 The objective here was to test an aspect of the utility function, hypothesised in earlier work of the author.

REFERENCES

Berkouwer, J. et al. (1978), *Alternative Specifications of Earnings Equations*, Institute for Econonmic Research discussion paper series, 7804/G, Erasmus University, Rotterdam.
Bouma, N. et al. (1976), 'Testing and applying a theory of utility', *European Economic Review*, 8, 181–91.
Frisch, R. (1932), *New Methods of Measuring Marginal Utility*, Tübingen.
Levy, S. and Guttman, L. (1975), 'On the multivariate structure of well-being', *Social Indicators Research*, 2, 361–88.
McKennell, A.C. (1978), 'Cognition and affect in perceptions of wellbeing', *Social Indicators Research* 5, 389–426.
Pareto, V. (1896), *Cours d'économie politique*, Paris.
Pen, J. and Tinbergen, J. (1977), *Naar een rechtvaardiger inkomensverdeling*, Amsterdam and Brussels.
Pigou, A.C. (1920), *The Economics of Welfare*, London.
Thierry, Hk., Zanders, H.L.G., Koopmans, E. and de Wolff, Ch.J. (1977), *Sociale indicatoren in beweging*, Deventer.
Tinbergen, J. (1977), 'Gerechtigkeit als gesellschaftliches Ziel', in *Soziale Probleme der modernen Industriegesellschaft*, Verhandlungen auf der Arbeitstagung des Vereins für Socialpolitik in Augsburg 1976, Berlin.
Tinbergen, J. (1980), 'Überdeckung von Wissenschaftsgebieten', in Küng, Emil (ed.), *Wandlungen in Wirtschaft und Gesellschaft*, pp. 17–30, Tübingen.
van Herwaarden, F.G and Kapteyn, A. (1979), private correspondence.
van Praag, B.M.S. (1975), *De verdeling van inkomen en macht*, Leiden (where previous English publications are quoted).

Part III
Welfare Functions

11 The Measurement of Social Welfare

11.1 IS MEASUREMENT POSSIBLE?

In this chapter the measurement of social (or national) welfare is discussed since this concept has often been used by Floor Hartog. As a tribute to him I shall try to express myself as clearly as he does, or at least to approach his clarity.

The first question that the subject raises is whether such a measurement is indeed possible. At present most of our colleagues, following Pareto (1897), think that it is not. As stated in his *Toegepaste welvaartseconomie* [*Applied Welfare economics*] (Hartog, 1963) Hartog shares this opinion. Regarding this issue the present author belongs to the Pigovian school, since he does not reject welfare measurability.

The acceptance of welfare measurability may be defended as follows. In social life, and especially in socioeconomic policy, decisions are taken continually which are only possible if the decision-makers have yardsticks to compare different individuals' welfare. This implies that if economists don't do so, less economically trained authorities will. These decisions have socioeconomic consequences, sometimes quite important ones. The latter can be estimated better by economists than by non-economists. As a minimum a close collaboration between economists and authorities is therefore desirable. Moreover, a good leader may be assumed to be characterised by the ability to think him- or herself in the situation of those on whom he or she has to make decisions. This capability is comparable with what in the past in Dutch law was called 'the behaviour of a good family father'. (Perhaps the behaviour of a good family mother or of good parents is even better.)

This capability may also be called the capability to put oneself in others' shoes, which implies a projection of different persons' welfare on a common yardstick, and therefore constitutes the measurement. Because of human imperfection it will be sensible, anyway, not to have one individual decision-maker, but rather a committee of representatives, and to have the decision made by majority vote.[1]

In addition to this argument in favour of welfare measurability three others can be offered. Van Praag (1981) and his colleagues express various welfare levels verbally, using terms from 'very bad', 'bad', 'very insufficient', etc. to 'good', 'very good' and 'excellent'—phrases which parallel school marks. (For varying *levels of schooling* attained fewer levels are distinguished, from three (primary, secondary and tertiary) to seven.) As with school diplomas, words are then replaced by figures. In view of the uniformity experienced with three methods for inquiries confidence in these proceedings is justified. It should be kept in mind that in meetings the discussions preceding a decision are usually also expressed verbally, rather than numerically. Later discussants may then refer back to the wording in which judgements were formulated.

A second method, alongside van Praag's, launched by this author (Tinbergen, 1980, 1984), is based on preferring observed behaviour to the words of the individuals under discussion, but this more solid basis has to be bought with the acceptance of an additional assumption.[2]

A third alternative—and hence a fourth—defence of measurability of welfare has been proposed by Morgenstern and von Neumann (1944) and is based on the element of uncertainty. In the simplest case two situations may occur with known probability. Welfare is supposed to be determined by the mathematical expectation of these two situations. Since the authors (as opposed to the others) have not done empirical research, a comparison with the other methods is not possible.

As observed, in practical politics many decisions are made which implictly assume measurability of the welfare of different persons or groups. An arbitrary example is the comparison of social welfare in different countries or in the same country at different times, measured in money of equal purchasing power. The figures are not explictly shown as a measure of welfare, but very often this is implicitly suggested. Examples may be found in Kravis *et al.* (1982) and in the time series for the Netherlands in the National Accounts, established by the Central Bureau of Statistics (1982). The figures offered are described correctly, and are used by many to illustrate welfare developments.

The aim of this chapter is to indicate a number of refinements in the calculation which enable us better to approach the differences in welfare. In section 11.2 earlier refinements will be discussed, and in sections 11.3–11.5 further possible improvements will be discussed. The latter are a refinement of the *concepts* and *aspects of reality* rather than actual calculations, since often the figures can be—but have not (yet) been—estimated. Sections 11.3–11.5 offer answers to criticisms made of earlier publications of the author (Tinbergen, 1981).

11.2 NATIONAL EXPENDITURES AS A MEASURE OF WELFARE AND THEIR ESTIMATION

The national accounts of many countries supply a survey of 'national means and expenditures' and have developed from what, at an earlier stage, was indicated as two alternative computations of national income, the objective and the subjective methods. A very good survey of estimates on the Netherlands carried out by various authors before the second world war was presented by Derksen (1939). The objective method started from the value of production and therefore was also called the *national product*. The subjective method started from individuals' incomes and hence was called the *national income*. In addition, two different price levels were used, indicated by *factor costs* and *market prices*. The latter consisted not only of factor costs (i.e. the amounts paid to production factors—wages, salaries, interest, rent) but in addition value-added taxes (net of possible subsidies paid).

The concept of expenditures has not yet been mentioned and in a way constitutes a third observation stage. Incomes are spent and the main categories are called *consumption expenditures* and *savings*. Together, in the absence of hoarding, they equal incomes.

If measurement of welfare is the aim, it will be clear that a large part of this is obtained from consumption expenditure, which serves to satisfy consumption needs, largely those satisfied in the same timespan. Savings may be said to help to satisfy the needs of future generations (especially children and grandchildren), responsibility for whom it is felt by those living in the period the income is earned. Part of the savings moreover serves to satisfy own future needs.

If a negligible interest for the future exists, savings may be disregarded in a first approximation of welfare; on the other hand, if a larger weight is given to the future one tends to consider total income, after deduction of direct taxes. In section 11.5 the relation between expenditure and welfare will be considered in more detail. Here we only want to state that there is usually a parallelism between welfare and expenditures (either consumption expenditures only, or total expenditures). Corrections on the computations of expenditures will be discussed in sections 11.3 and 11.4. Since expenditures can also be calculated through the means of national accounts the corrections will consist—perhaps somewhat unexpectedly—of corrections of the calculations of the means.

First, we shall discuss some corrections on earlier calculations of the means (i.e. of national product) which are now generally accepted, and at the same time illustrate a development in our thinking by offering in this chapter some additional examples.

In some countries, in the past, national product was calculated by adding up the value of gross output of all industries. It was soon discovered that this procedure contains duplications. For example, adding the product value of spinning (hence the value of yarns produced) to that of weaving (hence the value of tissues) evidently contains the value of yarns twice. Similarly, the value of *semi-manufactured inputs*, and possibly *raw materials*, must be deducted from the value of output. This also applies to *auxiliary* inputs (energy, lubricating oil, etc.) which are the products of energy plants, and so on. Finally, the value of worn-out machinery and other capital goods (buildings, transportation equipment) which have been replaced must be deducted for the same reason. We shall not deal with subtleties (e.g. the prices) which have to be used, although very interesting questions arise here also. We shall only summarise our argument by the well-known statement that we have to take for each industry the *value added* as its contribution to national product. All this is well known and generally accepted.

11.3 ADDITIONAL CORRECTIONS: ITEMS OVERLOOKED, COLLECTIVE GOODS AND PSYCHIC INCOME

We now propose to discuss some corrections still under debate. First there are *items overlooked*. Part of production is the value of *services not paid for*, including voluntary as well as compulsory services. Examples are the services performed in the *household*, mostly but decreasingly by the housewife, and *military service* (the latter being paid only in part in countries with conscription). Estimating the value of these is beset with difficulties. A market for household services cannot be organised as long as we accept the institution of marriage, which seems to be much more important. To put it more concretely: a good marriage (which is very important for the upbringing of the future generation) is based on many other criteria then the ability to be a good housekeeper. A market for military activities cannot easily be organised either, at least if one wants to maintain conscription as the system of organised defence. But here the question arises whether military activity itself is desirable. We have attained a stage of human development where military activities pose an enormous threat to welfare.

A completely different group of items so far overlooked are those of the so-called *black* or *informal* sector, (i.e. production by individuals who are not paying taxes or social insurance contributions). Increasingly attempts are now being made to estimate the size of this sector (cf. Tanzi (ed.), 1982, where the literature is given). For a country like Norway, where this sector is probably small, Isachsen *et al.* (1982) estimate figures between 2.3 and 6.3 per cent of national income (for 1979 and 1978, using two different methods).

In this context we shall ask: to what extent must the value of *collective goods*, which also contribute to the population's welfare, be measured by the value of production by the public authorities? For lack of a market that production value is measured by equating it to its cost of production, and hence to civil servants' salaries. But the following deviations between that production value and the salaries may exist:

1. Part of public services must be considered as *auxiliary goods* for their final output. To simplify matters it has been assumed that cost-increasing ('indirect') taxes are equal to these intermediary inputs, but this is a perfectly arbitrary assumption;
2. besides public authorities, *citizens* too may produce collective goods. This category so far has hardly been discussed. As a minimum it includes collaboration with the police in attempts to identify criminals. Many more examples may be suggested, i.e. abiding by the law—this varying from respecting traffic lights, to payment of all taxes according to fiscal legislation, to educating one's children to be law-abiding individuals (this last example was mentioned before as part of household services). Still another example recommended for discussion is the *maintenance of free competition*, instead of establishing monopolies or oligopolies characterised by several markets. The value to the community of the maintenance of free competition as an alternative to monopoly may be estimated approximately without too many difficulties.

    A last item omitted is that of *job satisfaction*. For some types of labour this may be considerable, for other types it will be felt to be negative. In fact, for a long time economists spoke only of the *disutility* of all labour. This was associated with the thesis that everybody will continue to work until the point is reached when labour disutility equals the utility of the remuneration received or the goods produced. This thesis is complemented by the thesis that leisure (i.e. not working) contributes positively to welfare. But a period like the present 'Long Stagflation' labour contributes positively to welfare for many unemployed people.

Incidentally, one of the suggestions adhered to by a number of economists for estimating the value of collective goods produced—namely, equalling it to the sum total of marginal utilities of all citizens—can only be accepted if utility is considered quantifiable.

11.4 CORRECTIONS FOR COUNTERPRODUCTION

Elsewhere I defended (as others did before) the idea that in our society not only production, but also *counterproduction* exists (cf. Chapter 4). From critical discussions of this idea in book reviews it appeared that a clearer formulation of the concept of counterproduction is desirable. Counterproduction occurs because a perfect society where no error is made cannot be realised, if perfect means that all activities are harmonised in the way proponents of central planning have imagined. This perfect society would be characterised by the following features (please, don't laugh):

On the road nobody ever violates any traffic regulations; no collisions occur; no accidents happen. Nobody leaves a bus at the wrong stop. In factories, no machine ever stops unexpectedly, not a single product is rejected by a quality test, and so on. Nobody drinks or eats more than is healthy. No illegal drugs (hard or soft) are taken.

Reality is different. Collisions do happen and make accident victims. As a consequence, the labour of nurses and doctors is needed, hospital beds are kept in reserve in order to deal with the collision's casualties. The driver whose error caused the collision contributes to counterproduction and, in the best case, his activities and the compensating ones of the nurses and the doctors together add a quantity of zero to social welfare. One can easily produce a large number of other examples. The importance of counterproduction is its growth in the last decades or half-century.

Partly, this is the consequence of the massive increase in the production of dangerous chemical and radioactive goods. New housing estates have had to be demolished because they were built on contaminated land—itself the consequence of illegal dumping of toxic waste products. Partly it is the consequence of increased vandalism and the use of violence. Finally, there are the old enemies of social welfare: alcohol, tobacco products and over-eating by those who can afford it, and lack self-discipline. Even seemingly 'innocent' foodstuffs such as meat and sugar are consumed in more than optimal quantities. The necessary corrections, *defensive expenditures* (see Leipert, 1982; Hagen, 1984), may be made by the simple deduction from national product as calculated before. (We shall come back to the question of whether other procedures may be better.)

A question of some importance seems to be where to start the measurement of counterproduction (i.e. where to choose the zero point). In the measurement of temperature this question can be answered elegantly: as is well known, it is at about $-273°$ C and defined as the temperature where molecules do not move anymore. Should we, in economics, start at the 'error-free' society? As a clarification it may be helpful, but the error-free society looks too unrealistic. For the time being it seems better to start from some empirical point, as done by Mishan (1967) and Nordhaus and Tobin (1972). Yet it seems worth while to put the question of the starting point on the agenda for further research.

A second problem is which of two compensating activities should be defined as production and which as counterproduction. In the case of the traffic accident it seems natural to call the accident counterproductive; and its compensating activities productive. In the case of chemical production polluting the environment, intuition gives a less obvious choice; but it is hardly a real problem since together the two activities don't contribute to national product.

A third question is whether the concept of *collective goods* should play a role in the treatment of counterproduction. That idea arises when the maintenance of the quality of soil, water and atmosphere is discussed. Such maintenance benefits all citizens and its 'use' by one person does not impair the possibility of others profiting from it. This is considered to characterise collective goods. In the example of the traffic accident, the nurses and doctors of a casualty ward are available to everybody and hence constitute a collective good. It may occur, none the less, if by coincidence a large number of accidents take place simultaneously, that that availability does not exist temporarily. We then speak of 'part-collective goods' (Tinbergen, 1984). This aspect of collective goods needs closer study and has only just started.

11.5 CORRECTIONS BECAUSE OF INCOME DIFFERENCES

So far we have assumed that national (or social) welfare can be measured and have used money values of expenditures (possibly consumption expenditures) as a yardstick. We added that comparisons are often made between different nations or between the welfare of the same nation in different periods. As a matter of course, corrections for price differences are included in such comparisons.

If we join the majority of economists' opinion that utility or welfare derived from the consumption of the last unit of a given quantity of some good equals the utility of its price, then implicitly we assume that the marginal utility of the money unit is the same for all citizens.[3] We also assume that the utility of £1 decreases the more pounds we spend. The last £1 of a high income is then spent on goods satisfying less urgent needs than the last £1 of a low income, unless a high-income recipient constitutes a person with a higher level of needs or a handicapped person. If that is what we believe, the unequal income distribution is justified.

If the actual income distribution deviates from that ideal distribution, then a *correction for the inequality of marginal utility* of income is necessary. The nation's population may then be subdivided into classes with the same marginal utility. The correction aimed at may be made in different ways, from the simple to the very complicated. One of the simple ways uses one function only, reflecting the relation between income and marginal utility. Such a function can be derived from Frisch's (1932) or from van Praag's (1981) work. More complicated corrections may also take into account the size of the household, give different weights to children of different age, or correct income for psychic income, or even for other indicators of welfare (e.g. health and other indicators used by Levy and Guttman (1975)). Most of these more refined methods require more research than is available at present. Mention should be made of the very valuable and concrete work done by Helmers (1979) for the evaluation of investment projects financed by the World Bank. As a consequence of such corrections, projects may be selected that do not yield the return required by the capital market. This is one of the justifications of IDA (The International Development Association) which provides soft loans to the poorest countries.

11.6 SUMMARY

This author believes in the measurability of welfare or utility and starts such measurement from national expenditures, possibly with a weight $\neq 1$ for savings. In national accounting, expenditures are considered identical to national product, which therefore can also be taken as the starting point. After having reminded the reader of *duplications* which have been discovered earlier and eliminated in today's estimates of national product, additional corrections are discussed. One category consists of *items overlooked*, such as voluntary or compulsory services (household or military) means originating in the *black* or *informal sector*, *collective* goods already included but perhaps incorrectly, and possible *psychic income* from labour (positive or negative). Furthermore, items have to be deducted as a consequence of *counterproduction*, defined as activities needed to compensate for many errors in the implementation of production plans. These deductions may also be considered as the value of a category of collective goods. Finally, a correction is needed if income *distribution* deviates from the ideal distribution where marginal utilities of income are equal. A person's welfare should then be derived from income corrected for psychic income by taking a function of it which reflects its decreasing marginal utility.

NOTES

1 In physics temperature is measured with the aid of thermometers, because it has been found that upon heating the majority of substances, these increase proportionally in volume. Some substances show a deviating behaviour (all substances at their melting and boiling points, and water between 0° and 4° C). Even here therefore a 'decision' is 'made' by 'majority vote'.
2 It is assumed that welfare depends on variables (of which some can be chosen freely by the individual considered, e.g. occupation, expressed by level of schooling required, or size of household), parameters (which indicate personal characteristics, e.g. actually attained level of schooling) and coefficients (which are equal for all individuals and indicate the impact of variables and parameters on welfare). With the aid of multiple regression analysis income y of all occupations earned by all employed is expressed as a function of variables x_i and parameters z_k:

$$y = \sum a_i x_i + \sum b_k z_k$$

A further assumption made is that welfare depends on income 'corrected' for the influence of variables $y - \sum a_i x_i$. Welfare may then be represented by the relation just mentioned, or by a freely chosen function of the latter relation. This author prefers a logarithm of corrected income, since that implies a diminishing marginal utility. With this assumption welfare does not depend on the parameters.

An alternative assumption of the welfare function is that the parameters appear in it, but only in the shape of the tension between a parameter and the value of that parameter required for the proper execution of the occupation. That tension is indicated by the square of the difference between the actual and required value of the parameter (deviations to both sides work out the same way). The most important example of such a tension for which measured data are available is that for level of schooling. This alternative assumption is not discussion in the *Kyklos* article.
3 We don't touch on the question of consumer surplus, although an interesting discussion would be possible on this concept as well.

REFERENCES

Centraal Bureau voor de Statistiek (1982), *Nationale rekeningen* [*National Accounts*] *1981*, The Hague, Staatsuitgeverij.
Derksen, J.B.D. (1939), 'Enkele berekeningen over het nationale inkomen van Nederland', ['Some calculations on the national income of the Netherlands'], *De Nederlandsche Conjunctuur*, Speciale Onderzoekingen, No. 2, Centraal Bureau voor de Statistiek, The Hague, Albani.
Frisch, R. (1932), *New Methods of Measuring Marginal Utility*, Tübingen.

Hagen, J.H. (1984 forthcoming), Ph.D. dissertation, University of Utrecht.
Hartog, F. (1963), *Toegepaste welvaartseconomie* [*Applied Welfare Economics*], Leiden, H.E. Stenfert Kroese.
Helmers, F.L.C.H. (1979), *Project Planning and Income Distribution*, Boston, The Hague and London, Martinus Nijhoff.
Isachsen, A.J. et al. (1982), 'The hidden economy in Norway' in Tanzi, V. (ed.), *The Underground Economy in the United States and Abroad*, Lexington Books.
Kravis, I.B. et al. (1982). *World Product and Income, International Comparison of Real Gross Product*, World Bank, Baltimore and London, The Johns Hopkins University Press.
Leipert, Chr. (1982), *Bruttosozialprodukt, defensive Ausgaben und Lebensqualität. Zur Notwendigkeit einer integrierten Wirtschafts politik* [Gross National Product, Defence Expenditures and Quality of Life. On the Necessity of an Integrated Economic Policy], IIUG, Wissenschaftszentrum, Berlin.
Levy, S. and Guttman, L. (1975), 'On the multivariate structure of well-being', *Social Indicators Research*, 2, pp. 361–88.
Mishan, E.J. (1967), *The Costs of Economic Growth*, London, Staples Press.
Morgenstern, O. and von Neumann, J. (1944), *Theory of Games and Economic Behaviour*, Princeton, N.J., Princeton University Press.
Nordhaus, W. and Tobin, J. (1972), *Economic Growth*, Washington, National Bureau of Economic Research.
Pareto, V. (1897), *Manuel d'économie politique*, Paris.
Tanzi, V. (ed.) (1982), *The Underground Economy in the United States and Abroad*, Lexington Books.
Tinbergen, J. (1980), 'Two approaches to quantify the concept of equitable income distribution', *Kyklos*, 33, pp. 3–15.
Tinbergen, J. (1981), 'Contraproduktie', in Eijgelshoven, P.J. and van Gemerden, L.J. (eds.), *Inkomensverdeling en openbare financiën*. Opstellen voor Jan Pen, Utrecht and Antwerp Het Spectrum (Chapter 4 of this book).
Tinbergen, J. (1984), 'On collective and part-collective goods', *De Economist*, 132, pp. 171–82 (Chapter 5 of this book).

12 The Allocation of Workers to Jobs

12.1 THE LABOUR MARKET TRANSACTION PROBLEM

The subject-matter of this chapter is part of the labour market problem. As for all markets, the equilibrium position is characterised by two aspects: what price will prevail and what the volume transacted is. For a complex of markets the prices and transactions of each sector characterise equilibrium. In this chapter only the transactions aspect will be discussed. This may also be called the allocation problem; i.e. which worker will be allocated which job? The number of workers will be assumed to be equal to the number of jobs. Here workers, as in the American and possibly other Censuses, stands for all who work: the self-employed as well as employees. Workers are characterised by personality traits, such as years of schooling completed, manual dexterity, IQ, social intelligence (e.g. the ability to deal with people), etc. The number of independent personality traits is hardly known, since many concepts used may partly overlap. Jobs are characterised by a set of requirements personality traits have to satisfy in order that the job can be done (more or less) satisfactorily. Some personality traits may be relevant to several job requirements (e.g. zeal or kindness) others may be irrelevant.

12.2 THE ALLOCATION PROCESS

The allocation of persons to jobs may take place in different ways, organised or more haphazardly. For job categories held by large numbers of persons, allocation will be the subject of negotiation, conducted by organisations of employers and employees. For less frequently held jobs personal negotiation or simply a personal choice will be decisive. In each of these processes employers or self-employed workers will tend to maximise profits, whereas employees or dependent workers will tend to maximise utility. Strictly speaking, profits are a proxy only for utility, but profits can be determined by calculations which facilitate the execution of negotiations. For large-scale negotiations production functions also enter the picture as helpful proxies to estimate the consequences of the decisions at stake. Thus, production functions enable the economist to estimate marginal productivities of various types of workers (cf. Gottschalk, 1978). It is often thought that the number of workers allocated depends on such marginal productivities and wage rates prevailing in equilibrium. Much empirical work on production functions is available.

12.3 UTILITY MAXIMISATION

As observed, a more precise picture of allocation should be based on utility rather than profit maximisation, since the latter approach implicitly assumes that money income is the only (or main) determinant of human welfare or satisfaction, phrases we shall use as synonyms for utility. The former approach assumes that, alongside income, other aspects of a job also affect satisfaction, positively or negatively. Thus, labour disutility is an aspect considered at an early stage of the development of economic theory. Somewhat later job satisfaction was recognised as a possible positive determinant of welfare. Whether the two aspects result, on balance, in a positive or a negative contribution to welfare depends very much on the nature of the job, as well as on the nature of the person.

As observed, the number of personality traits and job characteristics may be considerable and many of them may enter the utility or welfare function. In order to make progress in our understanding of the labour market empirical estimation of welfare functions is important. A considerable amount of research in this area has been done by van Praag and his school (cf. van Praag, 1973, for further references).

Another co-determinant of welfare was proposed by the present author (Tinbergen, 1956, 1959) and called 'tension'. It stands for the possible difference between the degree or level of an ability required (h) and the level actually attained, h' and the assumption implies that a positive and a negative tension are equally disliked. So a proper measure may be $|h - h'|$, or $(h - h')^2$ or a higher even power of $h - h'$. We chose $(h - h')^2$ where h and h' vary from 1 to H.

Empirical data on degrees required and degrees attained are rare. Recently Rumberger (1982) has produced a vast material on schooling required for the jobs of a large sample of the American labour force. Since actual schooling is known from the Censuses, we are now able to check empirically whether allocation of workers to jobs is co-determined by schooling tension. The variables h and h' will be measured in Rumberger's way, comprising six levels. Our empirical results will be

The allocation of workers to jobs

discussed in section 12.7, preceded by a theoretical frame (sections 12.4 to 12.6).

12.4 THE ALLOCATION MATRIX Φ AND THE ALLOCATION PROBLEM

Simplified by the use of one aspect only—schooling—our allocation problem may be illustrated by a matrix Φ whose elements $\phi_{hh'}$, represent the promilles of the labour force characterised by h and h'. It follows that $\sum_h \sum_{h'} \phi_{hh'} = 1000$. It is appropriate to add the borders of $\sum_h \phi_{hh'} = \phi_{.h'}$, the column totals and $\sum_{h'} \phi_{hh'} = \phi_{h.}$, the row totals. Both borders add up to 1000.

The matrix contains H^2 cells, which constitute a new concept needed and a smaller area than a labour market sector. The latter will not be used in the present chapter, since we are not dealing with the price aspect. But it seems useful to add a definition of sectors in order to illustrate the difference between cells and sectors. The latter are a set of cells showing the same earnings since sectors, being the smallest units considered, are supposed to be homogeneous. A labour market with one aspect only must be represented by a one-dimensional set (a vector) of sectors, numbering H in our example and a two-dimensional set (a matrix) of cells. Two aspects would confront us with more than two-dimensional sets of cells, tensors.

In addition to the definition of tension for one cell, $(h - h')^2$, we shall define *total tension* $T = \sum_h \sum_{h'} \phi_{hh'} (h - h')^2$.

The allocation problem consists of finding the unknowns, $\phi_{hh'}$, from the given border vectors, $\phi_{.h'}$, the *supply vector* and $\phi_{h.}$, the *demand vector*. As observed, we have simplified our problem by the assumption of equality of the numbers of workers $\sum \phi_{.h'}$ and of jobs $\sum \phi_{h.} = 1000$.

The number of relations that have to be satisfied equals $2H - 1$, expressing the definitions of the supply and the demand vectors, each numbering H, but one dependant, since $\sum_h \sum_{h'} \phi_{hh'} = 1000$.

The number of *degrees of freedom* appears to be $H^2 - 2H + 1 = (H - 1)^2$.

12.5 TWO PARTICULAR SOLUTIONS

With so many degrees of freedom the number of solutions is infinitely large to the power $(H - 1)^2$, unless more relations have to be satisfied. Among the many solutions two may be worth studying, which we shall indicate by t and p. The solution $\phi_{hh'} = t$ stands for the so-called northwest corner rule, used for the solution due to Hitchcock (1941) of a transportation problem. The procedure to calculate the t-value may be described as follows:

Step 1. For $h = h' = 1$ (the north-west corner of Φ) take:

$$\phi_{11} = \min(\phi_{1.}, \phi_{.1}) \tag{12.1}$$

Step 2. If $\phi_{1.} > \phi_{.1}$, $\phi_{21} = 0$ and $\phi_{12} = \min(\phi_{1.} - \phi_{.1}, \phi_{.2})$ (12.2)

If $\phi_{1.} < \phi_{.1}$, $\phi_{12} = 0$ and $\phi_{21} = \min(\phi_{.1} - \phi_{1.}, \phi_{2.})$ (12.3)

Repeat the same procedure for the remaining part of Φ. The solution obtained will have a minimum of non-empty cells.

In the particular case where $\phi_{h.} = \phi_{.h'}$, $h = h'$ for:

$$1 \leq h \leq H \tag{12.4}$$

(i.e., the vector $\phi_{h.} = \phi_{.h'}$ or 'educational equilibrium') (12.5)

only the main diagonal of Φ will be non-empty; all

$$\phi_{hh'} = 0 \text{ for which } h \neq h' \tag{12.6}$$

By solution p ('probability') we understand:

$$1000\, \phi_{hh'} = \phi_{h.} \cdot \phi_{.h'} \tag{12.7}$$

The solution resembles the calculation of the probability of the combination h, h' if the probability of value h is $\phi_{h.}$ and independent of the probability $\phi_{.h'}$ of value h', both expressed in ‰.

In the particular case where all $\phi_{h.} = \phi_{.h'} = 1000/H$ all $\phi_{hh'}$ will be equal to $1000/H^2$.

The two solutions constitute opposites in the sense that t concentrates all observations as closely to the main diagonal as possible, whereas p spreads them evenly over the square matrix Φ and so constitutes a 'minimum of concentration'.

Another case worth mentioning is the one where both vectors $\phi_{h.}$ and $\phi_{.h'}$ equal the binomium $H - 1$, i.e. the consecutive terms of 1000 $(1/2 + 1/2)^{H-1}$, a good approximation of the Gaussian or normal distribution. Matrix Φ will then be a good approximation of a two-dimensional orthogonal normal distribution.

12.6 SOLUTION t IS THE MINIMUM TENSION SOLUTION

In order to show that solution t constitutes the matrix with minimum total tension T as defined in section 12.4 we introduce a small decrease

$-\epsilon$ to the frequency $\phi_{hh'}$ of a cell on the t-path $h., h'$. In order not to violate the conditions imposed on the row and column totals we have to extend the variation to a 'variation quadruple', adding a positive increment $+\epsilon$ somewhere in the same row and the same column of h, h', plus an additional $-\epsilon$ to the cell $h+a, h'+a'$, if a and a' are the shifts to the reference cell where the first $-\epsilon$ is applied. The increase in total tension T then may be written:

$$\Delta T = -\epsilon \left\{ (\Delta h)^2 + (\Delta h + \Delta a)^2 - (\Delta h + a)^2 - (\Delta h - a + \Delta a)^2 \right\} \quad (12.8)$$

where $\Delta h = h - h'$ and $\Delta a = a - a'$.

Execution of the calculations yields:

$$\Delta T = +2\epsilon a a' \quad (12.9)$$

In order to interpret this result we have to be aware of the necessity that a variation $-\epsilon$ can only be applied to a non-empty cell, hence a t-cell. The two cells where $-\epsilon$ is applied must be t-cells, and a third cell may, but need not, be such a cell.

With regard to the signs a and a', four combinations are possible, since both a and a' can be >0 or <0. The corresponding configurations have been indicated below, where the t-cell started with has been italicised and the variation in $\phi_{hh'}$ been indicated by 'pos' or 'neg' according to its sign. Below each configuration the signs of a, a' and ΔT have been added:

I	II	III	IV
neg pos	pos *neg*	*neg* pos	pos *neg*
pos *neg*	*neg* pos	pos *neg*	*neg* pos
$a>0, a'>0$	$a<0, a'>0$	$a<0, a'<0$	$a>0, a'<0$
$\Delta T > 0$	$\Delta T < 0$	$\Delta T > 0$	$\Delta T < 0$

The t-path is characterised by movements between consecutive cells either to the right or downward (i.e. either h or h' or both increase); no movements to the left or upward are permitted. Since negative changes in $\phi_{hh'}$ must be in t-cells only, configurations II and IV are impossible. That implies that variations in $\phi_{hh'}$, away from t-cells (configurations I and III) always lead to $\Delta T > 0$, an increase in total tension. Solution t hence constitutes the *solution with minimum total tension*.

Although of no relevance to the present chapter, it may be added that if production per unit of frequency $\phi_{hh'}$ equals $(h+h')^\alpha$ or $(qh+q'h')^\alpha$ the t-matrix also constitutes an extremum of production, namely a minimum if $\alpha < 0$ (decreasing returns) and a maximum if $\alpha > 0$ (increasing returns).

12.7 EMPIRICAL RELATION BETWEEN $\phi_{hh'}$, p AND t

With the help of the empirical data on schooling required for a large sample of workers, collected and computed by Rumberger (1982), we shall now study the relationship between $\phi_{hh'}$ and t. The hypothesis we shall test is that $\phi_{hh'}$ is a weighted average of t and p, or:

$$\phi_{hh'} = \alpha p + (1 - \alpha)t \qquad (12.10)$$

In this relation the unknown is α and can be obtained from a simple correlation:

$$\phi_{hh'} - t = \alpha(p - t) \qquad (12.11)$$

implying that

$$\alpha = \sum(\phi - t)(p - t)/\sum(p - t)^2 \qquad (12.12)$$

A constant term needs not to be added to (12.11), since ϕ, p and t all represent frequencies in promilles of which the total is 1000 and hence the average $1000/H^2$. We have already mentioned that Rumberger used a schooling level system with $H = 6$.

Rumberger uses two alternative educational groupings 1 and 2. The results are shown in Table 12.1

Table 12.1: Regression equations and correlation coefficients

Educational groupings:	1		2	
Regression equations:	$\hat{\phi} = 0.7995\ p + 0.2276\ t$		$\hat{\phi} = 0.5513\ p + 0.4146\ t$	
Standard deviations:	(0.0721)	(0.0441)	(0.0923)	(0.0637)
Correlation coefficients:	$r^2_{\phi p} = 0.8784$,	$r^2_{\phi t} = 0.6913$	$r^2_{\phi p} = 0.8531$,	$r^2_{\phi t} = 0.8505$
	$R^2_{\phi.pt} = 0.9301$		$R^2_{\phi.pt} = 0.9531$	
	$\bar{R}^2_{\phi.pt} = 0.9258$		$\bar{R}^2_{\phi.pt} = 0.9502$	
	$r^2_{pt} = 0.5161$		$r^2_{pt} = 0.6517$	

These results are quite positive as a test of our hypothesis. The coefficients of determination, corrected for degrees of freedom, $\bar{R}^2_{\phi.pt}$ are remarkably high and the significance of the values found for α is very high as well.

The following interpretation is offered, which contains three options. The allocation of workers over jobs can be explained in *three alternative* ways.

(i) Using the explanatory variable the tension-minimizing variable t,

69–85 per cent of the variance in frequency distribution ϕ can be explained, as shown by the values of $r^2_{\phi t}$.

(ii) The assumption of independence of supply and demand vectors, leading to the solution p, is able to explain 85–88 per cent of the variance, as shown by the values of $r^2_{\phi p}$.

(iii) In the explanation of the allocation by t the random disturbances characteristic for an ordinary least-squares regression practically coincide with the term αp, since $R^2_{\phi . pt}$ is very close to 1 (93 and 95 per cent, respectively). (In fact, this is an elaboration of the first interpretation.)

12.8 SUMMARY

Labour market supply is assumed to depend on the maximisation of worker welfare. Welfare is assumed partly to depend on the 'tension' between schooling required by the job and actual schooling. Hence in the allocation of workers to jobs a tendency can be expected to minimise tension. Strict minimisation produces a matrix t obtained by Hitchcock's north-west corner rule. Recent material (Rumberger, 1982) allows an explanation of 69–85 per cent of frequency variance.

The remaining error term can be explained by the assumption of independence of demand and supply.

REFERENCES

Gottschalk, P.T. (1978), 'A comparison of marginal productivity and earnings by occupation', *Industrial and Labor Relations Review*, 31, no. 3, pp. 368–78.

Hitchcock, F.L. (1941), 'The distribution of a product from several sources to numerous localities', *Journal of Mathematics and Physics*, 20, pp. 224–230, in Mennes, L.B.M. *et al.* (1969) *The Element of Space in Development Planning*, Amsterdam p. 321.

Rumberger, R.W. (1982), personal communication, 1 November, University of Amsterdam.

Tinbergen, J. (1959), 'On the theory of income distribution', in *Selected Papers*, Amsterdam, North Holland, pp. 243–63. (N.B. formulae (7.1) p. 257 should read:

$$\lambda_{10} = \frac{\omega_1}{\omega_3}\left(\frac{\bar{s}_1 \tau_1}{\sigma_1} - \bar{t}_1\right)$$

$$\lambda_{01} = \frac{\omega_2}{\omega_3}\left(\frac{\bar{s}_2 \tau_2}{\sigma_2} - \bar{t}_2\right)$$

van Praag, B.M.S. and Kapteyn, A. (1973), 'Further evidence on the individual welfare function of income: an empirical investigation in the Netherlands', *European Economic Review*, 4, pp. 33–62; see also the numerous other publications of the Economic Institute, University of Leyden, Hugo-de-Grootstraat 32, 2311 XK Leiden, The Netherlands.

13 Some Neglected Determinants of Welfare Functions

13.1 INTRODUCTION

The welfare concept is central to economics and to some topical problems and requires interdisciplinary research. Psychology, biology and education may be important contributors. Economists have overemphasised economic (and among these consumption) aspects; a learning process to reduce unhealthy consumption remains topical; on the production side, the diversity of labour types has been neglected. Here a central problem is job choice by maximising welfare. Variables needed are the capabilities required for jobs and personality traits. We ignore the number of independent characteristics. Path analysis with inherited and learnable traits may be extended by data on grandparents and on non-cognitive capabilities. A more precise production function of education is badly lacking. Two methods of measuring welfare functions and the shape of the latter are discussed.

Economics as a science cannot do without some elements originating in psychology, since the satisfaction of human needs is one of its central issues. This was emphasised by the introduction of the subjective base of value almost simultaneously by Jevons, Menger and Walras more than a century ago (cf. Samuelson, 1947, pp. 90ff). Even more explicitly, and about a century ago, this relationship was brought out by Edgeworth (1881) in his treatise on (mathematical) economics, *Mathematical Psychics*.

The century that separates us from Edgeworth's standard work has been characterised by two, almost opposite, tendencies in scientific development. On the one hand, we have experienced a widespread specialisation. Most, if not all, sciences have been split up into specialities (astrophysics, economics of public finance, etc.) which have each been developed in more depth. On the other hand, and as a consequence of the first tendency, the need for interdisciplinary research has increasingly been felt. With some time-lag more interdisciplinary work—common already to all practical work—has been organised by scientific institutions. In the present chapter we shall extensively profit from one interdisciplinary analysis of welfare (Baerends et al., 1978).

The concept of welfare is one of the key concepts used by economic science. In de Groot's opinion (Baerends et al., 1978, p. 53) the problem of enhancing welfare—and hence what welfare signifies—is the fundamental problem of our time. A welfare function indicates how anyone's welfare depends on its determinants. Mathematically, this statement implies that what we are after, in economics and in other disciplines, is to know a list of variables entering into the welfare function and the shape of the mathematical function expressing some welfare indicator in terms of the values of these variables.

The psychology applied by the economist—we may call it economic psychology—for quite some time was rather primitive. It is natural that the picture an outsider has of any science, lags behind the actual state of that science: it takes some time for developments to reach the outsider. As we shall see later, this also applies to the picture of economics held by outsiders. Similarly, the methods used by—at least some—psychologists were unknown to (most) economists. As an econometrician I did not know that econometric model-building (started in 1936) has so much in common with what psychologists call path analysis (started some twenty years earlier).

The primitive character of economic psychology, as understood for a long time, made it desirable to start multidisciplinary research on the welfare concept. The initiative of the Foundation for Inter-disciplinary Research of the Behavioural Sciences (Stichting voor Interdisciplinair Gedragswetenschappelijk Onderzoek) to organise a seminar on 24 March 1977 at Apeldoorn, The Netherlands, deserves to be applauded: its report (Baerends et al., 1978) proved to be a source of inspiration to this author. The interdisciplinary character of that symposium reflects itself in the list of disciplines represented: mathematical philosophy, ethology, ecology, social psychology, technology of energy production, cardiology, philosophy, psychological theory of behaviour, social psychiatry, psychobiology, methodology, psychology, humanist psychology, cultural anthropology, family sociology, biology, international law, polemology, forensic psychiatry, child psychiatry, child medical science, comparative and physiological psychology, pharmacology, sociology, business psychology. This list is taken from the invited audience, with apologies to the reader for the random order of the disciplines. Clearly and correctly, psychologists of different specialisations participated; apparently no economist attended. To this author it was striking that in particular the ecologists' contributions appeared to be helpful in formulating this chapter's subject matter. Part of the explanation may be that their subject implies the behaviour of animals of different levels of evolution and hence presumably induces them to use models of different levels of sophistication. In addition, the models presented by Professor Baerends have a double similarity to economic problem models: they show similarities with the economics of individual behaviour, but also similarities with the economics of social systems, for instance organisational hierarchies.

13.2 THE WELFARE CONCEPT

In modern economics (cf. Samuelson, 1947) the concept of welfare, whether applied to individuals, households or a nation's economy, is much broader than, say, a century or even half a century ago. It is sometimes used as synonymous with 'happiness', even if the old term 'utility' is maintained. This implies at least that it is defined more broadly than well-being, which has a materialist connotation. It is an illustration of the lag between economists' and outsiders' use of a concept, that at the symposium mentioned, this more restricted definition of well-being was assumed to be the economist's present concept. The broadest interpretation, that of 'happiness', contains elements such as friendship, religion and love, which are sometimes excluded since they cannot be the subject of socioeconomic policies. Even then, economic science tends to overemphasise the economic determinants of welfare.

This may be illustrated with the aid of figures compiled in Spring 1973 by Levy and Guttman (1975) from 1940 inhabitants, twenty years of age and over, in the four largest cities of Israel. With the aid of the four determinants showing the highest single correlation coefficient with the respondents' 'happiness', 59 per cent of the variance in happiness could be 'explained'. None of these determinants was economic in character; they were indicated as a good family life, good health, satisfaction with leisure and satisfaction with town life. Using as determinants the three with an economic character (sufficient income, satisfaction with education, and good labour relations at work) the variance we could explain was only 18 per cent. Other applications of the same material confirmed that socioeconomic determinants, even if broadly interpreted, can only affect happiness in a limited way.

Levy and Guttman's findings have some relevance to the explanation of today's cultural crisis, by which we mean the state of mind of those who increasingly feel alienated from social life and show this by increasing use of violence, vandalism and drug addiction. The contribution to the variance in welfare of a good family life and of satisfaction with leisure is used is no less than 25 and 16 per cent, respectively. If we add the satisfaction derived from the life in town (8 per cent) close to one-half of total variance is connected—for the positive as well as the negative values of these determinants, it should be understood—with these determinants: a convincing piece of evidence that certainly not only good economic policies are what we need.

Some similar conclusions can be drawn from a second enquiry, conducted in Summer 1973, and reported in the same article.

Apart from being too closely connected with economic determinants, the welfare or utility concept as studied and applied by economists is also often too static: the fact of life is overlooked that a positive change over time of the determinants may make people relatively happy even if the absolute level of these determinants is low in comparison to the situation elsewhere. Even the prospect that their children will be better-off than they are themselves may lift people's welfare. This dynamic aspect is, of course, the base for development policies and is, to that extent, accepted by development economists. But it should be recognised that sociologists often have shown a better understanding for the forces at work here than the economic profession as a whole. The issue is connected with the well-known thesis that a revolutionary situation is more likely to result from a reduction of relatively high welfare levels than from a very low absolute level of welfare.

13.3 CONSUMPTION ORIENTATION OF WELFARE FUNCTIONS

Restricting ourselves—more or less in accordance with the present economists' attitude—to static, economically-oriented welfare functions, another shortcoming of the attitude will now be discussed. Welfare or utility functions have been studied more with the purpose of understanding economic man's consumption behaviour than production behaviour. Productive behaviour covers not only the supply of (immediately) productive labour and—as far as an object of personal possession—land and capital. It also implies the participation in the preparation of (later) productive contributions. Most economics textbooks hardly use the welfare function as a source of productive behaviour, whereas considerable attention is given to the welfare function as a source of consumer behaviour. Demand functions for individual consumer goods and groups of such goods receive treatment, as shown by Schultz (1938), Samuelson (1947) and Schneider (1948). The same rather one-sided application of the welfare function to the problems of the demand for consumer goods is reflected in econometric research, as is exemplified by Stone's (1967 and many other publications) impressive contribution to such research. Correspondingly, the availability of statistical information on consumer behaviour is abundant. Typical for this abundance are household expenditure statistics which already have a long history (cf. for The Netherlands, van der Goot, 1930); in the United States an even larger volume of information on consumer behaviour, extended to include consumer expectations, is currently being made available.

Even though the subject of consumer attitudes—including such concepts as planned and anticipated consumption alongside actual consumption, and the related use of the concepts of *ex-ante* alongside *ex-post* values of it—has been explored with great care, present circumstances require advancement in new directions. With the spectacular development of consumption on the one hand and the new scarcities (clean environment, energy) on the other hand, the divergence between the satisfaction of 'natural' or 'reasonable' needs, as distinct from actual behaviour, has become a key problem; also because a large number of human beings is being exposed to extreme shortages of essential consumer goods. Increasingly, the consumption of unhealthy goods (from the old enemies such as alcoholic beverages and tobacco products to new ones, the so-called soft and hard drugs) and the unhealthy quantities consumed of goods considered healthy (meat, sugar) requires further research. Advertising (absorbing, in the USA, 3 per cent of GNP) and keeping up with the Jones's are among the villains of the piece, but what is more fundamentally needed is what learning processes can be discovered and which of these can be stimulated by feedback in the individual and in society to reduce the divergence between healthy and grossly unhealthy behaviour. It is here that the interdisciplinary research mentioned in section 12.1 may find one of its applications. A simple and self-evident example is the input that medical experts can make; but various aspects of psychology will have to add their contributions, if only because any learning process will rightly attract their interest. Since we are coming back to this subject in a broader context, we may refer to the following sections for some elaboration.

13.4 PRODUCTION ORIENTATION OF WELFARE FUNCTIONS: THE SUPPLY OF CAPABILITIES

We are now entering one of the underdeveloped uses of welfare functions: how do human beings behave as potential participants in the production process? In economic science it is customary to think of the production process as the combined use of land, equipment or capital goods, and labour, called the three production factors. The combination may be said to be undertaken by the 'organisers of production', often called entrepreneurs. The supply of land and of capital goods may or may not originate from private individuals, depending on the social order. These two factors are not necessarily connected with the individuals: they can be owned by them but are not part of them. This is why we shall concentrate on the supply of labour, which itself contains a number of psychological aspects. It is correct, we think, to say that this side of the welfare function has long been neglected by economic science. A simple illustration is the fact that for a long time, in economic production theory, labour was treated as one homogeneous factor (cf. Schneider 1948, pp. 430ff.). In the last few decades a relatively small group of economists has joined those who had chosen job classification as a practical activity. Job classification is used to streamline the wage and salary structure as well as to facilitate the matching of demand and supply of services on the highly diversified labour market. In fact, it is better to speak of the many sectors of the latter, or of the complex of labour markets.

Each individual joining the labour market is characterised by a number of degrees to which a list of relevant capabilities is in her or his possession. In a direct sense this may be a BA or MA degree in chemistry, but the concept of degree is meant also to include an estimated level, often expressed in figures on a scale, of such capabilities as physical strength, manual dexterity or general or social intelligence. By the latter term the capability to deal with people is meant, which is important for jobs in which contact with other people is regular or intense. General intelligence may be measured by an IQ test. Most scales are the result of negotiations between representatives of labour and management, assisted by experts on job classification.

Each person, during his or her lifetime, goes through a process of learning which, from a certain moment, is combined with working and, as a rule, holding a succession of jobs, whose classification indicates the degree required to perform properly in that job. A simplified picture of the process of production, closer to what it was in the past than what it is at present, is that each person involved first goes through a process of schooling and then fills a job for the rest of her or his life until retirement. The main choice at stake is, in that picture, the choice of the job, implying an effort to obtain the degrees required of the relevant capabilities, plus the effort to perform in that job. These efforts give rise to positive or negative satisfaction, and are combined with the satisfaction derived from the consumption the income attached to the job permits. Examples of the development of this branch of economic science in the last few decades include work by Bowles and Nelson (1974), Corocan et al. (1976). de Wolff and van Slijpe (1972), Garfinkel and Haveman (1975), Hartog (1981), Taubman (1975) and Wise (1975) (this list is not definitive) who all introduced variables indicative of some type of capabilities.

A thorough treatment of the choice of a job would have to include the use of a welfare function in which job satisfaction or dissatisfaction is reflected. In this approach the choice is based on an attempt to maximise welfare, subject to a number of restrictions. This aspect of the approach is rarely dealt with explicitly, as is customary for consumption-oriented behaviour. From both the economist's and the psychologist's point of view, the ideal would be to express welfare as a function of income, representing the consumption possibilities, personality traits reflecting the person's tastes, and job characteristics expressing the impact of these characteristics on job satisfaction or dissatisfaction. A concrete theoretical example has been elaborated by this author some decades ago (Tinbergen, 1956), but attempts to check it econometrically were only undertaken after 1970. The essence of the 1956 thesis was the assumption that welfare or utility depends on the effort required by one's job and on what was called the 'tension' between the required and the actually available degree or intensity of the various capabilities, and that both a positive and a negative deviation between the two would reduce welfare. So far, the somewhat crude attempts to check this assumption have not been successful (Tinbergen, 1975; Bouma et al., 1976), but better results may now be anticipated.

A central question regarding the use of personality traits and job characteristics is the number that can be considered mutually independent. An interesting attempt made by Hartog (1978) concerning the number of mutually independent job characteristics, using factor analysis, seemed to suggest that that number might be rather modest—of the order of three only. This conclusion was considered provisional only and the issue deserves further research.

Another central question, to be elaborated below, concerns the variability of personality traits: which of these are unchangeable and which can be changed by some learning process. We shall indicate the (practically) predetermined traits as parameters: these are entities constant for a given individual, but different among individuals. In contradistinction, other arguments entering into the welfare function are variables. This is true in particular for the job, although within limits.

The number of arguments entering into the welfare function constitutes, on the basis of the preceding remarks, an as yet undecided issue. As an approximation we may simplify matters by some convenient mathematical combination—for instance, a linear expression in some variables considered relevant. An important example is the use of only one argument to be called income corrected for a number of inconveniences so as to keep utility equal. Thus, income may be corrected for the size of the household, or for heavy physical work. It may also be corrected upward for interesting or challenging work, such as scientific research or managerial work. Figures given by Burck (1976), showing that chief executives' incomes in real terms did not change between 1952 and 1976, whereas the average income in the USA rose by 30 per cent, may be interpreted to disclose that this group was overpaid in 1952 and probably enjoys a positive psychical income (cf. Tinbergen, 1980).

13.5 THE LEARNING PROCESS AND THE ROLE OF GENETIC FACTORS

As stated, the strict separation of learning from work has increasingly been replaced by processes where, from about the age of 15, working and learning are combined or alternate. Moreover, formal learning is preceded by informal learning from birth. For the entire lifetime, human beings are involved in learning processes and it is here that interdisciplinary research is particularly important. The work done by psychologists and geneticists, in cooperation with education experts (Jencks, 1972; Fägerlind, 1975; Dronkers, 1979; to mention a few only) may be taken as a starting point. The main problem dealt with is the estimation of the influences exerted by some genetic and some environmental determinants on occupation and income. The material used originates from enquiries sometimes made for their own sake and sometimes made for other purposes but useful for the problem at hand. Examples are tests taken from a school population all of the same age (as, for instance, in Malmö, Sweden), or tests taken from conscripts (cf. Husén, 1974, and later). The method used is known as path analysis, in which each endogenous variable is supposed to be determined directly by causal connections with a number of endogenous and exogenous variables. Here endogenous means unknown, and exogenous given, in the context of the problem set considered. As already observed, there is much similarity between models as used, for instance, in econometrics and path analysis. The latter always works with 'normalised' variables (i.e. variables with mean equal to zero and standard deviation equal to unity), which is not customary in econometric models, although perfectly possible and sometimes helpful. In econometric models the time lags between variables are specified which is not always done in path analysis.

The main problem dealt with by psychologists, geneticists and education experts does not necessarily contain the same variables in all its versions; often the availability of data limits their number. The variables standing for inherited determinants refer to the parents and may include their education, occupation or income; these data may refer to the father or the mother, or both. They are taken as data. Among the endogenous variables early cognitive ability, if known from enquiries, or cognitive ability at a later date (e.g. 20 years of age), or both, may appear. Schooling (or educational level attained), occupation (sometimes for both initial and later jobs), and income (or earnings only) are, in most cases, included.

Clearly much remains to be desired. Thus it would be desirable to include more information concerning inherited determinants. To begin with, data on grandparents are desirable since some genetical endowments of the parents would be a highly useful variable. Alongside cognitive abilities, non-cognitive abilities of all concerned should also be included (cf. Behrman *et al.*, 1980). Further, the educational process is represented rather poorly if only the number of years of schooling is considered (cf. De Wolff and van Slijpe, 1972). The last mentioned authors give different weights to years of different phases of education. In a few cases more data on the quality of education have been studied (cf. Morgenstern, 1973).

In a general way, and using economic terminology, we must confess that the production function of (formal) education is a badly neglected subject, especially if we compare its treatment with that of production functions for material production. And even in the latter realm engineers have often been much more sophisticated than economists (cf. Boon, 1964, and after). Of the sometimes decisive inputs into the formal education process (quality of teachers, type of school, curriculum, etc.), the impact on the output (split up into types of school-leavers) is a question for speculation rather than empirical research. An example of the lack of accurate information is the debate on the desirability or undesirability of the comprehensive school system (German: *Gesamtschule*; Dutch: *middenschool*). Clearly the definition of the data needed already constitutes a problem and, subsequently, the collection of (sufficiently representative) data. For socioeconomic policy more insight into the degree of learnability of some personality traits, such as leadership, is extremely important. If more people with managerial capabilities could be supplied through, say, business schools, their relative incomes may be put under pressure. If the relevant capabilities cannot be learned—that is, are genetically predetermined—these relative incomes cannot be easily reduced (cf. Tinbergen, 1979). Intuitive opinions vary as much here as about the genetical differences (or non-existence of differences) between races (cf. Husén, 1974). So do preferences with regard to the comprehensive school, even if the production function were exactly known.

One very general question may be raised here where interdisciplinary research might be very fruitful. Biologists tell us that the simple contrast of nature or nurture (genetically predetermined or learnable) is suggesting too simple an approach. There are more types of behaviour between the extremes. How can educational psychologists and economists profit from this biological sophistication (cf. Baerends *et al.*, 1978)? One of the aspects of the problems just discussed can also be formulated in a seemingly simple way: are there, and if so what limits to learnability (cf. de Groot, in Baerends *et al.*, 1978, p. 55)? Among the limits suggested by some is a time limit or generation limit: for certain degrees of capabilities a minimum time of ten years or of two generations may exist.

13.6 MEASUREMENT OF WELFARE

If welfare is a central issue of economic science or even (de Groot, in Baerends *et al.*, 1978, p. 53) of our times, the question of its measurability remains vital. Natural scientists are anxious to keep open the possibility of measurement (Groen, p. 48 and de Groot, p. 61, in Baerends *et al.*, 1978) but groups of philosophers hold that measurement is impossible 'in principle'. Economic science has oscillated between these two positions. At present the majority of the economics profession is still following Pareto's rejection of the measurability of welfare. An active minority has made attempts, in recent times, at measurement, however. As customary, two approaches have been followed. van Praag (1968, 1978 and in a number of publications between these dates) sent out questionnaires to some 2500 members of Consumers' Unions in Belgium and The Netherlands and plans to collect this type of information in other countries. Apart from information about age, occupation, schooling and family size he asks the interviewees to indicate the incomes with which they would feel 'very well-off', 'well-off', etc. down to 'very badly-off'. The verbally indicated scale shows eight levels, and hence nine intervals. It appears that, if numbered by a rising arithmetical scale, the welfare function of income shows practically the same form for all respondents, the cumulated log-normal curve, characterised by two parameters. Van Praag and his colleagues use these functions as welfare functions: one of the parameters appears to be a rather precisely determined function of family size and other objectively determinable parameters (cf. Bouma *et al.*, 1976). The advantage of this method apparently consists of the possibility in a political debate, the respondent may be quoted to have 'declared voluntarily that some income different from what they now have would be satisfactory or would constitute a rise by 10 per cent of their previous welfare level'. A well-known disadvantage of the method—extensively dealt with by the authors in a number of studies, including van Praag (1978)—is that people do not always react to a change in their situation the way they have told the interviewer; that is they have not forecast correctly their own behaviour or evaluation of their new situation: in our case a new income. Their welfare evaluation is subject to what is called a 'preference drift'.

The other approach to measure welfare is not based on what people think they will do, but what they are actually doing; hence on observation of their behaviour. This method has been followed by this author and set out elsewhere (Tinbergen, 1975, ch. 4). Work done so far is in its infancy still, and of restricted value for lack of the relevant data. One drawback of this method is that it needs at least one additional assumption—a compensation for avoiding the disadvantage of the first method. For further details of the attempts made along the lines sketched, the reader is referred to Tinbergen (1980).

A last point to be mentioned is the question: which mathematical form should be preferred in the approach followed by van Praag, and generally if only one composite argument is chosen (for instance, income corrected for a number of inconveniences)? This author is strongly in favour of choosing the logarithm of (corrected) income, one reason being that this function shows a decline in marginal utility with an increase in income. The function preferred by van Praag and his colleagues shows an increasing marginal utility for very low incomes, which diverges from what most economists (and psychologists?) would require. Interestingly enough, van Praag's results give an equally good fit to both functions.

REFERENCES

Baerends, G.P. *et al.* (1978), *Over welzijn*, Deventer, Van Loghum Slaterus. [On welfare].
Behrman, J.R. *et al.* (1980), *Socioeconomic Success*, Amsterdam, North-Holland.
Boon, G.K. (1964), *Economic Choice of Human and Physical Factors in Production*, Amsterdam, North-Holland.
Bouma, N. *et al.* (1976), 'Testing and applying a theory of utility', *European Economic Review*, 8, 181–91.
Bowles, S. and Nelson, V.I. (1974), 'The "inheritance of IQ" and the intergenerational reproduction of economic inequality', *Review of Economics and Statistics*, 56, 39–51.
Burck, C.G. (1976), 'A group profile of the Fortune 500 chief executives', *Fortune*, May, p. 173ff.
Corocan, M., Jencks, C. and Olneck, M. (1976), 'The effects of family background on earnings', *American Economic Review*, 66 (proceedings), 430–5.

de Wolff, P. and van Slijpe, A.R.D. (1972), *The Relation between Income, Intelligence, Education and Social Background*, Institute of Actuarial Science and Econometrics, University of Amsterdam.

Dronkers, J. and de Jong, U. (1979), 'Jencks and Fägerlind in a Dutch way', *Social Science Information*, 18 (4/5), London, Sage, pp. 761–81.

Edgeworth, F.Y. (1881), *Mathematical Psychics*, London.

Fägerlind, I. (1975), *Formal Education and Adults Earnings*, Stockholm, Almqvist & Wiksell.

Garfinkel, J. and Haveman, R.H. (1975), *Economic Inequality and the Utilization of Earnings Capacity*, Madison, Wisconsin, Academic Press.

Hartog, J. (1981), *Personal Income Distribution: a Multicapability Theory*, The Hague/Boston/London, Nijhoff.

Husén, T. (1974), *Talent, Equality and Meritocracy*, The Hague, Martinus Nijhoff.

Jencks, C. et al. (1972), *Inequality*, New York, Basic Books.

Levy, S. and Gutman, L. (1975), 'On the Multivariate Structure of well-being', *Social Indicators Research*, 3, 361–88.

Morgenstern, R.D. (1973), 'Direct and indirect effects on earnings of schooling and socio-economic background', *The Review of Economics and Statistics*, 55, 225–33.

Samuelson, P.A. (1947), *Foundations of Economic Analysis*, Cambridge, Mass., Harvard University Press.

Schneider, E. (1948), *Einführung in die Wirtschaftstheorie*, II. Teil. Tübingen, J.C.B. Mohr (13th edn., 1972, Paul Siebeck).

Schultz, H. (1938), *The Theory and Measurement of Demand*, Chicago, The University of Chicago Press.

Stone, R. (1967), *Spending and Saving in Relation to Income and Wealth*, Cambridge, University of Cambridge, Department of Applied Economics, reprint series no. 265.

Taubman, P. (1975), *Sources of Inequality in Earnings*, Amsterdam, North-Holland.

Tinbergen, J. (1956), 'On the theory of income distribution', *Weltwirtschaftliches Archiv*, 77, 155–75. Reprinted in *Selected Papers* (1959), Amsterdam, North-Holland, pp. 243–63.

Tinbergen, J. (1975), *Income Distribution*, Amsterdam, North-Holland.

Tinbergen, J. (1979), 'Hoogte en beinvloedbaarheid van inkomens van "managers" ', in van den Goorbergh, W.M. et al. (eds), *Over macht en wet in het economisch gebeuren*, Leiden, H.E. Stenfert Kroese, B.V., pp. 7–25. [Level of and possibility to influence manager income].

Tinbergen, J. (1980), 'Two approaches to quantify the concept of equitable income distribution', *Kyklos*, 33, 3–15.

van der Goot, W.H. (1930), *De besteding van het inkomen*, The Hague, Martinus Nijhoff.

van Praag, B.S.M. (1968), *Individual Welfare Functions and Consumer Behaviour*, Amsterdam, North-Holland.

van Praag, B.S.M. (1978), 'The perception of income inequality', in Krelle, W. and Shorrocks, A.F. (eds), *Personal Income Distribution*, Amsterdam, North-Holland, pp. 113–36.

Wise, D.A. (1975), 'Academic achievement and job performance', *American Economic Review*, 65, 350–66.

Part IV
The Optimal Social Order

14 The Dynamic Welfare Maximum

14.1 CHARACTER OF WELFARE ECONOMICS

The problem I want to discuss in this chapter is by what institutions and policy instruments maximum welfare over the foreseeable future for a nation or group of nations can be attained. This ambitious task is that of welfare economics, a sub-discipline of economic science that was shaped in particular by Vilfredo Pareto (1927). As one of the pioneers of mathematical economics Pareto formulated the problem considerably more accurately than was usual before him.

Even today, after a considerable development of Pareto's ideas, however, in the leading texts (e.g. Samuelson, 1947) the true nature of the problem is rarely mentioned. Often it is announced as the formulation of the conditions that the welfare maximum has to satisfy. In this way it is not very clear what are the real unknowns of the problem. In my opinion it is in particular the *set of social institutions* and the *instruments* of socioeconomic policy they apply. The problem is how these have to be chosen so as to yield the welfare optimum.

The emphasis has to be put on the word 'set' since it is the operation of the set as a whole that has to satisfy as well as make possible the maximum conditions. Even in the extremely simplified form which I shall deal with here, as it is often dealt with, it contains difficult methodological aspects. One of these is that the operation of the initially unknown institutions may imply *costs* which cannot be taken account of beforehand. Probably a process of successive approximations will be one of the few methods of solving this aspect of the main problem. Only if we neglect these costs—as we shall do, following the existing tradition—will it be possible directly to interpret the maximum conditions in terms of institutions. A suggestion about a better method has been made in the Foreword to this book. The set of unknown institutions as a whole may be called the optimal socioeconomic order.

As a rule, the unknowns of the problem are considered to be the quantities produced, consumed and exchanged of the goods and services considered; and of course they are. They take a sort of intermediary position between the problem's data and the basic unknowns.

14.2 THE STATIC WELFARE MAXIMUM

In economic science the static form of a problem is often started with, as an introduction to the dynamic form. Often the former already shows some features characteristic for the solution with the advantage of a simpler shape. For other problems the dynamic feature may be so essential that this method eliminates the essential. As we shall show, some static features of our problem are sufficiently characteristic to permit their treatment by way of introduction. In the static version all variables are constants over time and the question is which configuration maximises welfare. Constancy implies, for instance, no change in population and capital, whose actual changes are a few percent *per annum*; tastes are assumed not to change either. These assumptions are harmless in comparison to, for instance, differences in income and type of work among the social groups of our societies.

Our problem is now specified by, as a first step, formulating a *welfare function* for the nation considered, that is, to indicate which variables enter into it and according to what joint scale they affect welfare. Again it is logical first to ask this question for *one individual* and subsequently extend the answer to the population at large. Important variables among the determinants of one individual's welfare are the quantities of different goods *consumed* per unit of time and some measure for the *effort made* in the production process, which usually also determines the quantity of *leisure* enjoyed.

The simplest way of defining the nation's welfare consists of adding up the individual welfare figures, which implies that welfare can be *measured*. Although many economists do not adhere to this assumption, as discussed in Chapter 11, our scientific strategy will be to assume measurability.

From the very summary remarks made about the impact of consumption and productive effort one might deduce that welfare can be raised by raising consumption and reducing effort. This is not possible in the short run, and constitutes the main example of the *restrictions* imposed on the maximisation of welfare. In this case it is the *production function* for each of the goods considered; another frequently occurring example is some *balance equation* expressing that no more can be used or applied of any product or production factor than is available. Mathematically our maximisation or optimisation problem therefore constitutes a maximisation problem subject to restrictions. It is essential that relations derived from some socioeconomic order, such as a particular tax, not be used as a restriction: that would mean the presupposition of some institution instead of a search for the (set of) institutions maximising welfare, restricted only by laws of nature.

In our illustration of the problem we shall use the solution with the aid of Lagrange multipliers. More modern mathematical methods are those of programming, especially linear programming, using set theory (Koopmans, 1957).

14.3 SOME PREVIOUS RESULTS

Among the earlier versions of welfare economics some are very well known. Not only a large number of persons, but also many products produced in many enterprises (or production units) are considered and production processes use inputs of a few production factors (natural resources, labour and capital). Often the latter's number is not assumed to be large. Production functions are supposed to show diminishing returns, implying that marginal costs are rising functions of quantities produced. On the basis of these assumptions some well-known features of the optimum situation can be proven to apply:

(a) any two pairs of *products* have to be exchanged at the same price ratios (*uniformity of prices*);
(b) prices have to be equal to *marginal costs* of production;
(c) prices of production *factors* paid by enterprises are *uniform*: the same wage is paid by all enterprises and, similarly, the same interest rate.

Such results can be obtained by a *system of markets* where *free competition* between enterprises prevails. These markets are the institutions whose operation yields the welfare optimum. It is part of a social order often called *laissez-faire* and has long been the basis of liberal political programmes in the European sense ('Manchester School liberalism', and not liberal in the American sense).

The validity of these results is, however, restricted by the assumptions already mentioned and by the fulfilment of part of the conditions only that follow from the optimalisation process. Within this restricted framework some interesting policy conclusions can be drawn, however. Oligopoly and *monopoly* (and -opsony) are not optimal and *anti-trust legislation* and similar regulations are based on that non-optimality. Also, many forms of *discrimination* violate price uniformity; among them interference with foreign trade by import duties and export subsidies.

A very important maximum condition that has not been used yet in the preceding argument is the condition derived from varying income distribution (cf. section 14.11 for the corresponding mathematical operation). This deserves a special argument, since it is especially here that the tendency exists to adhere to a restriction valid in the existing order, but not a restriction imposed by the laws of nature. That restriction is the individual (or family, for that matter) *budget restriction*. The system of maximum conditions (cf. section 14.11) does not imply individual budget restrictions, or, in other words, *income redistribution is a feature of the optimum*.

14.4 THE INTRODUCTION OF EXTERNAL EFFECTS

For a number of productive activities the production laws assumed in section 14.3 do not apply. A first deviation consists of *external effects*. By it we shall mean the phenomenon that a certain production volume not only affects welfare of its producers, sellers and buyers, but also of others (Drewnowsky, 1961), to be called *outsiders*.

A first series of examples of external effects occurs when for technical or cultural reasons some products are obtained without payment. There are no buyers then and everybody is an outsider. In this category are a number of *collective goods* (cf. Chapter 5), such as the maintenance of the road network, internal and external security, and a healthy monetary system. Sometimes also quasi-collective goods are included but it remains a point of doubt whether rightly so.

A second type of example may occur even when some services in this group are paid for. The schooling of an individual may not only affect his own welfare but also the welfare of his colleagues. Clean air, soil and water have become very important examples of either the first or the second category.

A famous, although not very important, example (Meade, 1955) has become the one of 'mutual external effects' of apple-growers and bee-keepers. Expansion of an orchard furthers the production of honey and expansion of bee-hives the production of apples. In this case an optimum decision on the production of both apples and honey can be taken if the two branches are *integrated*. If, however, the external effects are widely spread, production by a public enterprise may be a solution. It depends on the way such an enterprise is organised whether public production is optimal indeed; this applies if no difference in productivity between public and private enterprises exists.

14.5 THE INTRODUCTION OF INDIVISIBLE MEANS OF PRODUCTION

Another deviation from the assumptions made on production processes in the simple model dealt with in section 14.3 consist of the existence of *indivisible means of production*: a bridge, a railway, an electricity plant. Many of these have a minimum size below which they would be considerably less productive. The phenomenon often is more complicated and one of its consequences is that marginal costs of production are decreasing, or at least marginal costs are lower than average costs. Equality of prices and marginal costs would then imply permanent losses. Free competition and private production are incompatible; if private production were maintained, enterprises will tend to cooperate and create restricted, possibly monopoloid, competition.

A solution may also be attained by the introduction of *two-part pricing*: consumers pay a fixed amount plus an amount proportional to the quantity consumed. The system is applied to energy, water and transportation. Application could be extended to more commodities whose production requires indivisible means of production. Its introduction raises two new questions, however. One is what criteria for the level of the fixed amount are optimal; consumers with different incomes should not pay equal fixed amounts. Theories have been developed which consider as the *raison d'être* of the fixed amount the 'availability' of the commodity and for electricity measure this by the number of lamps and plug connections. For other commodities other criteria are needed, of course.

The other question that arises is how the *collection* of the fixed amounts can optimally be organised. Essentially, for consumers the *total* of all fixed amounts for all commodities *plus* income tax is what matters. For the enterprises supplying the commodities it is only the *total* of fixed amounts received from all consumers that matters. If there are M consumers and N commodities each produced by one enterprise only, the number of fixed amounts (plus income tax) equals $M(N+1)$; but relevant are only $M+N+1$, which may be much less. Collection by one institution, say the Treasury, may be the optimal organisation of collection to be followed by distribution to the supplying enterprise. This organisation may also be in charge of the financing of new investments by the enterprises concerned (cf. section 14.8).

14.6 LABOUR OF DIFFERENT QUALITY

In the older versions of economic science, including welfare economics, labour is considered as one *homogeneous* factor of production and more attention is given to the *quantities* (length of working day, working week and working year) than to differences in quality. In the course of the last century the importance of decisions on quality has increased and that of decisions on quantities decreased. Working hours have become more uniform by legislation and the expansion of schooling and training has increasingly diversified the variety of occupations in modern societies. Great progress has been made in the *measurement* of labour quality: job evaluation and requirements on the demand side of the labour market, and screening of workers supplying labour, with the aid of their level of schooling and other personality characteristics on the supply side.

This implies that for a more precise description of the demand for labour production functions are needed in which the quantities of various types of labour entering as determinants (cf. Chapters 1, 2, 3 and 6) and for a more precise description of the supply of labour welfare or utility functions are needed in which job characteristics and personality traits enter alongside traditional determinants like consumption (cf. Chapters 8, 9, 12 and 13). The simplest example appears if only one figure characterises jobs and a correponding figure the type of worker. In fact the data available refer to the level of schooling of workers and level of schooling required for jobs. On other aspects similar data are needed but are often available to the enterprises only.

14.7 INTRODUCTION OF SCHOOLING PROCESS

In the simple example to be dealt with in section 14.11 we shall introduce the schooling process as an illustration of how the quality of labour complicates the social order. It is necessary to distinguish between inherited (*innate*) and (*learnable*) qualification components. (An early example is Correa, 1963.) In order to attain an optimal situation two choices have to be made: the choice of schooling and the choice of occupation. Schooling improves a worker's quality and consequently the occupation (job) that will maximise his (her) welfare. The latter will of course also be determined by the earnings. So welfare depends on innate qualities (including the individual's taste), the addition of qualities due to schooling, the nature of the occupation and earnings, which, after deduction of taxes, determine consumption possibilities.

The schooling process is, as a production process, characterised by a production function, expressing the increase in quality obtained as a function of innate quality and the quantity of schooling received. This function constitutes another restriction of the maximisation of welfare. The quantity of schooling will be measured (cf. Chapter 16) by the total cost, in terms of consumer goods, of those involved in the training process—teachers etc., goods used (buildings, books etc.)—and the loss of product if the student is of working age.

14.8 THE DYNAMIC WELFARE MAXIMUM

We now proceed to the dynamic formulation of our problems. To begin with, we no longer assume that variables are constant over time. We must assume that population size and capital may change, that knowledge of production and schooling processes increase, and that these processes, especially education, take time.

The formal changes in the setting of the problem may be characterised briefly as follows. Each individual's welfare may now be considered to depend on all relevant variables discussed before for a series of time units. A special form of this relation is the sum total of welfare experiences for the series of time units the community is interested in. The number of restrictions to be satisfied must be equal to their number per unit of time multiplied by the number of time units considered. The balance equation for commodities becomes somewhat more complicated since part of production may now be used for capital formation (physical as well as human capital formation, where the latter is another name for the schooling process). Some of the restrictions may now express the time-consuming character of some processes mentioned before.

The dynamic problem, similar to the static version, has as its main unknowns the institutions and the instruments they command; these may now change over time. The intermediary unknowns are no longer constant levels of production, consumption, and so on, but their development over time. In concrete cases it is possible now to formulate statements on the optimal rate of growth, although very simple assumptions have to be made on the production functions involved. One example has been discussed intensively, implying that the optimum growth rate should be equal to the percentage of national income attributed to capital (Phelps, 1961). Clearly, this subject disappeared from the agenda after all that happened after 1961.

Another type of problem whose relevance remained topical will be taken up after a simple mathematical formulation of our set-up has been shown. This problem may be formulated as follows: is the optimal redistribution of incomes found in our static model also valid in the dynamic setting? In other words, are the conditions to attain the optimal growth compatible with those to attain optimal distribution? Its topicality may be understood by a somewhat provocative reformulation: can the governments of Third World countries maintain that high income inequality is necessary for rapid development? This defence of strongly unequal distribution is usually based on the higher savings rate corresponding with unequal income distribution. It disregards the possibility of high *public savings*. Public savings do require a strict public finance discipline, but public savings need not be invested by the public sector; they may be used to subsidise private investments. As we shall see in section 14.11, the redistribution of incomes as found in our static models need not be changed under these assumptions.

A last example of the conclusions that may be drawn from a dynamic welfare optimum may be taken in the field of the investment in indivisible (bulk) equipment. Decisions in this field cannot be based on data from individual enterprises or even branches. They point to the necessity of central planning for this type of investment (cf. Tinbergen, 1964; and section 14.5).

14.9 THE OPTIMAL INCOME REDISTRIBUTION

In the preceding section we stated that, with appropriate public finance discipline, income redistribution is not only a feature of the static welfare optimum but also of the dynamic; in section 14.11 the mathematical formulation will be offered. In this section, a few more aspects of this feature of the optimum will now be taken up. Not all forms of *taxation* are appropriate to implement an optimal redistribution. Two of the most important taxes in existing social orders can be shown to be non-optimal, value added or other turnover taxes and income taxes. Both have the tendency to reduce production because they contribute to an over-estimation of the disadvantages of a production increase: they add something to the true costs of production. Of the more important existing taxes only profit taxes and (approximately) wealth taxes do not suffer from this drawback. Profit taxes only tax production on which a profit is being made and wealth taxes hardly affect current production, which is small in comparison to all past production. Theoretically, a tax on personal, innate capabilities would not lead to a wrong production decision. The implementation of such a tax on part of human capital is not yet clear; possibly we have here a case of an institution with very high costs (cf. section 14.1). The human capital tax would be in the interest of physical capital-owners, since it might make possible a reduction of the tax on physical wealth.

If costs of this institution are prohibitive—as we assumed—this may lead to the search for a second best. Another alternative is Kaldor's tax on consumption expenditure, which, however, is also suffering from its relatively high cost: the necessity for the state to have a closed system of national accounts in which each individual is represented.

The essential feature of the optimal tax system—neglecting the costs of collection—is that the capacity to produce be taxed but not the result of production.

The objection often made that in this way the incentive to produce is affected and reduced is not correct. It should not be overlooked that the full amount of a production increase remains income to the individual concerned.

14.10 WELFARE MAXIMUM AND SOCIAL EQUITY

So far we have discussed a welfare maximum (or optimum) on the basis of individual welfare functions in which only variables concerning each individual itself appeared; these individuals—typically for the *homo oeconomicus*—are supposed to be perfectly selfish. Even so, we found as characteristics of the optimal order some features which have often been recommended on the basis of equity. It is interesting to state that such characteristics appear desirable even if only a maximal total welfare is aimed at. Redistribution is not advocated for its own sake, but as a means to maximise total welfare.

It is also conceivable, however, that equity is one of the autonomous aims of a social order. Logically this may even be inserted into welfare economics: (a) because a number of individuals consider this as a desirable element, and introduce it into their personal welfare function; and (b) because the social (or national) welfare function need not only be seen as the sum total of individual welfare functions of all citizens, but also contain social equity. Both ways of enriching the concept of social welfare may well come down to almost identical generalisations. The next question arising then is that of the *definition of (social) equity*. Textbooks of ethics or the philosophy of law hardly pay attention to the concept (cf. Perelman, 1945). One aspect is emphasised clearly enough, namely that equity requires equal treatment of individuals who are the same or in the same circumstances; but the complement about people who are not the same or in the same conditions is lacking. One definition of equity, namely that there should be equality between what a person contributes to national income and what he (she) receives as income, seems to be obsolete. It implies that persons well-endowed by nature with capabilities receive higher incomes than persons modestly endowed; hence that the differences in endowment are equitable, that nature is equitable. This definition certainly doesn't appeal to most citizens.

Since everybody's ethical intuition contains ideas about what is equitable, we clearly find ourselves confronted with a lacuna. I have to admit that I cannot fill that lacuna to my full satisfaction, but I think I see a theoretical starting point. As the hard core I submit that equity means the *equality of welfare* of all individuals considered. There are difficulties to the extent that heavily handicapped individuals cannot, in all probability, be as happy as most other people. Excepting these cases, the idea only makes sense if welfare *can be measured* (cf. Chapters 11 and 13), an assumption we adhere to, even though the precision of such measurements is a subject of wide differences of opinion among economists. Even so another question arises: is a situation of maximal social welfare also one of equity or not? Since the former requires equaliy of marginal welfare among the members of a community, and the latter equality of welfare, maximum social welfare need not imply equity as we defined it. It may, however, imply equity; that depends on the mathematical shape of welfare functions assumed. Finally, in the situation where the social welfare maximum does not imply equity, it is possible to add as an additional restriction *equity as an autonomous element* of the optimum we search for. The additional restriction will, as a rule, reduce social welfare in the new optimum, with the limiting possibility of a zero reduction. With our present knowledge on welfare functions no precise answer to this question can be given.

14.11 MATHEMATICAL FORMULATION

In this section an illustration will be given of the formulation of the social welfare optimum using the method of Lagrange multipliers as mentioned in section 14.2. We shall restrict ourselves to what was dealt with in section 14.4 and after. We shall not, therefore, distinguish a number of goods and services and a number of enterprises; this has been done by many authors and been used to derive the features (a), (b) and (c) in section 14.3. (These aspects will be reconsidered elsewhere by the present author in a forthcoming book devoted to Professor Arrow, edited by Professor Feiwel.)

In the present illustration the aspects dealt with in sections 14.6, 14.7 and 14.8 are treated in a simple mathematical way. The variables appearing in this illustration are the following:

x_t^i: total consumption, measured in one composite good, of individual i during time unit t;

s_t^i: the quality of individual i's occupation in period t measured by some method of job evaluation;

v_t^i: the quality of individual i itself, measured in the same way as s_t^i; this quality having been attained during a learning process, described by:

u_{t-1}^i: the innate quality of person i in period $t-1$, and

e_{t-1}^i: the 'quantity' of education absorbed by person i during period $t-1$;

k_t: the stock of capital goods available at the end of period t;

The dynamic welfare maximum 155

ω_t^i: individual *i*'s welfare in period *t*;

Ω: total welfare of the community considered in the period considered relevant;

I: the number of members of the community.

It is assumed that

$$\Omega = \sum_i \sum_t \omega_t^i \qquad (14.1)$$

where $i = 1, 2 \ldots, I$ and t is summed over the relevant period. This formulation implies that future values of ω are not discounted in the usual way, but by considering part of the future irrelevant. (For other approaches cf. Inagaki, 1970.)

One type of restriction to be satisfied for each time unit t runs:

$$\xi_t(k_{t-1}, s_t^1, s_t^2, \ldots, s_t^I) = \sum_i x_t^i + k_t - k_{t-1} + \sum_i e_t^i \qquad (14.2)$$

where ξ_t represents production in period t, supposed equal to the total of: consumption $\sum_i x_t^i$, physical capital formulation $k_t - k_{t-1}$, and education quantity as defined in section 14.7.

The shape of ξ_t indicates how total production depends on the physical capital stock at the beginning of period t and the quality of the jobs held by all individuals.

The second type of restriction is:

$$e_t^i = \Psi_t(v_{t+1}^i, u_t^i) \qquad (14.3)$$

expressing that the education absorbed by individual *i* during period *t* depends on his or her innate quality u_t^i and the attained quality v_{t+1}^i at the end of period *t*.

The number of restrictions (14.2) equals the number of relevant time units and the number of restrictions (14.3) I times that number of time units.

This set-up implies that our problem consists of the maximisation of

$$\Omega' = \sum_i \sum_t i_t^i(x_t^i, s_t^i - v_t^i, u_t^i)$$
$$+ \sum_t \lambda_t \{ -\sum_i x_t^i - k_t + k_{t+1} - \sum e_t^i + \xi_t(k_{t-1}, s^1, s^2, \ldots, s^I) \}$$
$$+ \sum_i \sum_t \mu_t^i \{ e_t^i - \Psi_t(v_{t+1}^i, u_t^i) \} \ldots \qquad (14.4)$$

where λ_t and μ_t^i are Lagrange multipliers. We shall not discuss the existence of possible initial and final restrictions, basing ourselves on the intuitive opinion that a number of reasonable assumptions to justify such neglection can be formulated. For the large majority of time units the optimum will then have to satisfy the conditions obtained from putting the partial derivatives of Ω' equal to zero. The variables appearing in Ω' and the corresponding partial derivatives are listed below.

Variables	Optimum conditions	
x_t^i:	$\dfrac{\partial \omega_t^i}{\partial x_t^i} - \lambda_t = 0$	(14.5)
s_t^i:	$\dfrac{\partial \omega_t^i}{\partial s_t^i} + \lambda_t \dfrac{\partial \xi_t}{\partial s_t^i} = 0$	(14.6)
v_t^i:	$-\dfrac{\partial \omega_t^i}{\partial v_t^i} - \mu_{t-1}^i \dfrac{\partial \Psi_{t-1}}{\partial v_t^i} = 0$	(14.7)
e_t^i:	$-\lambda_t + \mu_t^i = 0$	(14.8)
k_t:	$\lambda_{t-1} - \lambda_t + \lambda_{t+1}\dfrac{\partial \xi_{t+1}}{\partial k_t} = 0$	(14.9)

From (14.8) we derive that all μ_t^i for the same t, but different i must be equal to λ_t.

For a given t we derive from (14.5), (14.6), and (14.7) that for each individual:

$$-\frac{\dfrac{\partial \omega_t^i}{\partial s_t^i}}{\dfrac{\partial \omega_t^i}{\partial x_t^i}} = \frac{\partial \xi_t}{\partial s_t^i} = \frac{\partial \Psi_{t-1}}{\partial v_t^i}\frac{\lambda_t}{\lambda_{t-1}} \tag{14.10}$$

The first of these two equations constitutes the *choice of occupation* (job); marginal productivity $\partial \xi_t/\partial s_t^i$ of the improvement of anybody's job must be equal to the marginal improvement of consumption $\partial x_t^i/\partial s_t^i$ (equal to the left-hand side of (14.10)), with given attained and innate qualities v_t^i of the individual considered obtained by a possible shift in occupation.

The second equation of (14.10) constitutes the *choice of education* (schooling). For the simplified shape of the welfare function we have chosen it indicates that the marginal schooling effort (i.e. the effort in order to raise quality by a unit) must be almost equal to the marginal product that may be obtained with the aid of the corresponding shift in job.

Equations (14.5) indicate that income (re)distribution must equalise marginal consumption welfare for all individuals; so this feature of our static model remains valid:

$$\partial \omega_t^1/\partial x_t^1 = \partial \omega_t^2/\partial x_t^2 = \ldots = \partial \omega_t^I/\partial x_t^I \tag{14.11}$$

Equations (14.7) and (14.9) link the successive time units. Equations (14.7), similarly to the second equation in (14.10), express that, as the consequence of the time required for some phase of schooling, in fact imply a comparison of schooling effort in $t-1$ with consumption increases later (t). Equations (14.9) establish a link between marginal product of capital and the rate of decrease in λ_t:

$$\partial \xi_t / \partial k_{t-1} = (\lambda_{t-2} - \lambda_{t-1})/\lambda_t \tag{14.12}$$

From (14.5) we see that λ_t is the marginal utility of consumption (or, in our simple setting: income). As a more specific illustration we may give to ω_t^i the shape $\ln x_t^i$. Then $\lambda_t = \partial \omega_t^i / \partial x_t^i = 1/x_t^i$. This transforms (14.12) into:

$$\partial \xi_t / \partial k_{t-1} = (x_{t-1} - x_{t-2}) x_t / x_{t-1} x_{t-2} \tag{14.13}$$

For a slowly developing x_t the expression $x_t / x_{t-1} x_{t-2} = (1 + 2\delta) x_{t-2}$ where δ is the rate of growth of x_t, assumed constant, and:

$$\partial \xi_t / \partial k_{t-1} = (1 + 2\delta)(x_{t-1} - x_{t-2})/x_{t-1} \tag{14.14}$$

which may also be approximated by:

$$\partial \xi_t / \partial k_{t-1} = \delta \tag{14.15}$$

Clearly, δ is an interest rate: it is the marginal productivity of capital.

REFERENCES

Correa, H. (1963), *The Economics of Human Resources*, Amsterdam, North-Holland.
Drewnowski, J. (1961), 'The economic theory of socialism: a suggestion for reconsideration', *The Journal of Political Economy*, LXIX, p. 341.
Inagaki, M. (1970), *Optimal Economic Growth*, Amsterdam, North-Holland.
Koopmans, T.C. (1957), *Three Essays on the State of Economic Science*, New York, McGraw Hill.
Meade, J.E. (1955), *Trade and Welfare*, Oxford, Oxford University Press.
Pareto, V. (1927), *Manuel d'économie politique*, Paris.
Phelps, E. (1961), 'The golden rule of accumulation: a fable for growthmen', *American Economic Review*, 51, p. 638.
Samuelson, P.A. (1947), *Foundations of Economic Analysis*, Cambridge, Mass., Harvard University Press.
Tinbergen, J. (1964), 'Economic development and investment indivisibilities', in *Problems of Economic Dynamics and Planning, Essays in Honour of Michael Kalecki*, P.W.N. Polish Scientific Publishers, Warsaw.

15 Some Remarks on the Optimal Tax System

15.1 OBJECTIVE AND LIMITATIONS OF THIS CHAPTER

This chapter constitutes an attempt to derive some features of an optimal tax system. For this purpose a simplified model of the economy has been used. The optimal tax system is considered to be part of an optimal order, defined as the state of the economy which maximises a social welfare function Ω to be specified later. The model used might be called semi-macro and concentrates on a number of features considered relevant to income distribution between groups of individuals characterised by different personality traits and working on jobs described by a number of job characteristics. The number of personality traits equals the number of job characteristics, and there is no restriction on this number. In this respect the model has a high degree of generality. The production function used is a function of capital used and of the quantities ϕ_a^b of employed persons, where a is a vector of the intensities in which each personality trait is available in the group considered, and b is a vector of the trait intensities usually required for the satisfactory execution of the job. The order of the components of the vectors a and b is the same, and components a_i and b_i therefore refer to the same trait or characteristic. In the language of job evaluation i is one of the aspects of a job and b_i the score of that aspect required for the job. It may or may not be equal to the value of a_i characterising the person on the job. If all $a_i = b_i$ we write $a = b$. The quantity ϕ_a^b is the proportion of the labour force characterised by a and b and the total of all ϕ therefore adds up to unity. In one version of the model the total number of people characterised by a given value of a has been considered given, that is:

$$\sum_b \phi_a^b = F_a \tag{15.1}$$

The total number of components of a and b is written A, hence:

$$i = 1, \ldots, A \text{ (number of aspects)} \tag{15.2}$$

Assuming that each aspect can occur in grades $g = 1, \ldots, G$, the total of all possible values of a_i or b_k amounts to AG. In what follows we shall omit indices i and k of the vector components. We shall indicate the set of all values which a or b can assume as: $a = 1 \ldots AG$ and $b = 1 \ldots AG$.

Personal welfare ω is supposed to be a function of $x_a^b - f(a, b)$, where x is income after redistribution and $f(a, b)$ a correction on x which represents the monetary compensation for all efforts made and inconveniences suffered in the execution of the job b.

Job satisfaction appears as a negative inconvenience. The mathematical shape of ω is such that $\partial \omega / \partial x$ is a (negatively) monotonous function of x.

The present chapter constitutes a generalisation of two earlier attempts to deal with the subject (cf. Tinbergen, 1975, 1977).

Among the many limitations of the model chosen four deserve special mention.

(i) The economy considered is a closed economy. No balance of payments is considered.
(ii) No breakdown into economic sectors has been made: the production function is supposed to apply to the economy's total output.
(iii) To begin with a social welfare function $\Omega = \sum \omega$ will be used, which in Sen's terminology (1977) is the 'welfarist approach'. This implies, among other things, that in the community considered no preference with regard to distribution is assumed to exist. It is interesting to observe that without such a preference some rather egalitarian features of the optimum prevail. In section 15.6 a simple example will be given of the direction in which the optimum is changed if a preference for less unequal incomes is assumed to prevail.
(iv) We assume that each household supplies one member participating in production outside the household. It would not be difficult to introduce alternatives, but it would unnecessarily complicate the model.

15.2 COMPARATIVE STATIC APPROACH CHOSEN: SOME IMPLICATIONS

The analysis to be presented is static. Its results will also apply to a developing economy provided the development satisfies a number of conditions. No attempt will be made to set out the full list of these conditions. This implies that no proof of the statement just made is provided either. The only attempt made in this section is to remind the reader in outline of the type of assumptions presumably needed to prove that our results have a somewhat wider applicability than for a strictly stationary state. The main determinants of slow, long-term development of an economy are the development of population, of total capital, of knowledge and its distribution over the most relevant groups of the population. We assume that these determinants are moving over time in a regular and slow way, comparable to a development without business cycles, catastrophes or sudden structural changes. Among the preconditions for such a development we mention the following, thought to be the most relevant.

The age composition of the population in total and the distribution of the school population must be such as to exclude sudden surpluses or deficits in the age group as well as the numbers of students of various levels of learning. Similarly the age composition of capital goods must be such as to let the total stock move regularly and in the proportion to the various parts of the active population required by the prevailing production functions, including the gradual changes in technology occurring. The use of scarce natural resources must switch gradually to the use of less scarce resources so as to avoid unexpected shortages.

In our model we do not consider the non-active part of the population, such as the student population or the pre-school and retired populations. We do not identify the distribution of expenditures over consumption and investment, but assume that the investments necessary to let the capital stock grow regularly in the desired way do take place. We assume that school-leavers find jobs fitting their education levels and that practical training on the job develops harmoniously. We do not specify the production function, which constitutes a wide applicability of our findings in respect with this aspect of development. Our assumption on individual welfare functions ω has already been specified. Although this constitutes a limitation on the validity of our findings, the arbitrary number of personality traits and job requirements offers the possibility of a compensation for this limitation. With our present very limited knowledge of welfare functions the procedure chosen seems permissible.

15.3 THE CENTRAL CASE CONSIDERED

The economy is supposed to consist of a number of households, each of which belongs to a relatively homogeneous group characterised by the vector values a and b mentioned in section 15.1. All members of such a group are supposed to have identical welfare functions, $\omega_{ab} = \omega\{x_a^b - f(a, b)\}$, also mentioned. Although a and b refer mainly to personality traits and job characteristics relevant to production, we may also consider traits relevant to welfare rather than production, such as family size. The inconvenience due to a large family must then be reflected in $f(a, b)$.

There are a few personality traits which depress ω to such an extent that for households of that kind—with a member having a serious physical or mental handicap—the level of welfare required by the optimum conditions cannot be attained. Some curves in the graphical representation of the nature of the optimum position may not have the point of intersection required, so that only lower welfare than that of all others may be possible for such groups, and a rather arbitrary level will as a rule be chosen.

Another difficulty in defining personality traits is that some of them can very easily be changed (e.g. the speed with which a given job (task) can be performed). We shall not deal with this difficulty in the present chapter, but it is not difficult to build into the model speed incentives, such as piece-rate payments.

As already observed, in the central case we shall use a welfarist social welfare function $\Omega = \sum_j \omega_j$, where $j = 1 \ldots J$ indicates a household. Even without adding distributive features into Ω, we shall arrive at rather egalitarian conclusions about the optimum order, as has also been observed. Apart from the introduction of distributive features, mentioned in section 15.6, something should be said about what can also be called an egalitarian feature of the welfarist choice made. That feature resides in the absence of weights given to the individual welfare functions ω_i in our sum. Clearly, various weight systems are conceivable as alternatives to our choice. Somewhat parallel to a method introduced by Cohen (1977), high weights could be used to reflect the social or political power of some groups and variations in these weights will affect the optimum. Also van Praag's (1975) idea of making a distinction between the social welfare function as perceived by various groups within society is related to variable weights and in fact a more sophisticated way of introducing social or political power. In this chapter we leave it to the reader to assess these alternatives.

The optimum order studied here is defined as a set of variables' values satisfying a conditioned maximum of the social welfare function. The conditions are the usual *restrictions* the economy has to satisfy. One set of such restrictions expresses the *availability* of households with given personality traits of the active member. The total portion of the productive population with personality characteristics a will be indicated by F_a and the restriction consequently is:

$$\sum_b \phi_a^b = F_a \tag{15.3}$$

As one alternative, applicable only for longer-run policies and even then within limits, we shall also assume that personality characteristics can be changed by *processes of learning* and that accordingly only one restriction remains to be respected, namely:

$$\sum_b \sum_a \phi_a^b = 1 \tag{15.4}$$

The next restriction to be satisfied by the optimum is the economy's *production function*, stating that total product y depends on the quantities of various types of manpower and on the quantity of (physical) capital K used:

$$y = \text{prod } f(K, \phi_a^b) \tag{15.5}$$

As already stated, it is not necessary in our model to specify the production function which has the advantage of a high degree of generality. We do assume, however, that the production function is differentiable with respect to all ϕ.

The last restriction we shall introduce concerns one aspect of how national income is spent. We assume two things only: (i) a given total net amount T of taxes minus subsidies has to be paid; and (ii) there is no hoarding or overspending. This implies that disposable incomes x_a^b have to satisfy the equation:

$$\sum \sum \phi_a^b x_a^b + T = y \tag{15.6}$$

15.4 INCOME DISTRIBUTION AND TAXATION IN THE CENTRAL CASE

From the preceding choices and assumptions made, it is easily seen that our problem is that of maximising:

$$\sum_{a=1}^{AG} \sum_{b=1}^{AG} \phi_a^b \omega \{ x_a^b - f(a, b) \}$$

$$+ \sum_{a=1}^{AG} \lambda_a \left(\sum_{b=1}^{AG} \phi_a^b - F_a \right) + \pi \{ y - \text{prod } f(\phi_a^b) \}$$

$$+ \varrho \left(y - \sum_{a=1}^{AG} \sum_{b=1}^{AG} \phi_a^b x_a^b - T \right) \equiv \Omega' \tag{15.7}$$

with regard to the variables ϕ, x and y and the Lagrangian multipliers $\lambda_a (a = 1 \ldots AG)$, π and ϱ.

As a special case we shall consider the choice $\lambda_a = \lambda (a = 1, \ldots AG)$.

Some remarks on the optimal tax system

Assuming that all solutions satisfy the conditions that $x_a^b \geq 0$ and $\phi_a^b \geq 0$ for all a and b the optimum will be described by the conditions $\partial \Omega'/\partial x = \partial \Omega'/\partial \phi = \partial \Omega'/\partial y = 0$. We will consider three cases:

(I) all x and all $\phi > 0$

(II) all $\phi_a^b = 0$ if $a \neq b$

(III) all $\lambda_a = \lambda$

In the present section the optimum conditions are:

$$\omega\{x_a^b - f(a, b)\} + \lambda_a - \pi \partial y/\partial \phi_a^b - \varrho x_a^b = 0 \tag{15.8}$$

$$\phi_a^b \partial \omega/\partial x_a^b - \varrho \phi_a^b = 0 \tag{15.9}$$

$$\pi + \varrho = 0, \text{ hence } \varrho = -\pi \tag{15.10}$$

Since for Case I we have assumed all $\phi > 0$, it follows from (15.9) that:

$$\partial \omega/\partial x_a^b = \varrho \tag{15.11}$$

Since we assumed $\partial \omega/\partial x_a^b$ to be a monotonous function of x_a^b it follows that:

$$\omega_a^b = \varrho_0 \tag{15.12}$$

Substituting (15.10) and (15.12) into (15.8) we get:

$$\varrho_0 + \lambda_a - \pi(y_a^b - x_a^b) = 0 \tag{15.13}$$

where y_a^b stands for income before tax of an individual or household (a, b).

Writing t_a^b for the optimal tax to be paid by such an individual it follows from (15.13) that

$$t_a^b = \frac{\varrho_0 + \lambda_a}{\pi} \tag{15.14}$$

or the optimal tax only depends on the personality traits a and *has to be independent from the job—and hence the income y_a^b—chosen* (cf. Chapter 14).

Taking up Case II, we find that all equations (15.9) where $a \neq b$ are automatically satisfied. Case II implies that only individuals (a, a) are present, meaning that everybody finds a job whose characteristics b coincide with her or his personal characteristics. This situation may be called one of *equilibrium between demand for and supply of* certain characteristics without implying an equality of prices (that is income before tax). Writing ϕ_a for ϕ_a^a and x_a for x_a^a we have:

$$\phi_a = F_a \tag{15.15}$$

and:

$$\partial \omega / \partial x_a = \varrho \text{ leading to } \omega_a = \varrho_0 \tag{15.16}$$

Equation (15.9) becomes:

$$\varrho_0 + \lambda_a - \pi(y_a - x_a) = 0 \tag{15.17}$$

or:

$$t_a = \frac{\varrho_0 + \lambda_a}{\pi} \tag{15.17}$$

Again taxes depend only on a, but since $a = b$ we can interpret the tax system, if we want to, as one in which taxes depend on the job. The relevance of this statement will be discussed in section 15.7.

Considering Case III, where all λ_a are equal ($= \lambda$), we find:

$$y_a = \varrho \tag{15.18}$$

and:

$$t_a = \frac{\varrho + \lambda}{\pi} \tag{15.19}$$

All individuals now pay the same tax:

$$T / \sum \phi = T \tag{15.20}$$

15.5 TAX REVENUE DEPENDS ON EDUCATION COSTS

So far total tax revenue T per working person was considered given. In Case III it is more realistic to assume that T depends on the costs of education which depend on the F_a. We shall give an example to show what changes have now to be introduced into our thesis. The example chosen is one with three levels i of education as the characteristics of individuals, and the same three levels as required for the execution of the job. As part of T we must now introduce costs of education. The latter will be assumed to consist of three items, namely:

(i) income forgone, which will be 0 for primary education, y_1 for secondary and y_2 for tertiary education per person educated;
(ii) cost of teachers which are, for the three levels, $n_1 \bar{y}_2$, $n_2 \bar{y}_3$ and $n_3 \bar{y}_3$ respectively, where n_i is the teacher–student ratio for education level i and $\bar{y}_i$ the teacher income at level i;
(iii) costs of buildings and other fixed assets to be represented by g_i. A realistic choice for n_i is $n_1 = 0.03$, $n_2 = 0.04$ and $n_3 = 0.08$

From Dutch sources we further estimate $g_1 = 0.018y$, $g_2 = 0.015y$ and $g_3 = 0.343y$, where y = average income per active person. Furthermore we estimate $y_1 = 0.9y$, $y_2 = 1.6y$ and $y_3 = 2.4y$. All cost figures quoted so far are, however, costs for 1 year's schooling of each type. Assuming an average active life of 40 years and schooling of 6 years at each level, we have to multiply the figures mentioned by 6/40, if we want to multiply them by the total active population ϕ_i of each type in order to arrive at the annual burden of education in the stationary state of the optimum.

Our example will be elaborated for Case III only, where $b = a$ (i.e. all jobs requiring an education level i are performed by people with that same education level). The spending restriction (15.6) will now have to be:

$$y = \sum \phi_i x_1 + T_0 + 0.010\, \phi_1 y + 0.17\, \phi_2 y + 0.080\, \phi_3 y$$
$$+ 0.15\, \phi_2 y_1 + 0.15\, \phi_3 y_2 \qquad (15.21)$$

As a consequence the optimum conditions for Case III are now changing. They become considerably more complicated. Not only are *interaction terms* such as those in $\phi_i y$, but the last two terms in (15.21) should be written $0.15\phi_2\, \partial\text{prod}\, f/\partial\phi_1$ and $0.15\, \phi_3\, \partial\text{prod}\, f/\partial\phi_2$, respectively. The most important conclusions which can be drawn, without going into the specification of the utility and production functions, are now that the values of the utility or welfare functions for the three groups no longer have to be equal in the optimum position. At least for some specifications we now find that welfare of the lowest income group has to be higher than that of the two other groups. Also the types of tax equalities found before no longer apply.

15.6 INTRODUCTION OF INCOME DISTRIBUTION INTO SOCIAL WELFARE

We now propose to leave our welfarist social welfare function and, restricting ourselves to Class II, add to it a term expressing that the more unequal incomes x_i are the lower social welfare function:

$$\Omega = \sum_a \phi_a \omega(x_a - f_a) - E\sum \phi_a(x_a - y')^2 \qquad (15.22)$$

where $y' = y - T$ constitutes the weighted average of x_a.

With this social welfare function the optimum conditions become:

$$\omega(x_a - f_a) = E(x_a - y')^2 + \lambda_a + \varrho(y_a - x_a) = 0 \qquad (15.23)$$
$$a = 1 \ldots AG$$

$$\phi_a \partial\omega/\partial x_a - 2E\phi_a(x_a - y') - \phi_a\varrho = 0 \qquad (15.24)$$

$$a = 1 \ldots AG$$

$$2E\sum \phi_a(x_a - y') + \pi + \varrho = 0 \qquad (15.25)$$

Since:

$$\sum \phi_a(x_a - y') = 0 \text{ we find again } \pi = -\varrho \qquad (15.26)$$

Since all $\phi_a \neq 0$ we obtain from (15.24):

$$\partial\omega/\partial x_a = \varrho + 2E(x_a - y') \qquad (15.27)$$

This means that marginal utility (which is negatively monotonous) falls with increasing a. Hence utility will rise with increasing a. The distribution will change to the advantage of low and to the disadvantage of higher incomes.

15.7 SUMMARY AND CONCLUDING REMARKS

Let us now interpret our findings. To begin with, in the important difference between Cases I and II on the one hand and Case III on the other, it should be kept in mind that in the former cases education costs are fixed because all F_a are taken as given. Only in Case III, where F_a may shift, do education costs have to be discussed, as was done explicitly in section 15.5. Our treatment of Cases I and II do not need the introduction of education costs as a variable.

It is noteworthy that the optimum positions found in Cases I and II coincide with equitable distribution situations, as defined in Tinbergen (1975a); all individual welfare levels are equal. This does not apply to Case III and to the alternative dealt with in section 15.6, where a preference for less inequality was introduced into the social welfare function.

The optimal tax system found can be characterised as follows: In Case I we found (cf. equation 15.14) that taxes have to depend only on personality traits and not on job characteristics. This is the type of lump-sum tax dealt with in Tinbergen (1975b). Its feasibility is doubtful, to say the least, and will depend on the development of psychotechnical tests.

In Case II we found (cf. equation 15.17) the same result, but since job and personality characteristics are identical here, the tax can also be based on job characteristics and hence on income; it is inversely proportional to π, the marginal utility of product and linearly dependent on λ_a, the marginal utility of labour category a.

The result of equal taxes for all (equation cf. 15.20) for Case III is valid only if education costs are assumed to remain unaffected by the shifts in manpower quality found. As mentioned in section 15.5, this result changes in favour of lower income groups at least in one specification investigated. A general treatment meets with considerable difficulties and has not been undertaken in this chapter. For a much more general and sophisticated treatment, the reader is referred to Ritzen (1977).

Finally, the introduction of a preference for less unequal incomes into the social welfare function shows that the solution found for Case II changes again to the advantage of lower income groups, whose welfare should now be raised in comparison to that of higher income groups. This result may be interpreted to mean that the egalitarian result found for Case II in the welfarist version is an understatement.

REFERENCES

Cohen, S.I. (1977), *Development Models with Different Decision-Makers*, discussion note for a conference on 'Future research, planning and decision-making', held at the Conference House of the Polish Academy of Sciences, Jablonna, Poland, 22 April EUR, Centre for Development Planning.

Ritzen, J.M.M.R. (1977), *Education, Economic Growth and Income Distribution*, Amsterdam, North-Holland.

Sen, A.K. (1977), 'On weights and measures: informational constraints in social welfare analysis', Walras–Bowley Lecture, Econometric Society, *Econometrica*, 45, p. 1539–72.

Tinbergen, J. (1975b), *Income Differences: Recent Research*, Amsterdam, North-Holland.

Tinbergen, J. (1977), *Die Internationale Neuordnung und ihre Machbarkeit*, Verein für Sozialpolitik [The New International Order and its Feasability].

van Praag, B.S.M. (1975), *De verdeling van inkomen en macht* [*The Distribution of Income and Power*], Leiden.

16 Optimal Education, Occupation, and Income Distribution in a Simplistic Model

16.1 FEATURES OF THE MODEL

The model used in the present chapter is extremely simple, and hence called simplistic. This will become clear from the list of its features:

(i) It is static and hence at most applicable to a sequence of slowly changing equilibria:
(ii) three levels of education are distinguished: $i = 1, 2, 3$;
(iii) individual welfare ω_i is assumed to be dependent only on disposable income x, education i and occupation j;
(iv) the labour market is in equilibrium (i.e. everybody has the education level i required by his or her occupation j) or $i = j$, with the consequence that ω needs only the index i;
(v) social welfare Ω is welfarist (Sen) (i.e. depends on individual welfare only); moreover it is assumed to be the unweighted sum of the ω_i;
(vi) the macro production function is a Cobb–Douglas function $F(\phi_1, \phi_2, \phi_3) = C_0 \phi_1^{\lambda_1} \phi_2^{\lambda_2} \phi_3^{\lambda_3}$ where the impact of physical capital is, together with the size of total active population and units used, hidden in C_0, ϕ_i is the proportion of active population with education and occupation i and $\sum_1^\lambda = 0.8$, reflecting that 20 per cent of national product constituted income from assets.

16.2 AIM AND SCOPE OF THE EXERCISE

In two previous publications on income distribution (Tinbergen, 1975; Pen and Tinbergen, 1977) a distinction between an equitable and an optimal income distribution was discussed. As an illustration, optimum distribution was calculated with two restrictions: first, the number of active population with education levels 1, 2 and 3 was assumed given for each level; second only the total of the three groups was given, and shifts in education levels admitted. Education costs were not considered, however, and this omission was rightly criticised by Haveman (1977). The present chapter constitutes a correction of this omission, and is offered as a modest tribute to Abram Bergson whose pioneering work in the field of social welfare functions is one among many facets of his contributions to economic science.

In order to maintain comparability with the previous approaches by the present author, this chapter concentrates on the case of the Netherlands in 1962. An application to other countries or years might not be too cumbersome but will be postponed until a later occasion.

16.3 MATHEMATICAL FORMULATION OF THE OPTIMUM PROBLEM

Symbols used are:

- i: level of education $i = 1, 2, 3$;
- ϕ_i: proportion of active population with education level i;
- x_i: disposable income *per capita* of working population with education level i;
- f_i: income correction reflecting (dis)utility of education and occupation i;
- $\omega(x_i - f_i)$: welfare of person with disposable income x_i and education and occupation i;
- $F(\phi_1, \phi_2, \phi_3) \equiv C_0 \phi_1^{\lambda_1} \phi_2^{\lambda_2} \phi_3^{\lambda_3}$: product *per capita* function;
- y: product *per capita* of working population;
- T': total tax revenue minus public and private expenditure for education;
- $\varkappa_i$: total annual cost of education *per capita* of stock of working population with education i expressed as part of product *per capita*. For a more detailed description cf. section 16.4 where the estimation is described;
- λ, π, ϱ: Lagrange multipliers.

Formulation of optimum problem: maximise social welfare $\sum_i \phi_i \omega (x_i - f_i)$ with restrictions:

$\sum \phi_i = 1$ (balance equation)   (A)

$y = F(\phi_1, \phi_2, \phi_3)$ (production function)   (B)

$y = \sum \phi_i x_i + T' + y \sum \varkappa_i \phi_i$ (destination of product)   (C)

Using Lagrangian multipliers we have to maximise:

$$\sum \phi_i \omega(x_i - f_i) + \lambda(1 - \sum \phi_i) +$$
$$\pi\{y - F(\phi_i)\} + \varrho\{y - \sum \phi_i x_i - T' - y \sum \varkappa_i \phi_i\} \quad (16.0)$$

In this expression the f_i, T' and $\varkappa_i$ are figures to be estimated, as are the λ_i and C of the production function. Differentiation of (16.0) with regard to the variables appearing in (16.0) yields:

$$\omega(x_1 - f_1) - \lambda - \pi \partial F/\partial \phi_1 - \varrho x_1 - \varrho y \varkappa_1 = 0 \quad (16.1)$$
$$\omega(x_2 - f_2) - \lambda - \pi \partial F/\partial \phi_2 - \varrho x_2 - \varrho y \varkappa_2 = 0 \quad (16.2)$$
$$\omega(x_3 - f_3) - \lambda - \pi \partial F/\partial \phi_3 - \varrho x_3 - \varrho y \varkappa_3 = 0 \quad (16.3)$$
$$\phi_1 \omega'(x_1 - f_1) - \varrho \phi_1 = 0 \quad (16.4)$$
$$\phi_2 \omega'(x_2 - f_2) - \varrho \phi_2 = 0 \quad (16.5)$$
$$\phi_3 \omega'(x_3 - f_3) - \varrho \phi_3 = 0 \quad (16.6)$$
$$\pi + \varrho - \varrho \sum \varkappa_i \phi_i = 0 \quad (16.7)$$

The solution of our problem may start by reminding ourselves that the $\phi_i \neq 0$ and deriving from (16.4), (16.5) and (16.6):

$$x_1 - f_1 = x_2 - f_2 = x_3 - f_3 = g(\varrho) \quad (16.8)$$

Substitution into (16.1)–(16.3) using

$$\partial F/\partial \phi_i = \frac{\lambda_i}{\phi_i} y$$

provides us with:

$$h(\varrho) - \lambda - \pi y \lambda_1/\phi_1 - \varrho x_1 - \varrho y \varkappa_1 = 0 \quad (16.1')$$
$$h(\varrho) - \lambda - \pi y \lambda_2/\phi_2 - \varrho x_2 - \varrho y \varkappa_2 = 0 \quad (16.2')$$
$$h(\varrho) - \lambda - \pi y \lambda_3/\phi_3 - \varrho x_3 - \varrho y \varkappa_3 = 0 \quad (16.3')$$

Subtraction of (16.2') from (16.1') and of (16.3') from (16.2') yields:

$$\pi y(\lambda_2/\phi_2 - \lambda_1/\phi_1) = -\varrho(x_2 - x_1) - \varrho y(\varkappa_2 - \varkappa_1) \quad (I)$$
$$\pi y(\lambda_3/\phi_3 - \lambda_2/\phi_2) = -\varrho(x_3 - x_2) - \varrho y(\varkappa_3 - \varkappa_2) \quad (II)$$

Equation (16.7) can be used to eliminate π from (I) and (II) and rewrite them, using (16.8):

$$(L_1 =) \lambda_1/\phi_1 - \lambda_2/\phi_2 = \frac{-f_2 + f_1}{y(1 - \sum \varkappa \phi)} - \frac{\varkappa_2 - \varkappa_1}{1 - \sum \varkappa \phi} \quad (III)$$

$$(L_2 =)\lambda_2/\phi_2 - \lambda_3/\phi_3 = \frac{-f_3 + f_2}{y(1 - \sum \varkappa\phi)} - \frac{\varkappa_3 - \varkappa_2}{1 - \sum \varkappa\phi} \qquad \text{(IV)}$$

Equations (A), (B), (III), and (IV) contain four variables, namely the three ϕ_i and y and can be numerically solved, as will be discussed in section 16.5.

16.4 DATA-BASE USED

In our model three sets of data (given coefficients) appear:

(a) those characterising the production function, written λ_i and C;
(b) those characterising the welfare function, written f_i; and
(c) those characterising the costs of education, indicated by $\varkappa_i$.

The coefficients λ_i of the production function have been taken from the admittedly crude estimations shown in more detail in Tinbergen (1975); they are $\lambda_1 = 0.648$, $\lambda_2 = 0.088$ and $\lambda_3 = 0.064$. As is well known for a Cobb–Douglas function, these figures constitute the shares (in total income) of labour of levels 1, 2 and 3 of education. As stated in section 16.1, they add up to 0.8, supposed to have been the share of earnings in total income. With the units chosen for income (thousands of guilders per working person) this amounts to 9.123 for 1962. This implies a value of $C_0 = 15$.

The estimates of the compensations f_i for net labour disutility have been derived from the same source, extremely crude indeed and amount to $f_1 = 0.45$, $f_2 = 0.90$ and $f_3 = 1.35$.

The cost of education figures have been derived from the annual public expenditure per student at each of the three levels of education, since in the Netherlands private expenditures are almost negligible. They amount to 518, 1508 and 10,167 fl. for levels 1, 2 and 3, respectively (Central Bureau of Statistics, 1966). What we need in the model is not annual costs per student in the year observed, however, but annual costs per members of the labour force in a static situation. Assuming the number of years' schooling to be 6 for each level, which is very close to practice in 1962, and further assuming an active life in production of 40 years, the figures have to be multiplied by $6/40 = 0.15$. In order to express them as a portion of y, as chosen in section 16.3, we have to divide through 9.123 and accordingly obtain 0.009, 0.025, and 0.167, respectively.

Finally, the question must be answered whether these figures should not be raised by income forgone by students at the second and third level, amounting to, respectively, the average earnings of the first and second level, which equals, according to Tinbergen (1975), 6.75 and 9.70. Since in Equation (C), indicating the destination of product, on the left-hand side, we have actual production value, not including income forgone by students, we must not, however, include income forgone on the right-hand side. The argument may be restated by rewriting the destination of product equation verbally as follows:

> potential production = production forgone + actual production = production available for private spending + production available for government spending (both for other purposes than education) + total costs of education. (C')

Here the last item constitutes the usual definition of costs. Since, however, on the left-hand side, we have production forgone, this term must be deducted if, on the left-hand side, as in (C), we want to retain actual production.

For those who might not agree with our argument, we also mention the numerical estimation of the cost coefficients using the conventional definition: they amount to $\varkappa_1' = 0.009$; $\varkappa_2' = 0.136$, and $\varkappa_3' = 0.327$.

16.5 NUMERICAL SOLUTION FOR ϕ_2 AND ϕ_3

In this section two sets of figures will be shown. The first set (Table 16.1) refers to the solution neglecting education costs (i.e. taking $\varkappa_i = 0$ for all i). Equations (III) and (IV) can now be written in numerical form:

$$L_1 = \lambda_1/\phi_1 - \lambda_2/\phi_2 = -0.05 \quad \text{(III')}$$

$$L_2 = \lambda_2/\phi_2 - \lambda_3/\phi_3 = -0.05 \quad \text{(IV')}$$

This is based on the results of two numerical orientations which show that both y and $\sum \varkappa_i \phi_i$ are almost insensitive to the relevant variations in ϕ_i, that is the variations around the solution values.

Table 16.1 Values of the expressions L_1 and L_2 around the solution values for ϕ_2 and ϕ_3, for $\varkappa_i = 0$, per cent

ϕ_3 \ ϕ_2	0.10		0.105		0.11	
	L_1	L_2	L_1	L_2	L_1	L_2
0.07	−10	−3	−5	−8	−1	−11
0.072	−10	−1	−5	−5	−1	−9
0.075	−9	+3	−5	−2	−0	−5
0.08	−9	+8	−4	+4	0	0

The second set of figures (Table 16.2) is based on the values for $\varkappa_i$ discussed in section 16.4 leading to Equations (III′) and (IV′):

$$L_1 = \lambda_1/\phi_1 - \lambda_2/\phi_2 = -0.06 \tag{III″}$$

$$L_2 = \lambda_2/\phi_2 - \lambda_3/\phi_3 = -0.19 \tag{IV″}$$

Table 16.2 Values of the expressions L_1 and L_2 around the solution values for ϕ_2 and ϕ_3, $\varkappa_i = 0.009;\ 0.025;\ 0.167$ respectively, per cent

ϕ_3 \ ϕ_2	0.10 L_1	0.10 L_2	0.105 L_1	0.105 L_2	0.11 L_1	0.11 L_2
0.06	−11	−19	−6	−23	−2	−27
0.062	−11	−15	−6	−*19*	−2	−23
0.065	−10	−10	−6	−15	−1	−18

As indicated by the values in italics, the optimum values for ϕ_2 and ϕ_3 are 0.105 and 0.072 or 10.5 and 7.2 per cent of the labour force, if education costs are neglected. Inclusion of education costs changes these values for ϕ_3 only, and not for ϕ_2, The optimum level of tertiary educated manpower now goes down by 1 per cent.

Clearly the results depend on the coefficients of the production function. As shown elsewhere (Tinbergen, 1975, Ch. 6) technological development can be represented by changes in these coefficients and during the twentieth century λ_3, if a Cobb–Douglas production function is assumed to be valid must have risen considerably. This will also change the results for the ϕ_i as calculated in this note.

REFERENCES

Haveman, R.H. (1977), 'Tinbergen's income distribution: analysis and policies—a review article', *Journal of Human Resources*, XII, 1977, pp. 103–14. (Also published in the Dutch journal *De Economist*, 125, pp. 161–173; and as Reprint Series of the Institute for Research on Poverty, University of Wisconsin.)

Pen, J. and Tinbergen, J. (1977), *Naar een rechtvaardiger inkomensverdeling* [*Towards a More Equitable Income Distribution*], Elsevier, Amsterdam and Brussels.

Tinbergen, J. (1975), *Income Distribution: Analysis and Policies*, Amsterdam, North-Holland.

17 Ways to Socialism

17.1 DEFINITIONS OF SOCIALISM

Originally a very simple definition of socialism as a social order was used: namely *public property of the means of production*. This definition was associated with Marx's analysis of the operation of a society in which *private property* of the means of production or capital goods prevails. It was on the basis of this definition that the first country aiming at a socialist society, the Soviet Union, saw as its first priority the socialisation of the means of production. Various experiences and many discussions since 1917 have introduced tendencies to revise the original definition. There still exist, even in the Soviet Union, privately-owned means of production—among them private lots of land. Not only do they exist, but the usefulness of this form of private enterprise is expressly underlined by the authorities. This is only one of the ways in which the Soviet authorities are—quite naturally—after 60 years still experimenting with their social order.

Recent events in Poland illustrate that not only the ownership matters in a country adhering to socialism. Before these events other Eastern European countries had been facing huge problems. In addition, there are a large number of countries whose population preferred to introduce elements into their order *suggested by socialist criticism* of the capitalist (private enterprise) society. All western industrialised countries belonging to this category are considered to be *mixed economies*: that is, there is a mixture of free enterprise or market elements with an often considerable element of public intervention in favour of the low-income groups in the population. As a rule, it was the initiative of social democratic parties and the trade unions which has led to this transformation; in some cases other parties did so in competition with democratic socialist parties. Considerable experience and discussion in these countries also led to the questioning of the definition originally given for a socialist order. First, ownership was not the *only* relevant aspect. Secondly, the *way* in which non-private ownership was conceived became the focus, especially in the case of Yugoslavia. Thirdly, it became increasingly clear that ownership of the means of production was a *means* rather than an objective and this raised the question of how to define the aims of a socialist order.

There are some very good reasons to take up this last question. First, Marx explicity claimed that we should aim at *scientific* socialism; and science is a continuing process of *posing questions*, and trying to answer them, testing the answers by *empirical research* and then posing *new questions*. Secondly, and wholly in line with a scientific approach, Marx always declined to give 'recipes' for the future. In other words, a truly Marxian attitude is to join the process of *scientific research*, using all new evidence available, to develop new insights. The greatest enemy of science is a *doctrinaire attitude* or adhering to an *ideology* (cf. section 17.7).

In an attempt to start a discussion on the deeper aims of a socialist order I would suggest that two elements are of great importance: (i) a *low level of welfare* or happiness of a considerable portion of the population; and (ii) large *differences in welfare* between individuals or households. Both elements are considered unacceptable by socialists whose aim is to eliminate them as much as possible. Accordingly a socialist order aims at *raising the average level of welfare* and *reducing the differences*. Correspondingly, we can speak of a combination of *efficiency* and *equity* as the fundamental aim of a socialist society. Put in this way, we may arrive at an *objective* or *aim function* for society to be maximised under all the restrictions nature (and possibly other external factors) impose on human life. This aim function will be called the *social welfare function*, given by the symbol Ω when desirable for clarity of exposition. Ω will only become useful to our analysis after we have specified, within limits, its 'building blocks'. Mathematically speaking, we must specify (i) the *variables* or phenomena [*Erscheinungen*] entering into Ω; and (ii) the *functional form* of Ω in terms of these variables. As a contribution to the latter we may use the *individual* welfare (or happiness, satisfaction, utility all considered synonymous) functions ω of all citizens (or all households) following Bergson (1938). We may also add *corrections by the community* based on the necessity to protect individuals against their own myopia.

The variables entering into individual ωs will be the flows of *material* and *spiritual* commodities available to the individual. Examples of material commodities are *consumer goods* (food, clothing, housing, health care); examples of spiritual commodities are access to *education*, *recreation*, *cultural processes*, the pursuit of *equity* (in courts of law or through the distribution of jobs and incomes) and the *satisfaction derived from work*. Individual (dis)satisfaction may depend on commodities available to the person considered but also on those available to others—through envy or solidarity feelings; it also depends on relations with other individuals at work or in society.

Important examples of topical issues in the respects mentioned are Bahro's (1977) contentions that the existing ratio between *material* and *cultural* goods produced in the GDR is biased in favour of material goods (which applies to most western countries as well); and that *too large hierarchies* of supervised work exist, causing unnecessary irritation (again applying to most western societies).

We may conclude with the statement that the ability to establish individual or household ωs is low, though some pioneering work of considerable importance has been done by Levy and Guttman (1975) and van Praag and his colleagues (1971, and after).

17.2 THE RIGHT OF EACH COUNTRY TO CHOOSE ITS OWN SOCIAL ORDER

An important milestone in the development towards socialism was reached in 1976 at the Berlin Summit Conference of European communist-ruled countries, where the right of each country to choose its own path to socialism was recognised. Among western countries a similar right has long been recognised, which may be formulated as the right of each sovereign nation to choose its own mix of 'capitalist' (or 'market') and 'socialist' (or public intervention) elements. Under colonialism this right was not recognised by the colonial powers; but colonialism is nearing its end. The two comparable rights have their limits, which will be discussed later.

There are important arguments to justify this (limited) *autonomy*. A people's choice will depend on its *geographical* environment, as exemplified by the Dutch constitution which gives particular power to those functional authorities needed to combat floods.

A people's choice also depends on its *history*; thus, the extreme *decentralisation* of public authorities in Switzerland as well as the extremely high degree of *centralisation* in Russia can both be understood from a study of these countries' history. Relatively speaking, France, until recently, was also a centralised country. It is significant that a socialist government is now accelerating the process of decentralisation started by preceding governments.

A third reason for a different choice of order amongst countries is difference in *tastes*. The people of the USA originate mostly from Europe, but are by no means a representative sample of the European population. It is a selection biased in favour of *active* and *enterprising migrants*. This explains the relatively low level of socialist elements and the late start of the (limited) social security the American people seem to prefer. Differences of taste also exist between Latin, Germanic, Anglo-Saxon, Slavonic and Arab peoples. Latin and Arab peoples seem to be more individualist, Germanic peoples somewhat more community-oriented (it has been said about some Germanic people(s) that—astonishingly—they 'like to obey'); Slavonic peoples have been said to be somewhat fatalist.

So far we only mentioned ethnic groups within the aryan race. Comparing them with other races we find, as a matter of course, more obvious differences. In discussing these we must be cautious not to mix geographical and historical differences and differences in taste or preference; and even more not misinterpret productive capabilities: the wrong evaluation of Japanese capabilities some fifty years ago is now crystal-clear. As a consequence it seems appropriate to remind the reader that this chapter was written by a European and, in all probability, is Europe-biased.

The simplest way of summarising this argument scientifically is to state that the *weights* given to the various elements of the welfare function *differ among peoples* and *nations*. As a consequence we observe differences in the social order, and in the socialist order preferred by various nations. Even within the Communist bloc the extent of the private sector varies, as is the extent to which market forces are used or power of decision-making given to factory directors.

The autonomy of sovereign nations in choosing their own path to socialism is a very important principle. Yet its applicability has limits, because sovereignty as seen by many students of international relations is of limited use for an optimal management of our planet. Recent developments in population size, energy reserves and environment as well as political rigidity (cf. section 17.7), have become a threat to human survival and make *proper management* of our planet a matter of urgency. Such management requires the transfer of sovereign rights *to higher than national levels*.

17.3 DEVELOPMENT OVER TIME OF THE OPTIMAL SOCIAL ORDER

Apart from national differences about what constitutes a socialist order we must expect this order—the optimal social order—*to change over time*. Various—if not all—elements determining social welfare are subject to change. This applies to the geographical factors mentioned: *climate* is not a constant and has changed, showing various cyclical movements. Moreover, it may be affected by the increasing carbon dioxide content of the earth's atmosphere (the 'greenhouse effect').

Other environmental factors, such as the purity of air and water, are changing as well. Partly this is the consequence of scientific and technological development; in Marxian terminology the *development of productive forces* (*Produktivkräfte*). In recent decades we have seen impressive *changes in scientific knowledge*—one of them, the considerable development of chemistry and, as a consequence, the chemical industries. Another is the perhaps even more phenomenal developments in the field of electronics. The *processing of information* has developed to such an extent that we often speak of a new *information society*. Automatisation has attained a potential that may change the *role of work* in the distribution of time between work and leisure, in their various manifestations, in an unprecedented way. An additional example of changes in knowledge is the possibility of new techniques needed for *taxation* which may be elaborated in the future (cf. Tinbergen, 1975).

Parallel with these forces, but to a considerable extent independent of them, tastes (an economist's term) are changing. In fact this somewhat down-to-earth economic phrase covers many more fundamental issues. We are living in a *cultural crisis* which by itself may undermine human happiness. New *spiritual foundations* of life are felt to be urgently needed. The education process is being destroyed by selfishness, indifference, superficiality and shortsightedness. Elementary human values are increasingly offended—in the macrosphere of international politics as well as in the microsphere of personal and family life.

Socialist policy, if it wants to shape a future human race living in happiness, needs a *more profound basis*—either religious or humanist, and if religious, Christian, Islamic, Buddhist, or otherwise. Recent developments in policies and propaganda have been based far too much on materialist (in the practical sense of that phase) components of human needs. For a full development of human beings this is an insult to what characterises the human races. Man (and certainly the female part of humankind) *cannot live by bread alone* is an old saw: far from being 'opium of the people' religion or a philosophy of life (*Weltanschauung*) is a necessary source of inspiration for developing an individual's spiritual and moral potential. Serious mistakes have certainly been made by religious leaders. If their behaviour is to be representative of religion, Marx's dictum about opium can be understood. But the best of men have always been inspired by some philosophy of life, from which they derive the impetus to compassion and solidarity, for equity and for higher levels of understanding—understanding others as well as the physical environment.

Some of the finest socialists have been inspired by Christianity, others by humanism. Recently, an increasing number of Muslims have started thinking about which economic order they have to choose on the basis of the Koran (Naqvi, 1981). Socialist thinkers should not ignore this process: they may even be able to contribute to it. Neither should they be absent in neo-Christian manifestations such as—to mention only one example—the Evangelische Kirchentage [Protestant Christian German Church Days].

We shall now return to some topical aspects of this necessary innovation of socialist discussion (sections 17.7–17.9). To begin with, some basic subjects should be considered from a broader outlook.

17.4 FUNCTIONAL SOCIALISM

The concept and term of *functional socialism* were introduced by Adler Karlsson (1967), who chose as a sub-title to his book 'an alternative between communism and capitalism'. Perhaps the simplest way to introduce the concept is to start with the definition of the socialist order given in section 17.1. According to this definition community ownership of the means of production is the central characteristic of socialism. In reports of the Dutch Social Democratic Workers' Party devoted to the way to socialism (SDAP & NVV, 1921) the process was seen as shifting ownership from private to public ownership branch-by-branch, and an issue of importance was the time sequence: i.e. which key industries should first be socialised? should the banks be the first or the last? and so on. Similar discussions took place elsewhere (especially in Austria: cf. Bauer, 1919 and many other publications). In 1981 the political shift in France has, almost surprisingly, brought this question to the fore. As an alternative to this socialisation in a branch-wise order Adler Karlsson (1967) reminds us of the possibility, currently applied, to socialise one *function* after the other, and then for all—or many—branches simultaneously. The long series of Social Security Acts, introduced over the last century in most north-western European countries, show what is meant. Child labour, unhealthy work, old age pensions, statutory working hours and many other functions of the production process have been regulated by law, and brought under public control.

The importance of considering functions rather than ownership underlined by Adler Karlsson, was introduced into a different area by Mann-Borgese (cf. Tinbergen *et al.*, 1976, p. 312), who introduced the concept of *functional sovereignty* as distinct from geographical sovereignty in order to promote mutual understanding among the parties negotiating the new Law of the Seas. Geographical sovereignty has a good deal to do with ownership—in this case, of parts of the seas—by certain nations, and the parallel with Adler Karlsson's concepts is clear. A common element in the positions taken by the two authors is the limited relevance of ownership compared to the *management of processes*.

The functional approach also has elements in common with the distinction made between aims and means. Means usually constitute processes, a concept related to functions. Ownership as a means is too partial an answer to the question of how to attain the aims. It depends a good deal on the way ownership is used (i.e. on management), whether the aims are attained. *Management is a function.*

17.5 EXISTING ORDERS ARE TOO UNEQUAL

In the preceding sections we have dealt with the search, by various nations, for a better social order, and in particular by those nations striving for a socialist order, defined in a broader way than is customary. It seems appropriate to justify this search by stating that in practically all countries inequalities are still too large to be satisfactory.

This is true for western countries even though considerable reductions in equality of welfare have occurred over the last century. Statements of this kind cannot be based entirely on scientific evidence: they have a political character, and political decisions cannot wait until the problem has been solved by scientists according to the latters' standards: 'final' solutions do not, in fact, exist.

Political statements at best must not be in contradiction to the *state of scientific thinking* at the time of the statement. With this principle in mind we can state that, according to recent research, the incomes paid to the main occupational groups in the USA deviate from their marginal productivities in such a way as to be too high for capital (Thurow, 1968), managers and sales workers, and too low for manual workers and farmers (Gottschalk, 1978; Tinbergen and Kol, 1980). This means that, even according to the criteria of Manchester School liberalism (i.e. liberalism in the European sense), incomes are *more unequal than is equitable*. This statement refers to the USA and partly to Japan (Tinbergen and Kol, 1980), and is based on the assumption that production functions are Cobb–Douglas functions; an assumption that leaves open the possibility that the use of other production functions lead to a different statement. It is, as observed, based on the 'state of the art' of econometrics around 1980.

A number of European countries show less inequality of incomes. We shall quote the results of some comparative studies to illustrate this; but comparisons with marginal productivities are not available. Smolensky, Pommerehne and Dalrymple (1979) arrive at figures which show considerably less inequality in income distribution for the Federal Republic of Germany (1969) than for the USA (1970), the average of five different

Gini ratios being 0.264 and 0.366, respectively. The five ratios correspond with five definitions of incomes. Using a different definition, van Ginneken (1981) finds a figure of 0.308 for Germany (1974) and comparable figures of 0.261 for the United Kingdom (1979) as against 0.560 for Mexico (1968). Wiles (1978) arrives at some figures which compare several western and eastern countries and constitutes the ratios of the upper decile to the median and the lower decile to the median. This is shown in Table 17.1.

Table 17.1 Ratios of upper (U) and lower (L) decile income to median income for five western and four eastern countries around 1970

Country	GB(69)	H(72)	PL(71)	CS(65)	USSR(67)	S(71)	CDN(71)	USA(74)	D(69)
U	204	173	167	167	179	183	227	229	209
L	52	57	58	53	58	51	38	37	55
U/L	3.9	3.0	2.9	3.2	3.1	3.6	6.0	6.2	3.8

Abbreviations:
GB: Great Britain; H: Hungary; PL: Poland; CS: Czechoslovakia; USSR: Soviet Union; S: Sweden; CDN: Canada; USA: United States; D: Federal Republic of Germany. For details and footnotes the original publication should be consulted.

The ratio U/L has been added by the present author. In this table the UK and Germany show less difference than in van Ginneken's estimates. The USA clearly shows more inequality than Western Europe, where, as might be expected, Sweden comes out best, but somewhat less well than Eastern Europe. Bahro (1977), nevertheless, judges that in Eastern Europe (his country being the GDR) there is still too much inequality.

When it comes to developing countries this judgement is shared by a large number of observers from the North—the industrialised world.

17.6 IMPROVEMENT OF SOCIAL ORDER BY LEARNING FROM OTHERS

A social order is not only determined or characterised by its income inequality. There are many other criteria. We shall deal with some of these in order to illustrate the thesis we wish to defend in the present section.

One is the *decision-making* process for the community's most important issues. An overwhelming majority of citizens in western countries prefers decision-making by majority vote (sometimes a qualified majority) and where necessary by secret ballot. Bahro, a convinced communist, shares this preference; and recent events in

Poland show that an overwhelming majority in that country also share this preference. Its not being fulfilled constitutes a minus for the Eastern European nation's social order.

Majority voting is not the ideal system, but rather the least bad we know, as Sir Winston Churchill expressed it. It may be bad if ignorance or shortsightedness leads the citizens or Members of Parliament to make decisions which will be deplored later. Ignorance may be reduced by learning from the experience of other countries. With all its disadvantages the diversity and *Kleinstaaterei* [being subdivided into a large number of small units] of Europe at least has the advantage that many details of the social orders they have established are different and that some of them operate more satisfactorily than others. Thus in the Netherlands social benefits such as unemployment or sickness benefits which are higher than in other European countries may be too high, since the incentive to work or to work well is lower than elsewhere. (When we mentioned a minus for Eastern Europe on the issue of democratic voting, we should have added a plus (cf. Ellman, 1979) for them having limited open unemployment.)

In contrast to the advantages of democratic voting we observe grave disadvantages in the *cultural crisis*, characterised by vandalism, personal violence *vis-à-vis* fellow-citizens exerted 'for fun' and making an increasing number of victims. Among the causes we may assume a tendency to too slack education, or ignorance about how to bring up children, partly due to ignorance about the nature of children, partly due to taking it easy or to plain egotism (cf. Ortlieb, 1971).

Another serious aspect of degeneration in western culture is its *overconsumption*. By this we mean a larger volume of consumption than what is needed for a healthy life. Hard drugs are the worst example, associated with a complicated psychological and social background: this type of consumption is often all but imposed on weak victims of societal degeneration. Soft drugs, alcoholic beverages and tobacco products are the second group of commodities the consumption of which is much higher than a healthy life requires, even if some luxury is accepted as healthy. (Consumption of tobacco has now started to diminish thanks to better information.) The third group consists of foods such as meat and sugar. Here the consequences are not only unhealthy for the consumers, but, much worse, they harm the interests of the poor in developing countries (cf. Chapter 4).

In a more general way the industrialised countries are at the crossroads: which life-style is optimal in a broad cultural pattern? Probably we should be listening more to what leaders from the three developing continents have to tell us (Gandhi, 1948; Herrera *et al.*, 1978; Tévoédrjè, 1978).

Some of the instruments needed for the re-education of the West are the units in which our private life takes place: the family or its alternatives; and the system of formal education.

The main point we want to make in this section is that in order to choose better and to decide on these fundamentals of our order it is wise to look at what other communities are doing.

17.7 TOLERANCE NEEDED TO LEARN FROM OTHERS

Learning from other orders is part of a scientific attitude; but it is more than this. Science is the means by which we learn intellectually. But, as observed, learning has other, moral or ethical components. Even so let us first deal with the intellectual element, and hence with the scientific way of choosing an optimal social order.

Discussions on this subjejct have too often stopped short at a situation of *conflicting opinions*. Group A—standing for a group of scientists or of citizens or for a political party—adheres to Thesis I: (e.g. let the market system work freely without intervention by public authorities). Group B—another school of scientists or political party—adheres to Thesis II (e.g. prices should be regulated by public authorities). Scientifically, such a conflict situation constitutes a *non-finished thinking process*. An additional process is needed to complete the process. The final stage must be of the form: there are two or more types of markets; let us call them a and b. If a applies, Thesis I is correct; if b applies, Thesis II is correct. This new statement is a higher level of knowledge; the scientific process has been advanced and made compatible with what previously seemed to be incompatible. In other words, a *synthesis* has been reached. Of course, it need not be the final truth for all times. New complications may be discovered or may occur. But for the time being the state of the art is to distinguish a from b. As a concrete example a may stand for stable markets and b for unstable markets.

The scientific attitude requires understanding for the existence of both a and b. This understanding is a form of *tolerance*. Defined in this way tolerance is a prerequisite for scientific work and for a scientific attitude, including a scientific attitude *vis-à-vis* socialism. For the choice between social order this implies *convergence*. If in the past Group A wanted all markets to be free and Group B wanted all markets to be regulated there seemed to be two different orders. If at present it is understood that stable markets can be left to themselves, but unstable markets need regulation, a new order has been defined which is better than either of the two previously adhered to: these two orders have *converged*. It is in the interest of both old orders to proceed to the new integrated order.

Of course, the example chosen is highly simplified. This was done for reasons of exposition. We all know that in 1960 Sorokin started the discussion of the phenomenon of convergence. A large literature on the subject has grown. However, we have become stuck in a situation where indeed some convergence was stated to have taken place, but where for other elements of the choice new Groups A and B—and even more (cf. Adler Karlsson, *op cit.*)—had chosen their rigid positions. In the process the word *coexistence* was coined, to stand for the simultaneous existence of different social orders whose leaders have not completed an attempt to learn from each other. Of course, even if they had learned all they could learn from each other, they need not adhere to the same order as their optimal choice. But they remain farther apart than is necessary, since *information is limited on purpose*, thereby preventing the scientific process to find the optimum for each of them. The process is kept incomplete and the opinions expressed cannot be called scientific. Such opinions, based on deliberate withholding of information, may be called *ideologies* (cf. section 17.1).

It is significant that coexistence was aimed only at the material conditions of countries with different orders. It was denied *a priori* to apply to ideologies. Here the situation of incomplete scientific learning from other nations was maintained, blocking the learning process, and blocking the attainment of synthesis.

17.8 TOLERANCE NEEDED TO AVOID WAR

In section 17.7 we described the present state of world affairs, especally regarding the choice of an optimum social order as one of coexistence of nations with different social orders. An additional feature is the limitation of information on other orders. That constitutes the non-completion of the scientific process of choice as dealt with in section 17.6. This limitation of information has been accompanied by an increased use of military means to impose the choice.

This tragic development has been accentuated and become a deadly threat to mankind by the technological development of weaponry. The human race finds itself on a knife's edge. In this position the utmost caution is needed. In addition a true picture of what the real forces at work are is needed, especially concerning the question of whether it is indeed the choice of social order which is the central issue or whether, alternatively, it is a simple geopolitical power-struggle between the superpowers. In this context it may be significant that in the second world war the Soviet Union chose not to call their efforts against the German Nazis defence of the social order, but defence of the homeland (The 'Great Patriotic' War). Neither did the USA ask its soldiers to defend their social order—which American leaders call, rather proudly, capitalist. Could it be that Russian soldiers from rural areas were not that devoted to collectivist agriculture and that the American soldiers were not that enthusiastic about capitalism?

This chapter cannot claim, of course, to bring the solution to this great nightmare. It only ventures to add some modest additions to the arguments used in this debate. They concern the danger of non-scientific, extremist attitudes. Extremist attitudes lead to polarisation and the illusion that a new war could be won. What we need is tolerance, middle-of-the-road philosophies and synthesis in the sense of the scientific attitude described in section 17.7. In simple political terms there is an enormous task for democratic socialism, which, in this author's opinion, is closest to a scientific attitude as exemplified—in an oversimplified way—in section 17.7. The reader may also be reminded of the incompatibility of militarism and socialism. Militarism is not necessarily connected either with private business, except in the case of arms trade. It is far more connected with nationalism and feudal elements. It is significant that at this moment European democratic socialist governments are arguing intensively to convince the extremist superpowers that negotiation has top priority.

REFERENCES

Adler Karlsson, G. (1967), *Funktionssocialism*, Oskarshamn, Prisma (also available in English).

Bahro, R. (1977), *Die Alternative*, Cologne and Frankfurt, Europäische Verlagsanstalt.

Bauer, O. (1919), *Die Sozialisierungsaktion im ersten Jahre der Republik* [*Socialisation in the First Years of the Republic*] Vienna, Wiener Volksbuchhandlung; and many other publications.

Bergson, A. (1938), 'A reformulation of certain aspects of welfare economics', *Quarterly Journal of Economics*, LII, pp. 310–34; and later publications.

Ellman, M.J. (1979), *Full Employment*, Leiden and Antwerp, H.E. Stenfert Kroese.

Gandhi, M.K. (1948), *Constructive Programme, Its Meaning and Place*, Ahmedabad, Navajivan Publishing House.

Gottschalk, P.T. (1978), 'A comparison of marginal productivity and earnings by occupation', *Industrial and Labour Relations Review*, 31, pp. 368–78.

Herrera, A.O. (1978), ¿*Catastrophe o Nueva Sociedad*? [*Catastrophe or a New Society?*] Modelo Mundial Latino-Americano, Fundación Bariloche.

Levy, S. and Gutman, L. (1975), 'On the multivariate structure of well-being' *Social Indicators Research*, 2 pp. 361–88.

Mann-Borgese, E. in Tinbergen, J. *et al.* (1976), *Reshaping the International Order*, New York, Dutton, p. 312.
Naqvi, S.N.H. (1981), *Ethics and Economics, An Islamic Synthesis*, Leicester, The Islamic Foundation.
Ortlieb, H.-D. (1971), *Die verantwortungslose Gesellschaft,* [*The Irresponsible Society*], Munich, Wilhelm Goldmann Verlag.
SDAP & NVV (1921), *Het socialisatierapport* [*The Socialisation Report*], Amsterdam, Arbeiderspers.
Smolensky, E. *et al.* (1978), 'Postfisc income inequality: a comparison of the USA and West Germany', in Moroney, J.R. (ed.), *Income Inequality*, Lexington, and Toronto, D.C. Heath.
Tévoédjrè, A. (1978), *La pauvreté, richesse des peuples*, Paris, Editions ouvrières (also available in English).
Thurow, L. (1968), 'Disequilibrium and the marginal productivity of capital and labor', *Review of Economics and Statistics*, 50, pp. 23–31.
Tinbergen, J. (1975), *Income Distribution, Analysis and Policies*, Amsterdam, North-Holland.
Tinbergen, J. and Kol, J. (1980), 'Market-determined and residual incomes—some dilemmas', *Economie Appliquée*, XXXIII, pp. 285-301 (Ch. 1 of this book).
Tinbergen, J. *et al.*(1976), *Reshaping the International Order*, New York, Dutton.
van Ginneken, W. (1981), *Generating Internationally Comparable Available Income Distribution Data*, Evidence from the Federal Republic of Germany (1974), Mexico (1968) and the United Kingdom (1979), ILO Employment and Income Distribution Programme.
van Praag, B.M.S. (1971), "The welfare function of income in Belgium: an empirical investigation', *European Economic Review*, 2, p. 337; and several other publications, some in the same journal.
Wiles, P. (1978), 'Our shaky data base', in Krelle, W. and Shorrocks, A.F., *Personal Income Distribution*, Amsterdam, New York and Oxford, North-Holland.

18 Coexistence: from the Past to the Future

It is about twenty years ago that the idea was launched that countries with different social systems could and should coexist. To reflect this idea a journal was established: *Coexistence*. I was invited by the editors to set out, in that journal, how I feel about the development of this concept during the last two decades and how it might develop in the future. This chapter was the result.

So far, the impact of the idea has been limited. Coexistence has been restricted by the Soviet and and the rightist western leadership to the fact of physically living within their territories. The social order in East and West were themselves considered given, and indicated by the inexact names of capitalism *vs.* socialism, or democratic *vs.* authoritarian regimes. These terms are inexact because they are used to characterise ranges of social orders as different as the ones prevailing in 1850 in, say, Britain (when Marx wrote) and in 1950, or, for that matter, 1980. They were also used to characterise orders as they exist at present in the Soviet Union, Hungary, the Baltic states and China. Democracy was used to indicate parliamentary procedures of nations where voting rights were restricted to tax-payers, and nations where all adults have these rights. Some countries are said to be democratic when power is held mainly by feudal landowners; and alongside democracies the tautology 'people's democracies' has been created.

Not only were the social orders considered as given; discussing them was not considered to be integral to coexistence. The exchange of ideas took place by adhering to slogans and the effect of such a game is, of course, polarisation. This was exactly what Soviet leaders and rightist western politicians wanted, and divergence was the consequence. If an exchange of ideas is only permitted in the form of election slogans, and a really free intellectual debate is discouraged, the resulting opinions can hardly be called scientific, the qualification proudly claimed by Marx and not unjustifiably. And the process of scientific discussion stops completely if arguments are replaced by guns. These, in some well-known socialist songs, are called 'barbarians' weapons', and rightly so.

If the search for a better society has to be organised that way the norms and values we adhere to have degenerated into the principle that all means are permitted which contribute to reaching the predetermined aim. Does that lead to a better world? To pose the question implies answering in the negative. Never has it been clearer that the neglect of basic human virtues undermines the quality of human existence than in the last two decades.

Be that as it may, now that political thinking has increasingly been submerged by military thinking two questions seem to require answering. The first is: with what arguments did the superpowers motivate their soldiers to fight in the second world war? Interesting enough American soldiers were not asked to defend capitalism; neither were Russian soldiers asked to defend socialism. The majority of American soldiers, being workers, and the majority of Russian soldiers being, at that time, farmers, such slogans would not have been productive. The Americans fought authoritarianism; they 'fought for freedom'. This could not be the Russian soldiers' motivation. They were asked to fight the 'Great Patriotic War'. Let the reader draw his own conclusions about the use and non-use of social ideals under military rule.

The second question is: how did the two superpowers treat the countries they occupied after the war? The countries occupied, for the most part, by the USA were Japan and part of West Germany. The main countries occupied by the Soviet Union were the Eastern European countries and East Germany. Quite recently the USA has occupied Grenada; and the Soviet Union, somewhat earlier, Afghanistan. Again the answer to the second question may be left to the reader.

If we try to summarise the reaction to the idea of coexistence and accept my characterising it as a process of polarisation rather than convergence we have to state that this reaction resulted in an armaments race of unprecedented dimensions and in a far lower quality of human happiness than would be possible without the excessive level of armaments.

Let us now turn to the future. In principle there are two ways of dealing with the future: one is to speculate about the most likely future; the other to discuss the most desirable future. The former is the more difficult. In order to arrive at a picture of the most likely future one has to know the most likely unforeseen events. An example is the escalation of one of the existing military conflicts to a nuclear war; another is that the use of nuclear weapons is triggered by coincidence. Such forecasts are not only difficult to make, but many are of little use. They offer little help to the construction of an optimal world order. Our two examples— escalation or coincidental nuclear conflict—illustrate the lack of use. The former, moreover, is also based on an erroneous estimate, namely that even to be forced to live in the other party's social order is less attractive than to 'live' in a war. Finally, a nuclear war would eliminate the possibility to change the world order in whatever way.

So I propose to discuss the most desirable social order; and to discuss it, as far as possible, in a scientific way. Whatever the meaning of socialism, I join the Marxian endeavour to deal with it in a scientific way. The advantage we have in comparison to Marx is that there are now a number of countries living in an existing socialist order. We are thus able to observe the various orders in existence; we can compare their positive and their negative aspects. Such comparative studies have become recognised disciplines, and in both the East and the West we have some outstanding experts: I am thinking in particular of Bahro, Bergson, Ellman, Šik, Vanek and Wiles, just to mention a few.

Among the features characteristic for eastern and western regimes let me mention a few as an illustration of what comparative studies may teach us. Eastern countries don't have mass unemployment and their income distribution is less unequal than in western countries. Their citizens are 'supervised' by three hierarchies: production units, government and the Party. Western countries periodically face mass unemployment, but their average material consumption is higher because of higher efficiency and creativity. They also have access to more information and are freer to form voluntary associations. Eastern countries have various forms of private property of the means of production (e.g. agricultural land) and western countries have various forms of collective property (e.g. energy and transport). In other words, the Eastern bloc don't have a maximum of public ownership; and western countries don't have a maximum of private property of the means of production. This illustrates the difference between the maximum and the optimum. We don't find the most desirable order at the extremes of centralisation or at decentralisation; at the extremes of collective property of the means of production (all or nothing). In practice, all existing orders are mixed; and the question to be answered is: *which mixture is best* in a given country at a given time? Adler Karlsson (1967) introduced the useful concept of functional socialism: rather than socialising the ownership of all the means of production a number of *functions* going with ownership may be socialised, that is, regulated by the community.

Comparative studies are the empirical part of a scientific approach.

A theoretical part is also necessary, if only to discover what future empirical studies are most urgent. Moreover, the approach must be multidisciplinary, since in real life we cannot restrict ourselves to the discrete aspects considered by each science. This reflects itself in management science and cybernetics; the central problem we have to consider might well be defined as how to manage the planet so as to *maximise humankind's welfare*. The means to be used have a substantive and an organisational component. Moreover, both require the human attitudes to be discussed after these components have been indicated.

The *substantive component* contains a number of usual socioeconomic policy items (optimal efficiency, optimal distribution of both employment and consumption) as aims, and a corresponding number of means, especially in the field of taxes and subventions, and a number of regulations, including those on health care, schooling and training.

The *organisational component* includes the choice of an optimal hierarchy: a large number of decisions will have to be taken at low levels (the family, the production unit, the municipality, etc.), but a limited number of decisions must be taken at higher levels, including some at world level. It depends on the type of problem where the optimal level of decision-making is to be chosen.

We may distinguish between authorities at each of the levels from lowest to highest. In today's world national authorities have more than optimal decision power. Problems affecting people outside one authority's responsibility should not be decided by that authority. The optimal level of decision-making should be high enough to imply negligible external effects, that is, effects on people beyond an authority's jurisdiction.

A clear and rather recent example of external effects is *pollution*—for example, acid rain. In order that optimal decisions on pollution be taken the level of pollution legislation has to be continental, if not global. This example illustrates how a cybernetic or management–scientific approach must be followed to define an *optimal set of authorities* at various levels in order to maximise world welfare.

We now come to the fundamental question of what *attitudes* are required to establish the structures indicated and needed to maximise world welfare. From past experience we have learned that the polarising interpretation given to the idea of coexistence has lead us to a dead-end. Instead of accentuating the divergent elements of the two main alternative orders, it is the converging elements we should stress. This is equivalent to a scientific attitude which, in principle, aims at deriving a synthesis from a thesis and an antithesis.

Observation shows that a number of views in both East and West have already been converging. Market elements have been introduced into East European economies, and planning elements into Western societies. Capital has been rediscovered as a production factor in eastern economies and employment of labour as a necessity in western economic policies. Both East and West have discovered the *scarcity of energy* and the need for an *unpolluted environment*. Both are faced with the dangers of nationalism, and in particular of the armaments race. It is not necessary—nor even desirable—for the process of convergence to imply that the two main social orders become identical. Geographical, historical and cultural elements differ, and so will optimal orders (cf. van den Doel, 1971).

Among the many problems not yet solved (e.g the voting systems of the Bretton-Woods institutions, and the means to be made available to them) by far the most urgent is that of *world security*: can we agree on a Security Council *without a veto?* on a much stronger United Nations Peace Force? and so on. Will the attitudes of the leadership of the superpowers become tolerant enough to arrive at a solution of this pressing problem? Merging two previously competing big corporations is known to be an extremely difficult operation – especially for the sales managers. The initiative has to be taken by the chief executives. Such an initiative to cooperate in order to create an optimal world order would be by far the greatest contribution to the welfare of mankind that could be made—much larger than sticking to rigid slogans. The question of life or death will be decided only if the chief executives of East and West discover this before it is too late.

REFERENCES

Adler Karlsson, G (1967), *Funktionssocialism*, Oskarhamn (also available in English).

van den Doel, J. (1971), *Konvergentie en evolutie*, Assen, Van Gorcum en Comp., N.V. (Dutch, with extensive English summary).

19 Restructuring our Societies: International Coordination Policies

19.1 POLICY AIMS

The main subject of this chapter must be understood as the search for a better socioeconomic policy than has been pursued by most countries during the last decade. An orderly discussion of socioeconomic policies consists of a consecutive discussion of the aims to be chosen and the means to be applied (cf. Tinbergen, 1956, 1961, 1968). In section 19.1 the aims will be discussed; section 19.2 deals with the means to be recommended; section 19.3 discusses the level at which policy decisions are best taken and the most desirable orders of magnitude of the quantitative means; while in section 19.4 a rew remarks are made on the changes in attitude needed in both politicians and the electorate to escape global disaster (cf. Brandt *et al*, 1980).

Starting our discussion of the *aims* of a better socioeconomic policy, we submit that the highest priority should be given to a *high level of employment*, especially for young people. In the face of the non-fulfilled needs in today's world it is unacceptable that between 10 and 20 per cent of the developed western countries' labour force is unemployed. It is unacceptable both for those who are starving in the Third World and for those who want to work and are unemployed. The latter applies especially to school-leavers who, upon finishing their schooling, find that they are not wanted. Psychologists in particular can explain what damage is done to these young persons and to society if frustration builds up.

The aim of a high level of employment not only applies to industrial countries but also to *developing nations*. Although the latter have been accustomed to high levels of unemployment and poverty, their standard of life is deteriorating and an increasing number of people are getting into a hopeless situation. Conditions differ widely among regions and localities, but not only has the Brandt Commission emphasised the need for quicker development; even the Morgan Guarantee Trust (1980) does.

A third aim of socioeconomic policy is to reduce the *deterioration of the environment*. The awareness of the need for a cleaner atmosphere, water supply and land is spreading quickly as a reaction to the rapid accumulation of chemical and radioactive wastes as by-products of the chemical and nuclear energy industries. Protest actions in a number of countries illustrate the accumulation of problems we are facing.

A fourth aim remains the *reduction in income inequality*, both in and between nations. Since this constitutes a long-standing problem—a continuous struggle for over a century—we do not need to explain why this aim is on our list. Rather, we must mention a fifth aim, namely the *reduction of the rate of inflation*. This concerns a problem that has assumed unusual forms in industrial countries for the last decade or so. All citizens and politicians of western countries agree that inflation must be reduced. What we do not agree on is the degree of urgency to be given to this aim. That this aim appears fifth in this chapter is deliberate; however, many of our fellow citizens and politicians consider it to be the most pressing aim. Although my preference is to have no inflation—or 1 to 2 per cent *per annum* only—I think unemployment at present constitutes a much more serious problem, and that it is a misunderstanding to argue that reduction of the rate of inflation constitutes a necessary condition for a revival of production and employment. It has been rightly pointed out that Brazil, for example, has developed considerably in spite of continued inflation. Of course, this pattern is certainly not optimal, but for the Third World it is less abnormal than for developed countries.

19.2 POLICY MEANS

It seems appropriate to remind ourselves of some of the lessons from the past concerning the use of means of socioeconomic policy; in particular, the policies pursued in order to overcome the Great Depression of the 1930s provide cases in point: some means tried out fifty years ago have made us sadder and wiser. Generally speaking, in that period each nation attempted to solve its own problem. Many of the policies used were *beggar-my-neighbour* ones. This applies to the succession of devaluations as well as to the various types of protectionism practised. Space doesn't permit to go into details. Suffice it to say that the experiences of the 1930s were the main grounds for the establishment during or after the second world war of the Bretton-Woods institutions (The International Monetary Fund and the World Bank) and, for lack of better, the General Agreement on Tariffs and Trade.

Several countries emphasised, during the Great Depression, the need to *reduce government expenditures* in order to equilibrate government accounts. However, it remains an open question whether the attempts to economise on government expenditures had a favourable impact on production. There was certainly a revival in 1937, but in 1938 a setback followed. The real recovery was produced by Nazi Germany's massive spending, first on motorways (*Autobahnen*) and subsequently on armaments. Once the war had started all nations involved maximised government expenditure, and once the war was over reconstruction and development produced the 1950–70 boom which, somewhat like the period 1923–29, made us believe that we had learned to live without trade cycles. Soon enough we experienced that this was not correct.

Among the lessons from the past we may also count the experience that all protective measures we took could not counter the *shift of labour-intensive industries to the developing countries*. The few exceptions are the ones where some particular skills played a role—for example *haute couture*, which kept a small section of the clothing industry in Europe.

We shall now take up the discussion of the *means* of socioeconomic policy which seem to be effective, keeping in mind the lessons from the past. They are the main topic of this chapter. It is beginning to be understood that we have to *change our industrial structure*. One way of formulating an essential feature of an effective restructuring policy is that *no support should be given to activities without a future* and temporary support perhaps to activities with a future. This confronts us with the question of what activities these are. On the basis of the well-known Heckscher–Ohlin principle, I submit that the activities in which developed countries are able to compete are those using the production factors we are best endowed with. The most important among these, and common to all developed countries, are the two main types of capital: *physical* and *human*. Individual developed countries may have additional production factors codetermining the activities in which they are able to compete: a favourable geographical location, general capabilities such as the habit to work hard or 'liking to obey', accuracy or liking team work. *Innate creativity* should be mentioned in particular.

The phrase *human capital* stands for knowledge and skill, developed by (formal and informal) schooling. Another way of indicating the activities in which developed countries are able to compete therefore is knowledge-intensive activities. Today's standard example is that of microprocessors, used in automation, automisation or computerisation. Characteristic of many of these processes is the utilisation of numerically-controlled machine-tools.

The development of the activities just mentioned may be furthered by temporary subventions to be phased out according to a predetermined scheme, in order to train or *retrain the workers* needed. This training process will be more successful if a tradition of accuracy and hard work exists. Japan is an impressive example, but within Europe Germany,

Sweden and Switzerland stand out in comparison to several other western countries.

Knowledge-intensive activities are not restricted to manufacturing. In some countries considerable specialised knowledge in agriculture or horticulture is available. Services may also be knowledge-intensive; and not only traditional services such as marketing but today scientific research, both fundamental and applied, constitutes an important example. Particular types of research are required in order to keep the environment clean, and in this area some future activities may also be found.

Several of the possible future activities listed so far are also described by the phrase 'informatics' and our economies are said to pass through a third stage of transformation; we are said to become an *information society*. It is ironical that for quite some time economic science was built on the assumption that every agent or 'actor' had available all the information relevant to his or her activities. Step by step we have learned that the collection and processing of information constitutes a major problem. One of the hotly debated issues today is the question of what *degree of decentralisation of information* is optimal. The issue is particularly important in the discussion between proponents of central planning and their adversaries. Industrial espionage and trade restrictions on technological knowledge are now weapons used by the competing superpowers.

Japan's competitive strength has become one of the topics intensively discussed this last decade. Amongh the causes, one phenomenon is believed to play a role (and is believed to have started to do so in European internal discussions): employer–employee discussions (as well as a discussion launched by GDR dissident Bahro, 1977). This is the style of management, and more particularly the type and degree of participation of employees in management. Briefly expressed, the *effectiveness of supervision* is under discussion. Supervision produces irritation, and growing irritation when the supervised employees have become more educated. Smaller decision units, with team work rather than work ordered by the foremen, contribute to job satisfaction and hence to productivity. In Japan as well as in Sweden—in many respects socially the most advanced European country—such forms of participation exist and are experimented with. It seems to be natural that, *pari passu* with more education, such forms of management replace the more rigid forms of the past.

At the same time various forms of *reduction of working hours* make sense, at least as a general tendency. Over the last century and a half we have experienced a rise in productivity and real incomes, implying a rise in the utility of leisure, and as a consequence a shortening of work hours.

The latter takes various forms: reduction in the number of hours per working day, reduction of the number of working days per week, of the number of weeks worked per year and, finally, the number of years worked during one's lifetime. In recent years Emmerij (1978) has drawn attention to yet another type of lifetime working, made desirable by the development of technology: an option should be given on *educational leave* from time to time, in order to adapt an employee's knowledge of new technologies to his work.

A related issue is the increased supply of those who prefer to have a *part-time job*. Economically considered, it is attractive if this is combined with a longer time per day capital goods are operating, (e.g. two-shift working, one of normal working hours and one part-time). Such an arrangement will reduce fixed costs per unit of product and contribute to keeping prices competitive.

Alongside some types of *decentralisation* already discussed, others are studied and have been implemented. In France, traditionally a country with a rather centralised government, a number of functions have been shifted from Paris to regional centres. Italy too only recently gave more decision power to its regions. Various experiments are being made in these and other countries.

A related, but different, tendency is known as *deregulation*. This is the handing over of government tasks to private organisations. Recent examples are the handing over of refuse collection by German city authorities to private firms. If the latter are able to perform this task at a lower cost than the municipal services it is hard to oppose such a transfer. A few concrete examples may stimulate municipal authorities to become more efficient and so make further transfers unnecessary. Sometimes regulation as such is rejected because it raises costs of production of private firms. This is said of regulation of *polluting* activities, for example. Such a statement is not convincing, though, because environmental pollution harms the quality of life. A convincing argument on the topic can only be that a cheaper way of keeping the environment clean is possible, which means that the regulation itself can be made more effective.

The application of some of the means discussed requires expenditure, such as subsidies to promising activities or measures to regulate the quality of the environment. Since most countries suffer from a deficit on government revenue and are already in debt there is much hesitation about raising government expenditure. It goes without saying that a periodical screening of existing expenditures so as to eliminate waste is useful, if only to avoid inertia in the necessary adaptation to changing situations. The same applies to the forms of financing applied.

A particular category of expenditure—namely, transfers of unemployment benefit—has been critically considered by Rehn (1975), who holds the view that the amounts at stake can be used in a better way. Rehn advocates the use of these amounts for subsidising the employment of additional workers at normal hourly wages, either for full-time or for part-time jobs. The system requires some controls in order to avoid abuse, but is preferable to simply paying benefits and *prohibiting* the recipients from working.

Another problem of financing is *money creation* in the Keynesian sense. In the first few years of 'stagflation' some good reasons existed for not applying a Keynesian policy too readily. Now that unemployment continues to stay at undesirably high levels a reorientation towards Keynesian methods makes sense. The best argument in favour of it is that evidently a continual process of hoarding is taking place. This hoarding is partly located in OPEC countries and partly in countries whose citizens have sold assets to OPEC citizens. Among others the one-time director of the IMF, Dr H.J. Witteveen (1982) supports such a shift. Meanwhile the IMF has raised its total capital by 47 per cent, but the Brandt Commission (the Independent Commission on Internaitonal Development Issues) advocates doubling it.

The resistance against a Keynesian element in the optimal policy package originates from those who fear increased inflation as a consequence. Although the increasing under-utilisation of production capacity reduces this danger, it remains desirable to keep inflation under strict control. Among the means to be added is an *incomes policy*. A clear argument in favour of this is the increased organisation of interest groups. Whereas at the beginning of the century only manual workers were unionised, today almost all social groups are: office workers, farmers, the professions. We are living in a world of oligopolies (cf. Lesourne, 1981). Claims for salary increases follow each other at an increasing rhythm. Here a restructuring is also needed. In theory it can be avoided, but in practice the attitude of restraint is hard to find. Space prohibits the elaboration of the numerous problems which have to be solved; so reference may be made to other contributions (Tinbergen, 1983). An incomes policy may also help to reduce income differences, one of the aims of socioeconomic policy listed in section 19.1.

19.3 THE LEVEL TO BE APPLIED; ORDERS OF MAGNITUDE

Policy decisions can be made at various levels, from individual households or enterprises to the world level. In today's world a very large proportion of decisions are made at the level of national governments.

It remains to be seen whether this is an optimal structure. In order to formulate recommendations on the optimal level of decision-making two criteria seem to be important: (i) *maximum participation*, which requires a low level; in fact, as low as possible, provided that other interests are not seriously damaged for that would mean the non-participation of others whose interests are relevant; (ii), *minimal external effects*, which requires that the level be chosen so as to make external effects negligible. External effects of a political decision are effects on the welfare of individuals for whom the decision-makers have no responsibility. As an example, decisions on anti-pollution measures should be taken at a level responsible for all affected by the pollution in question.

As a first application of our criteria we take decisions on *employment policy*, such as the subsidisation of promising enterprises, reduction in working time, or the financing of additional investment. Both the experiences of the 1930s and recent experiences in France show us that the national government level is too low for an optimal employment policy. We therefore propose to discuss in the following paragraphs what supranational levels seem to be optimal.

Before doing so a few examples will be discussed where national or lower levels may be more appropriate. This may be so for management reforms, because of the differing traditions around this subject, and for incomes policies, because of the differing rates of inflation among nations. Clearly measures of decentralising government also belong to this category, as are many policy decisions with a strong cultural component, such as education.

If, in principle, we agree that some important policy decisions have to be taken at levels higher than the national government, the question arises which among the existing international organisations are able to take decisions. Evidently, neither the United Nations' institutions nor the OECD are decision-making bodies: they are advisory organisations only. Discussions held in their meetings, studies made by their secretariats, and recommendations made to member-governments contain a lot of precious information and wisdom, but national governments are free not to take the decisions suggested. There are no sanctions against such an attitude and this negative attitude often prevails. The sense of international responsibility of most national governments is very limited.

Almost the only institution endowed with a potentially strong decision-making infrastructure is the European Community of ten nations. Its structure contains a Parliament, a (potential) government, the Commission, a (for the time being overly powerful) Senate (the Council of Ministers) and a (fairly powerful) Court. As a consequence of nationalist pressure the decision-making power of the Council is, on the one hand, stronger than the Rome Treaty's spirit would have implied and, on the other hand, weaker because of the Luxembourg Arrangement which gave veto power to a member country if it considers a proposal damaging to the 'vital interest' of that nation. In line with the Treaties concerned, the Community does possess some supranational power and uses part of it. (In the field of transportation policies that power has not yet been used but the Court may decide that such policies must be introduced.) In the fields of agriculture and international trade an EC policy does exist, but one that is non-optimal in various respects. This can be changed, however, by using the competences in the hands of the various organs. In recent years the European Parliament has clearly shown the will to use its competence.

A modest but positive innovation has been agreed upon by the Commission concerning the *development cooperation* with developing countries (Document Com. (82) 640 Final). The percentage of the Community's income to be spent on such cooperation will be doubled by 1990, and more countries will be assisted. A better coordination of policies *vis-à-vis* Mediterranean countries (member countries as well as others) will be carried out. Changes in the Community's social policy, and in particular its employment policy, are in preparation.

It is this subject which is in need of a far stronger policy than pursued so far. There is a growing awareness of this need. Perhaps it is insufficiently understood that the link between this policy and development cooperation is stronger than usually realised. Amounts spent on development projects in the Third World will, to a considerable extent, be spent in Europe and so contribute to a European recovery.

It is a truism that the quantitative aspect of any goal of socioeconomic policy and that of the means to be applied are related and should be of a *comparable order of magnitude*. In the period of the Great Depression this has been often overlooked. It is a human characteristic to think qualitatively rather than quantitatively—at least a feature of people not immediately accountable for some concrete project or policy. I am afraid that this statement also applies to Document Com. (82) 640, mentioned before. The amount spent on development cooperation by the Community is 0.05 per cent of total income and this is far too small. Similarly the Budget for social and regional policies of the Community is not of the order of magnitude needed, once we agree that a much larger part of these policies must be pursued at a higher than national level. In other words, we are faced here with a clear example of too nationalist attitudes of member governments—an attitude incompatible with the longer-term interests of the nations concerned.

For those who are familiar with the subject this attitude is no surprise. The usual subjects of discussion testify to this sort of myopia. One of these subjects is that an upper limit is set to the member countries' contributions to budgets which is *far below the optimum*. We may illustrate this by comparing ratios existing within each nation between the central government's expenditures and those of the lower authorities' spending. For the EEC, with a population comparable to that of the United States, it might be useful to compare the Federal Budget of the USA with that of the EEC, both as a percentage of GNP. Taking into account American and European philosphies about government intervention it would be natural to expect, for a fully integrated Community, a *higher* percentage than for the USA. There are good arguments, therefore, for raising the EEC Budget considerably; but it will take time to convince Europeans of the desirability to move to a Budget 2 or 3 times the present Budget. The urgent need for a more active employment and restructuring policy constitutes a convincing argument to that effect. A strong argument in favour of a higher Budget is the fact that the American Federal Budget (excluding military expenditure) is about 10 times as high as the EEC Budget, both as percentage of national income.

19.4 A NEW ATTITUDE

It was Sir Winston Churchill who introduced the definition of *statesmen* as compared with politicians. The latter, he said, in their thinking look at the next elections, but the former look at what the next generation needs. Presumably the founding fathers of the European Community— Monnet, Schumann, Adenauer, De Gasperi, Spaak, Beyen—all belong to the category of statesmen. Today, in Mansholt's words, we are eagerly waiting for a new group of statesmen, to give guidance. So far they have not yet shown up. Rather, we have large crowds of politicians, proud of being *realists*. One of their favourite definitions is that politics is the 'art of the possible'. In order to know what is possible they canvas the electorate. They are looking in the wrong direction—backwards. Their guidance is based on the recent past compared with the present. They have no vision of a better future. They suffer badly from myopia.

Examples of myopia abound. Why do we have obligatory schooling? Because we know that later on those forced to go to school will be grateful. This is the true justification of forcing human beings to do something they don't like in the short run: in the long run they will be grateful. The example refers to children. But something childish remains with many of us for quite some time. There are other examples applicable to adults. In the Netherlands we have closed some factories and regretted it three years later: in Munich 1938 we thought we had 'peace in our time'.

Myopia means the *deliberate exclusion of some information—*

information about what is beyond the short horizon we have chosen. Is information exclusion a good thing to do in the information society? If we opt against myopia, what are we opting for? Not only a wide horizon in order to have more information—we must also opt *against rigidity*. Important aspects of today's crises—in plural—are connected with rigidity. Rigidity in wages, but also in fees to the professions: rigidity with regard to social rights for which we fought in the past; rigidity in military power. Rigidity makes for disaster. In military matters it is not possible for both sides to be stronger than the other. In all these cases tolerance and flexibility are the way out of inconsistency. Tolerance means being interested in the other's viewpoint. How can we innovate, how can we be creative, without being tolerant and flexible? We need statesmen for guidance. But we cannot accept guidance if we are rigid ourselves. So our attitudes also need flexibility and tolerance. We too must want a clean environment, for us too *quality of life* must rank higher than mere quantitative changes. We must even accept less quantity in exchange for better quality. As a matter of fact we are overeating, we drink more than is healthy, we smoke too much, and some of us have become drug addicts.

It is interesting to note that Bahro criticises his (communist) country for giving too little attention to cultural aspects, and too much to material welfare. The restructuring we need is not economic only, it is much broader. Leadership, citizens and political parties all need a new attitude if a new structure has to be created; and, in particular, to think more internationally if we want to overcome our multiple crises. It is not only by chance that the subtitle of the Brandt Report is *A Programme for Survival*.

REFERENCES

Bahro, R. (1977), *Die Alternative*, Cologne and Frankfurt, Europäische Verlagstanstalt.
Brandt, W. *et al.* (1980), *North–South: A Programme for Survival*, London and Sydney, Pan Books.
Emmerij, L. (1978), 'Restructuring industrialized countries and the new international order', in Dolman, A.J. and van Ettinger, J., (eds.), *Partners in Tomorrow*, New York, Dutton, pp. 149–62, esp. p. 161.
Lesourne, J. (1981), *Les mille sentiers de l'avenir* [*One Thousand Paths to the Future*], Paris, Seghers, p. 237.
Morgan Guarantee Trust (1980), *World Financial Markets*, New York.
Rehn, G. (1975), *The Fight against Stagflation*, University of Stockholm, mimeo, August.
Tinbergen, J. (1956), *Economic Policy, Principles and Design*, Amsterdam,

North-Holland (also available in French (Dunod, Paris, 1961), and German (Rombach, Freiburg. B. 1968).

Tinbergen, J. (1983), 'The future of incomes policies', in: Taylor, L. (ed.) *Economic Structure and Performance*, Academic Press for World Bank, Washington.

Witteveen, H.J. (1982), Interview, in *NRC-Handelsblad*, 11 December, p. 12.

Appendix

The chapters were originally published as

Part I
1. 'Market-determined and residual incomes—some dilemmas' (with J. Kol) (1980), *Economie appliquée*, tome XXXIII, no. 2 revue publiée par l'ISMEA, Paris, et les Editions Droz, Genéve.
2. 'Fonctions de production à plusieurs facteurs', *Cahiers du Département d'économétrie de l'Université*, no. 81.03., Genève.
3. 'Constraints on production functions: essential *vs.* non-essential factors', *Economic Essays in Honour of Jørgen H. Gelting*, Danish Economic Association.
4. 'Contraproduktie', in Eijgelshoven, P.J. and van Gemerden, L.N. (eds), *Inkomensverdeling en openbare financiën*, Het Spectrum, Utrecht and Antwerp.
5. 'On collective and part-collective goods', *De Economist* (Groningen), Stenfert Kroese, Leiden.
6. 'Production functions: research lacunae', Professor A. Simões Lopes, Universidade Tecnica, Lisbon.

Part II
7. Zu einem makroökonomischen Modell der Einkommensbildung' (with E. Wegner) (1983), *Schweizerische Zeitschrift für Volkswirtschaft und Statistik* pp. 69–78, Volkswirtschaftliches Institut der Universität Bern.
8. 'The role of occupational status in income formation', (1976) in Cramer, J.S., Heertje, A. and Venekamp, P.E. (eds), *Relevance and Precision, Essays in Honour of P. de Wolff*, 1976 Samson/North-Holland.
9. 'Hoogte en beïnvloedbaarheid van inkomens van managers', in van den Goorbergh, W.M., van de Klundert, Th. C.M.J., and Kolnaar, A.H.J. (eds), *Over macht en wet in het economisch gebeuren. Opstellen aangeboden aan Prof. Dr. D.B.J. Schouten*, H.E. Stenfert Kroese, Leiden and Antwerp.

10. 'Two approaches to quantify the concept of equitable income distribution' (1980), *Kyklos*, pp. 3-15, Institut für Sozialwissenschaften, Basle.

Part III
11. 'De meting van het volkswelzijn' (1983), in Maks, J.A.H. and Wester, E. (eds), *Met het oog op de werkelijkheid, Opstellen over economie en beleid voor F. Hartog*, H.E. Stenfert Kroese, Leiden and Antwerp.
12. 'Allocations of workers over jobs', *De Economist* (Gronigen), H.E. Stenfert Kroese, Leiden.
13. 'Some neglected determinants of welfare functions', (1981) *Journal of Economic Psychology*, Amsterdam, North-Holland.

Part IV
14. 'Over het dynamische velvaartsmaximum (1965), *Mededelingen der Koninklijke Nederlandse Akademie van Wetenschappen, afd. Letterkunde, Nieuwe reeks*—Deel 28—no 4, Amsterdam, Noordhollandsche Uitgeversmaatschappij.
15. 'Some remarks on the optimal tax system', (1977), in van Bochove, C.A. et al. (eds), *Modelling for Government and Business, Essays in Honour of Prof. Dr. P.J. Verdoorn*, Leiden, Martinus Nijhoff Social Sciences Division.
16. 'Optimal education, occupation and income distribution in a simplist model' (1981), in Rosenfielde, S. (ed.), *Economic Welfare and the Economics of Soviet Socialism: Essays in Honour of Abram Bergson*, Cambridge University Press, Cambridge.
17. 'Ways to socialism', *Coexistence*, Martinus Nijhoff, The Hague.
18. 'Coexistence—from the past to the future', *Coexistence*, Martinus Nijhoff, The Hague.
19. 'Restructuring our societies: international coordination policies', Gottlieb Duttweiler Institut, Rueschlikon.

Author Index

Adler Karlsson, G., 179, 189
Adler, L. D., 95
Arrow, K., 57, 58

Baerends, G. P., 132, 133, 140
Bahro, R., 93, 181, 195, 201
Balassa, B., 17
Barron, C. W., 93
Bauer, O., 179
Behrman, J. R., 139
Bergson, A., 175, 189
Berkouwer, J., 101, 105
Berndt, E. R. 26, 57
Boon, G. K., 58, 141
Bouma, N., 101, 108, 137, 140
Bowles, S., 26, 78, 80, 136
Boyes, W. J., 89
Brandt, W., 192, 201
Brown, C. V., 44
Burck, C. G., 88, 89, 95, 98, 138

Chamberlin, E. H., 37
Christensen, L. R., 26, 57
Chung, W. K., 14
Cochrane, W. W., 14
Cohen, S. I., 57, 161
Corocan, M., 136
Correa, H., 150

Dalrymple, R. E., 180
De Boer, P. M. C., 25, 28, 62
De Groot, A. D., 132, 140
De Hoogh, J, xii, 3
De Jong, U., 142
De Kam, F., 40
Denison, E. F., 14, 26
Derksen, J. B. D., 115
Deutsch, K, xii
De Wolff, Ch.J, 110
De Wolff, P., 78, 136, 139
Diewert, W. E., 57
Douglas, P. H., 4, 26, 92

Drewnowsky, J., 148
Drèze, J. H., 44
Dronkers, J., 138
Drucker, P. F., 7, 91
Duesenberry, J. S., 15
Duncan, B., 78, 83
Duncan, O. D., 78, 83

Edgeworth, F. Y., 131
Ellman, M. J., 182, 189
Emmerij, L., 196

Fägerlind, I., 138
Featherman, D. L., 79, 83
Fidder, J. A., 17
Frank, M., 39
Frisch, R., 102, 120
Fromm, G., 15

Gandhi, M. K., 182
Garfinkel, J., 136
Gelting, J. H., 25
Goedhart, C., 44, 51
Goldberger, A. S., 98
Gottschalk, P. T., 20, 41, 59, 61, 75, 124, 186
Griffin, T. J., 8
Groen, J. J., 140
Guttman, L., 109, 120, 133, 176

Hagen, J. H., 118
Hannah, L., 17
Harkema, R., 27
Harrell, T. W., 93
Hart, R. A., 24
Hartog, F., 113
Hartog, J., xii, 25, 62, 95, 136, 137
Haveman, R. H. 137
Helmers, F. L. C. H., 120
Hennipman, P., xii, 45
Herrera, A. O., 182
Hibbert, J., 8

Hitchcock, F. L., 125, 129
Huppes, J., 4, 38
Husén, I., 78, 138, 139

Inagaki, M., 155
Isachsen, A. J., 117

Jackson, P. M., 44
Janus, N., 99
Jencks, C., 78, 138

Kapteyn, A., 107, 130
Kay, J. A., 17
Klein, L. R., 15
Kloek, T., xii, 3, 25
Koike, H., 14
Kol, J., xiii, 3, 20, 26, 59, 75, 180
Kolm, S.-C., 87
Koopmans, E., 110
Koopmans, T. C., 147
Kravis, I. B., 114
Kreijger, R. G., 54
Kuh, E., 15
Kuipers, S. K., xiii
Kuznets, S., 11

Leipert, Chr., 118
Leontief, W. W., 28, 61
Lesourne, J., 197
Levy, S., 109, 120, 173, 176
Lewellen, W. G., 87, 88, 89, 98, 99
Lindblom, C. E., 13, 91
Lydall, H. F., 96

Maccoby, M., 93
Macrae, N., 17, 99
Mahmood, M., 60
Mann Borgese, E., 179
Marcus, L., 17
McKennell, A. C., 107
Meade, J. E., 64, 148
Miller, R. L., 60
Mincer, J., 79
Mishan, E. J., 60, 119
Morgenstern, O., 114
Morgenstern, R. D., 139
Mukerji, V., 57
Muller, H., 93
Myers, N., 40

Nadeem ul Haque, 60

Naqvi, S. N. H., 178
Nelson, V. I., 78, 80, 136
Newcomer, M., 87, 95
Nieuwenhuysen, J., 17
Nordhaus, W., 13, 119

Olneck, M., 141
Olson, M., 15
Ortlieb, H.-D., 182
Owen, W. F., 14

Pareto, V., 102, 113, 140, 145
Pen, J., xiii, 3, 4, 36, 91, 101, 168
Perelman, Ch., 153
Peseau, D. E., 89
Phelps, E., 151
Pigou, A. C., 102
Pommerehne, W. W., 180

Rehn, G., 197
Ritzen, J. M. M. R., 167
Robb, A. L., 24
Robinson, J., 37
Roncagliolo, R., 39
Rumberger, R. W., 33, 62, 124, 128, 129
Ryan, M. E., 14

Samuelson, P. A., 44, 131, 133, 134, 145
Schim van der Loeff, S., 27
Schneider, E., 134, 136
Schultz, H., 134
Schumpeter, J. A., 93
Sen, A. K., 159, 168
Šik, O., 189
Smolenski, E., 180
Smyth, D. J., 89
Stokes, B., 4
Stone, J. R. N., 134
Sturdivant, F. D., 95

Taubman, P., 136
Tévoédrjè, A., 182
Thierry, Hk., 107
Thurow, L. C., 180
Tinbergen, J., 26, 36, 49, 59, 69, 75, 81, 102, 119, 124, 137, 152, 159, 168, 180, 192
Tobin, J., 13, 119
Tuck, R. H., 91

Ullman Chiswick, C. J., 26
Van den Doel, J., xii, 3, 15, 37, 93, 191
Van der Zwan, A., 38
Vanek, J., 189
Van Ginneken, W., 181
Van Herwaarden, F. G., 107
Van Praag, B. S. M., 101, 107, 108, 109, 114, 120, 124, 140, 161, 176
Van Slijpe, A. R. D., 78, 136, 139
Varga, E., 17

Von Neumann, J., 114
Von Stackelberg, H., 37

Walker, R. L., 8
Wegner, E., xiii, 25, 69, 96
Wiles, P., 181, 189
Wise, D. A., 136
Witteveen, J. H., 197
Wolfson, D. J., xiii, 44
Wood, D. O., 26

Zanders, H. L. G., 62, 110

Subject Index

Ability to deal with people, 93, 123
Advertising costs, 13, 39
Aggregation, 61
Aims of economic policy, 192
Aim function, 175
Allocation
  of part-collective goods, 50
  of workers to jobs, 123
Antitrust legislation, 147
Auxiliary goods, 117

Balance equation, 146
Benefit principle, 51
Berlin Science Centre, xi
Budget equation, 52, 147
  government, 50
Bureaucracy, 37, 40
Business school, 95, 139

Capabilities required, 62, 93, 103, 124, 137
Capital, 8, 92, 194
  human, 58, 194
  proxies for, 8
Cell, 125
Centralisation, 176, 189
Central planning, 40, 152

CES production functions, 27, 74
Chief executives, 87, 191
Choice of education, 156
Choice of occupation, 156
Coefficients of utility function, 103
Coexistence, 184, 187
Cognitive elements of well-being, 107, 139
Collective goods, 43, 116, 148
  Part-collective goods, 43
  Quasi-collective goods, 44
  Semi-collective goods, 44
Competition, 41, 62, 91, 117
Comprehensive school, 139
Constraints on production functions, 27
Consumer goods, 175
Consumption, 39, 134
  Unhealthy, 39, 135
Control span, 96
Convergence, 183, 188
Costs of institutions, x, 145, 152
Counterproduction, 35, 60, 118
Cultural crisis, 182

Decentralisation, 99, 176, 189, 196
Decreasing returns, 5, 127

Subject Index

Degree, 103, 124, 136
Demand factors, 79, 95
Deregulation, 196
Dictionary of occupational titles, 95
Diminishing returns, 51, 147
Discrimination, 147
Distribution, income, 25, 147
Doctrinaire attitude, 175
Duplication of work, 38
Dutch State Mines (DSM), 43, 63
Dynamic welfare maximum, 151

Earnings equation, 95, 104, 108
Earnings function, 78
Education, 47, 138, 164, 168, 175
  actual, 26
  choice of, 156
  levels of, 26
  process, 139
  required, 26, 105
Educational equilibrium, 72, 126
Efficiency, 175, 189
Effort, 78, 101, 136
Elasticity of substitution, 27
Embodied technological change, 57
Energy, 26
Entrepreneurs, 4 (see also: managers)
Environment, 61, 177, 192, 196
Equitable income distribution, 91, 101
Equity, 101, 153, 175
Essential production factors, 25, 28, 62
Executives, chief, 87
Experience, job, 79, 105
External effects, 148, 190, 198

Factor costs, 115
Family size, 103, 108, 140
Farm workers, 14, 24, 60
Functional socialism, 179
Functional sovereignty, 179

Genetic factors, 138
Goods, ix, 41, 46
  auxiliary, 117
  public, 41

Helicopter view, 94
Hierarchy, 7, 25, 40, 86, 91, 176, 190

Hierarchy models, 75, 96
Household size, 138
Human capital, 58, 69, 194
  exploitation by, 75

Ideology, 184
Illegal activities, 37
Income, 137
  distribution, 25, 59, 165, 168
  market-determined, ix, 3
  from power, 4, 91, 97
  redistribution, 148
  optimal, 152
Incomes policy, 59, 197
Increasing returns, 5, 127
Indivisible means of production, 149
Inflation, 193
Informal sector, 116
Information, 38, 47, 184, 189
  incorrect, 38
Innate (inherited) capabilities, 63, 94, 103, 108, 150, 194
Input-output method, 58
Institutions, x, 145
Instruments of economic policy, 145
Integration, 148
Intensity, 103
I.Q., 123, 136

Job, 92
  characteristics, 158
  choice of, 131, 136, 156
  classification, 92, 136
  evaluation, 62, 92, 150
  satisfaction, 37, 41, 78, 117, 124, 136, 159, 175, 195
Job-oriented model, 70, 73
Justice, theory of, 81
Justifiable income differences, 79, 81

Knowledge-intensive industries, 195
Kuhn-Tucker device, x

Labour-intensive production, 25
Labour market, 123, 136
Labour types, 8, 23, 26, 58, 63, 131
Lacunae, 56, 131
Lagrange multipliers, 147, 155, 162
Laissez faire, 40, 147
Leadership, 105
Learnable capabilities, 63, 94, 103, 139, 150

Learning process, 98, 103, 136, 138
  formal, 138
Legal activities, 37
Liberalist definition of equity, 101
Logarithmic utility function, 107

Macro returns to scale, 5
Manager disease, 41
Managers, ix, 3, 15, 29, 85, 98
Manchester School, 147
Marginal costs, 147
Marginal productivity, 12
Marginal utility, 104
Market, 41
Market-determined incomes, 3
Market equilibrium, 72
Market prices, 115
Means of economic policy, 192, 194
Measurability of welfare (utility), 102, 113, 140
Measurement, direct or indirect, 104
Militarisation, xi, 188
Military expenditure, 38, 116
Mixed economies, 174
Monopoly, 40, 87, 91, 93, 97, 117, 147, 149
Monopsony, 147

National accounts, 115
National expenditures, 115
National income, 115
National product, 115
Nature or nurture, 140
Non-cognitive elements of well-being, 107, 139
Non-schooling capabilities, 96
Northwest corner rule, 125

Objective function, 175
Occupation, 28, 92, 150, 168
  parents', 138
Occupational status, 78
Oligopoly, 47
Order, social, ix, 143, 176, 177
  optimal, ix, 143, 177
  world, xi, 190
Organisers of production, 4, 5, 36, 92, 135

Parameters of utility function, 103
Part-collective goods, 43
  continuum of, 47

Path analysis, 80, 131, 138
Personality traits, 102, 123, 137, 158
Physical strength, 136
Pollution, 190, 196
Power, 4, 91, 97, 184
Preference drift, 141
Production, ix
  factors, 25, 92, 135
  function, ix, 5, 20, 25, 53, 92, 124, 146, 158
  of education, 139, 150
  organisers of, 4, 5, 36, 92, 135
Productivity, marginal, 12
Psychical income, 78, 99, 116, 138
Psychology, economic, 132
Profit sharing, 7
Property
  private, 174
  public, 174
Public goods, 43
Public savings, 151
Pyramid, 86, 96

Qualitative concepts, 103
Quantification of welfare, 102
Quantity vs quality of labour, 149
Queuing, 51

Rationing, 50
Recipe form of production function, 57
Recipes for the future, 175
Required capabilities, 62, 93, 103, 124, 137
Restrictions imposed on welfare maximum, 146
Restructuring, 192
Retraining workers, 194
Returns to scale, 5
  diminishing (decreasing), 147
  increasing, 5, 127
Revealed utility, 104

Satisfaction, 91
  from job, 37, 41, 78, 117, 124, 136, 159, 175, 195
Satisficing production, 51
Savings, public, 151
Scarcity, 91
Schooling, 26, 44, 69, 79, 93, 114, 123, 150
  required, 81

Scientific socialism, 175
Seas, Law of the, 179
Security, 47, 191
  social, 47
  world, 191
Set of institutions, 145
Social insurance, 87
Social intelligence, 123, 136
Social order, ix, 143, 176, 177
  optimal, ix, 143, 177
Social security, 47, 179
Social welfare, 113, 175
Socialisation, 174
Socialism, 174
  scientific, 175
Sovereignty, xi, 177
State economic enterprises, 43, 63
State farms, 43, 63
Supply factors, 79, 94
  non-cognitive, 79
Synthesis, 183

Tax
Taxes, 49, 152
  cost increasing, 117
  evasion, 39
  expenditure, 152
  income, 90, 152
  on innate capabilities, 152
  profit, 152
  system, optimal, 158
  value added, 115, 152
  wealth, 152

Technical progress, 92, 178
Technology, 178
Tension, 124, 137
Tolerance, 183
Traditional sectors, 26
Traits, personality, 102, 123, 137
Translog production function, 28, 94
Transportation, 47
Two-part pricing, 149

Unembodied technology change, 57
Unemployment, 193
Uniformity of factor prices, 147
Uniformity of prices, 147
Utility, 91, 124, 131, 137, 175
  function, 53
  marginal, of public goods, 45

Variables, endogenous, 138
  exogenous, 138
  in welfare function, 103, 138
  normalised, 138

War, 184
Welfare, 91, 124, 131, 137, 175
  economics, 145
  function, 146
  maximum, static, 146
    dynamic, 151
  social, 113
Working hours, reduction of, 195